RIDE GUIDE TO AMERICA

AMERICAN MOTORCYCLIST ASSOCIATION

RIDE GUIDE TO
AMERICA

EDITED BY GREG HARRISON

Whitehorse Press
Center Conway, NH

To the End of the Road, Pennsylvania Crude, Island Hopping in Georgia, Into the High Sierras, Loaded for the Road, Ride Smart, and selected excerpts from 33 Secrets for Smart Touring; Copyright © 2000–2004 by The American Motorcyclist Association/*American Motorcyclist*. Reprinted from *American Motorcyclist* with permission.

Into the West; Copyright © 2004 by Dr. Gregory Frazier. Reprinted from *American Motorcyclist* with permission from the author.

Trips 1–6 (Northern Country Notches, Northern Green Mountain Loop, Higher Northern Gaps, Lake George Loop, Northern Berkshire Loop, and Bay Loop) Copyright © 2003 by Martin C. Berke. Reprinted from *Motorcycle Journeys Through New England* with permission.

Trips 7–13 (Pennsylvania Heartland, In Search of Prospect Peak, Skyline Loop, Seneca Rocks, Search for the Swiss, Roan Mountain Mystery; and Old As The Hills) Copyright © 1995, 2004 by Dale Coyner. Reprinted from *Motorcycle Journeys Through the Appalachians* with permission.

Trips 14–16 (Jasper to Jefferson or Shreveport, Fredericksburg to Austin, Galveston to Rockport) Copyright © 2004 by Neal Davis. Reprinted from *Motorcycle Journeys Through Texas* with permission.

Trips 17–24 (Dead Horse Point to La Sal Mountains Loop, Grand Canyon (North Rim) to Glen Canyon (Dam), Continental Divide Loop, Top of the Paved Continent, Rocky Mountain High Loop, Cache la Poudre Trail, Gila Cliff Dwellings Loop, New Mexico's Rocky Mountains) Copyright © 1994 by Martin C. Berke. Reprinted from *Motorcycle Journeys Through the Southwest* with permission.

Trips 25–28 (Christmas Valley Confession, Hood River Loop, Packwood to Cashmere, Portland to Mt. St. Helens) Copyright © 2005 by Bruce Hansen. Reprinted from *Motorcycle Journeys Through the Pacific Northwest* with permission.

Trips 29–31 (The Big Sur Highway, Badwater & Death Valley Jct., Over the San Bernardino Mountains) Copyright © 2000 by Clement Salvadori. Reprinted from *Motorcycle Journeys Through California* with permission.

Whitehorse Press books are also available at discounts in bulk quantity for sales and promotional use. For details about special sales or for a catalog of motorcycling books and videos, write to the publisher.

Whitehorse Press
107 East Conway Road
Center Conway, New Hampshire 03813
Phone: 603-356-6556 or 800-531-1133
E-mail: CustomerService@WhitehorsePress.com
Internet: www.WhitehorsePress.com

ISBN 1-884313-51-5

5 4 3

Printed in China

Other Books in the Motorcycle Journeys Series
from Whitehorse Press:

Contents

Foreword

by Greg Harrison

SHE WAS ALL bonnet and dress—all three feet of her. As I rode by, she waved shyly, her palm stationary while her fingers wiggled in the late-morning sunshine.

The little Amish girl and her mother had set up a roadside business in the family's buggy. A handmade sign proclaimed "Fresh Baked Goods." I caught a captivating whiff of cinnamon and apples as I raised my left hand to wave back. Then the little girl, and the moment, disappeared over my right shoulder.

It was a perfect late-summer day for a ride, made better by the fact that I was on an old favorite of a road that I hadn't found time to ride all season. Clearly, my priorities needed straightening out, along with those delicious curves ahead.

This summer marks my 25th year at the American Motorcyclist Association. For most of that time, my job has been to edit the AMA's monthly magazine, American Motorcyclist. That makes me one of the luckiest people on earth. And believe me, I know it.

Every day, I get to think about, write about, photograph, and study motorcycles—and I get paid for it! Plus, I work at a place where I'm surrounded by people who are equally passionate about motorcycling. More importantly, I'm able to work for an organization I really believe in. The AMA is a leader in every aspect of motorcycling. We sanction thousands of road-riding and racing events all over the country. We put together a great package of benefits and discounts for our members. We publish a magazine (from which several of the stories in this book were drawn) and produce a website that offers an ever-expanding universe of motorcycling information.

But what the AMA really does for you (and me) is work tirelessly to defend our right to ride. Sometimes, that means fending off harmful legislation at the federal, state, and local level—laws that allow employers to cut off insurance coverage for their workers who ride motorcycles (and not even tell them about it!) or bike bans that keep motorcyclists out of parks and off roads, for instance. Sometimes it means working with insurance companies to eliminate blacklists against certain types of bikes. Sometimes it means promoting legislation to fund studies of motorcycle safety or help pay for the development of trails.

Those accomplishments—which benefit every motorcyclist in America—make me proud to be an AMA member. And prouder still to do this work on a daily basis.

My job at the AMA has given me opportunities to see more of the world on two wheels than I ever believed possible. And it's left me a rich collection of unforgettable motorcycling memories.

Some of the most vivid are from famous roads like Skyline Drive and the Blue Ridge Parkway in Virginia and North Carolina. The peaceful mountains and spectacular fall colors never fail to inspire me. Or seeing the sunset from the seat of a bike in Key West. Or a gorgeous Carolina dawn after a day of rain, sleet, and misery on a ride down to Daytona.

How about the great roads of the West—Colorado's Million Dollar Highway, Montana's Going to the Sun Road, California's Pacific Coast Highway? Each has its own special magic. And I've found remote spots on the Baja Peninsula of Mexico where you can look in any direction and see nothing but cactuses all the way to the horizon. It's a place as remote and beautiful, in its own way, as Newfoundland on the opposite end of North America.

I'm a big fan of retracing some of this country's earliest routes. I've learned more about American history and geography by leading other riders in search of remaining stretches of Route 66 between Chicago and Los Angeles than I accumulated in 16 years of school.

And for packing a lot of riding experiences into a day, it's hard to beat the morning I woke up early in Ohio and rode to Syracuse, New York, by way of Montreal to log 1,000 miles before stopping.

But that's just scratching the surface. Some of my best memories aren't from major cross-country rides to exotic locations. They're snapshots from the seat of a bike—unexpected moments, like that Amish girl waving as I passed, only an hour from my home. Or that afternoon of crystal-clear sunlight filtering through the trees on a deserted road whose name I can't even remember in Tennessee. Or pulling up at a perfectly preserved diner after a long day's ride in Vermont.

I hope the "AMA Ride Guide to America" gives you plenty of inspiration for memorable rides of your own. We've pulled together touring stories from American Motorcyclist editors and other top writers covering every region of the country. Plus, we've added some tips and tricks to make your ride even better.

Assembling all that information in one place inevitably got me to thinking about which ride is the best. Is it a cruise along the coast of Down East Maine or a trip into the high Sierras of California? Can you find it in Pennsylvania, or Georgia, or Montana? Does it involve infinite mountain views or endless forested curves?

What's the best motorcycle ride? After 25 years here, I can let you in on the secret: It's the next one.

Greg Harrison
American Motorcyclist Association

How to Carry Stuff on Your Motorcycle

By the staff of American Motorcyclist

YOU. YOUR MOTORCYCLE. The open road.

It's all you'll ever need, right? Well, clean underwear for tomorrow might be nice. And a few shirts, and a toothbrush, and maybe a camera. Plus a mobile phone, a book to read, and a sweater to wear to dinner.

You know, come to think of it, another pair of pants and some shoes to replace your motorcycle boots would come in handy. So would a rainsuit . . . just in case. You need more than you think. And pretty soon, it starts to add up.

The fact is that whether you're headed out on a two-week trip or just picking up a box of cereal and a loaf of bread after work, there are times when you really need to carry stuff on your bike. And it's instantly obvious when you look at most motorcycles that they weren't designed to haul large quantities of anything.

Fortunately, you aren't the first person to discover this. Lots of riders have faced the dilemma of getting something from here to there over the past century or so. And they've come up with plenty of innovative ideas—some of which are likely to be right for your bike.

In this chapter, you'll find a rundown of the major categories of motorcycle luggage, from cramming stuff in your jacket to high-end hard saddlebags, and everything in between.

BACKPACKS

Sometimes you're not riding coast-to-coast. Sometimes, you're just headed to the office, or out on a day-trip.

All you really need at times like those is a way to carry some files and computer disks, or a rainsuit, some water, and snacks for a midday break. That's where backpacks shine.

One advantage of a backpack is that you don't have to worry about attaching anything to your motorcycle, either with straps that could cut into your paint, or with brackets that clutter the clean lines of your machine. Backpacks are luggage you wear, and when you get off the bike, your stuff goes with you.

Standard backpacks, like those every kid wears to school, work reasonably well on a motorcycle, but there are drawbacks. The straps can be hard to get over bulky riding jackets, and many packs tend to flop around at speed.

■ *A short metal cable with loops on both ends (like those made to keep people from stealing bicycle seats) is perfect for securing a jacket and helmet to your bike's helmet lock.*

Several companies have adapted the backpack design to the motorcycle market with beefier straps that are more widely spaced to accommodate jackets and helmets, plus unique clasping systems to keep everything in place. Some even incorporate drinking-water bladders that can be used on the move.

Another innovative twist on the backpack theme is the courier bag, based on packs popularized by bicycle messengers. With a single strap, a courier bag goes on more easily over your helmet, and you can pull the pack around to the front to get at its contents. In addition, many courier bags are waterproof.

Drawbacks? There are a few. Soft items like clothes can cushion your fall if you crash wearing a backpack or courier bag, but you don't want to fill them with sharp or hard objects. Plus, anything you put in them is weight

Courier bags: an alternative to the traditional backpack.

Rear-seat bags are usually expandable to accommodate different loads.

■ *Take a tip from off-road riders and carry a backpack hydration system so you can drink water while you ride. A must for arid weather.*

Traveling alone? Use your rear seat to haul your stuff.

you have to carry on your body, not the bike. And they can get in the way if you're trying to carry a passenger. Still, if you're only carrying a light load of something soft, it's hard to beat a backpack.

REAR-SEAT BAGS

If you're traveling alone, one of the most logical places to carry clothing or gear is on the passenger seat. A number of companies offer rear-seat haulers to make this process convenient.

There's plenty of variation in this class, so it pays to look around for a rear-seat pack that fits your needs and your bike. Some are as small as an office briefcase, while others qualify as full-fledged luggage.

Besides size, the major differences between bags is in the attachment system. Many rear-seat bags use standard bungee straps, while others use nylon webbing with clips that hook under the seat itself.

Bungee-cord systems can work fine, as long as your bike offers a place to hook them. But be careful where you route the bungee straps. Over a long ride, they can wear through the paint on any body parts they touch.

Seat clips work on most seats, although they can be a little trickier to connect than bungees. And if your bike has nothing more than a small pad for a passenger seat, you may need to look for alternate connection points.

Rear-seat bags made specifically for motorcycles are convenient, but there's nothing to prevent you from using a bag you already own. Several companies make innovative systems to attach almost anything to the rear seat of a motorcycle. Nets of bungee cords can secure odd-shaped loads—even helmets—while adjustable bungees and flat spring-tension straps give you the capability to cinch down a small duffel bag or gear bag.

The main thing is to avoid overloading the attachment system. Heavy loads may fit inside a rear-seat bag, but that doesn't mean you can safely transport them that way. Most bag and cord makers offer guidelines on how much weight they can carry.

There are two other issues to keep in mind: Most rear-seat bags are not waterproof, so look for one with a rain-shedding cover, and remember that a rear-seat bag can get in your way when you go to swing a leg over your machine. Get used to propping your bike on its sidestand, then standing alongside it and kicking your leg straight out over the seat.

TANKBAGS

Tankbags are religion. Those who've been converted will tell you they do everything from making sure you don't get lost to curing baldness.

In fact, tankbags are pretty wonderful. The tank-top location means that any weight you carry is close to the center of the motorcycle, where it's least likely to upset your handling.

■ *A simple map case attached to your bike's tank (like the magnetic map holder from Roadgear, available from the Whitehorse Press website: www.whitehorsepress.com) can keep you on course without the bulk of a tankbag.*

Tankbags: Convenient storage; plus a great spot for a map.

Plus, it means you can get to your stuff easily at a rest stop.

In addition, most tankbags double as map holders, making them worthwhile even if you don't have much to carry. And larger models can be as effective as some low fairings in keeping wind off your chest. Also, many models come with straps that turn them into backpacks when you want to wander around off the bike.

No, tankbags aren't perfect. Their carrying capacity is limited, most have to be removed when you go to fill the gas tank, and they don't adapt well to many cruiser-style bikes or tight-quartered sportbikes. But a good tankbag can carry everything you need for a day-trip and makes an ideal starting point for touring luggage.

There are two basic mounting systems—straps and magnets. Magnetic bags can be incredibly convenient, but they don't work on all tanks, and you need to be careful if you're carrying computer disks, memory cards, digital cameras, cassette tapes, or even magnetic bank cards. With strap systems, you need to find a way to cinch the load down securely on your bike—there is nothing worse than a tankbag that tries to fall off every time you turn.

Despite that, tankbags are addictive. Once you try them, you'll never want to travel without one again.

■ *Carry a spare key. Zip-tie or duct tape it somewhere hidden on your bike, or better yet, give it to a traveling companion for safer-keeping.*

Soft saddle bags are available in styles to match your cruiser . . .

. . . Or in sizes to fit the tight spaces on a sportbike.

SOFT SADDLEBAGS

When most people think of adding luggage to a motorcycle, they think of soft saddlebags. These versatile carriers have been around since before the Pony Express riders were hauling mail in the Old West.

So many companies have built soft saddlebags that it seems just about every conceivable configuration has been attempted, from tiny nylon wedges designed to fit sportbikes to big leather bags with the right look to finish off your cruiser.

There are two keys to buying soft saddlebags—the fit and the attachment system. Upswept exhaust pipes on sportbikes can destroy a set of saddlebags in no time, and could even catch fire while you ride. Make sure you buy a set with ample clearance between your muffler and the bag.

Dual-sport and adventure-touring machines, with their high-mounted pipes, can be even tougher to fit. Some companies sell metal guards you can install to keep the bag and the muffler from making contact.

Saddlebags for cruiser bikes, too, often come with metal guards to keep the bags from making contact with the drive chain or belt. Don't use these bags without their guards.

Besides that, proper fit comes down to making sure the bags won't get in the way of your rear turn signals and that they won't block access to footpegs if you're planning to carry a passenger.

If you're headed out on a long, complex trip, you should consider keeping organized with the envelope system. Before you leave, prepare one envelope for each day on the road. Mark the dates on the outside, then stuff things like hotel reservation info and lists of things to see inside. Instead of juggling your entire stack of literature to find the piece you need, you can just open up the appropriate day's envelope.

Mounting soft bags is usually easy. Typically, you'll have a pair of straps that go over the rear seat. These may be adjustable with Velcro strips to determine the height of the bags when mounted. A clip-on strap usually extends forward from the bottom front corner of each bag to a secure mounting point like the passenger footpeg mount. Another strap usually goes around the back of the bike to connect the two bags. Once you have everything adjusted for your machine, removing the bags is often as simple as disconnecting three clips and picking up the bags.

Some systems attach via a harness that stays on the bike. You then disconnect the bags from the harness, which leaves all your adjustments in place.

Either way, the major drawback to soft saddlebags, like all strap-on luggage, is that they can't be locked. This can present a problem if you want to leave your bike parked somewhere while you're sightseeing. You can use a cable lock to secure the bags to the bike, or you could carry your valuables in something more portable, like a tankbag with backpack straps, and figure that no one will want your extra shirts and underwear enough to take them.

Two other considerations are moisture (most soft saddlebags aren't waterproof and will require rain covers) and comfort, since the straps that hold up soft bags usually sit on top of the passenger seat (and therefore under your passenger's seat) and the front straps can get in the way of your passenger's feet.

But if you find a set of soft bags that properly fit your bike (and with the wide range of choices available, chances are you can), they could provide all the luggage you'll ever need.

Aftermarket hard bags can provide waterproof, lockable storage you can live with for the long haul.

ALL-IN-ONE BAGS

Own a cruiser? Want to turn it into a touring bike? Then you probably already know about one type of all-in-one luggage known as back-rest bags.

These are rectangular bags that ride vertically on the rear of the bike, providing storage space either in place of, or behind, the passenger. Since the bags are shaped like small suitcases, they're easy to pack, and some come with backpack straps or even wheels for tranporting them off the bike.

To use this kind of luggage on your cruiser, you'll need a securely mounted back rest and a luggage rack. Typically, these bags come with a wide strap that slides over the back rest, and a pair of nylon-webbing straps that secure them to the rack.

Attachment is easy, and there's plenty of space available, but don't let that fool you into thinking that you can carry anything on a back rest. The mounting position—far up and to the rear of the bike—is exactly where any added weight will have the greatest impact on the handling of your motorcycle. Check the load limits on the bags and your luggage rack before packing, and think light.

Other considerations are pretty standard. Make sure your bags come with waterproof covers, and if you're concerned about security when you leave the bike, at least buy a zipper lock and a cable lock to keep someone from opening the bag or walking off with it.

Recently, some companies have started bringing the rear-mounted bag concept to the rest of the motorcycling world with designs that let you install a supporting rack and bag on your sportbike or standard. These can be a great solution

Loaded for the Road

for bikes that don't lend themselves to soft saddlebags, although they typically leave some brackets behind even when you're not using the bag.

Other companies offer a different take on the all-in-one bag design, with strap-on luggage that combines a rear-seat bag with a couple of mini saddlebags. There's a lot of storage available if these fit your bike.

HARD SADDLEBAGS

If you're really serious about touring, you've probably at least thought about buying hard saddlebags at one time or another. Indeed, back when airhead BMWs roamed the earth, hard bags were at the top of the touring food chain.

These days, fewer companies are in the hard-saddlebag business, but the products they make are more functional than ever, rivaling the integrated luggage you'd get on a full-dress touring bike for both carrying capacity and convenience.

To add hard bags, you'll have to purchase mounting hardware specifically for your machine. Some of these brackets will also give you a luggage rack or a mounting point for a touring top box, to boot.

Bolting this stuff on shouldn't be too difficult, although it will likely require you to relocate your rear turn signals. Then, once you have the hardware in place, you can simply pack the saddlebags and clip them into place on the machine.

The advantages of hard bags are many. All should be waterproof and lockable for security. And when you get to a hotel, you can unclip your bags and carry your luggage inside—just like you arrived in a car.

■ *On high-mileage days, you'll feel a lot better if you carry eyedrops and use them every time you stop for gas.*

■ *A wireless phone can be a lifesaver. Dial 911 for help anywhere you find wireless service, but remember to tell the dispatcher where you are. Keep track of route numbers, interstate exits, towns you've passed, mileposts—anything that can save emergency officials time in getting to you.*

It's not all beer and skittles, though. Hard bags may appear huge on the outside, but some are oddly shaped, leaving you with little nooks and crannies that aren't particularly useful. And unlike soft bags, they won't expand as you keep cramming stuff in. Plus, the mounting brackets can position the bags pretty far out, adding significantly to the width of your motorcycle. And even with the bags off, you're left with brackets that might not be your idea of fashionable.

Still, life is full of compromises, and if you want the greatest convenience for long-haul touring, you at least need to consider getting a set of hard saddlebags.

■ AND HERE'S WHERE TO GET IT

Aerostich/Rider WearHouse	(800) 222-1994	www.aerostich.com
CycleVenture	(800) 688-6439	www.cycleventure.com
GIVI USA	(877) 679-4484	www.giviusa.com
Held/Intersport Fashions West	(888) 311-5399 ext. 321	www.held-usa.com
LadyRidersWear	(888) 857-7989	www.ladyriderswear.com
Mag's Bags	(888) 723-1504	www.magsbags.com
Marsee Designs	(800) 293-2400	www.marseeproducts.com
Nelson-Rigg	(714) 850-1811	www.nelsonrigg.com
RKA Motorcycle Luggage & Accessories	(800) 349-1752	www.rka-luggage.com
Roadgear	(800) 854-4327	www.roadgear.com
Spakman Products	(866) 765-3799	www.spakman.net
CDL T-Bags	(800) 957-6288	www.t-bags.com
Touratech	(206) 323-2349	www.touratech-usa.com
Travelcade/Saddlemen	(800) 397-7709	www.saddlemen.com
Whitehorse Press	(800) 531-1133	www.whitehorsepress.com

INTEGRATED LUGGAGE

None of the above is quite good enough for you? There's still one more choice—let the motorcycle manufacturer incorporate carrying capacity into your bike.

A big, fully equipped touring bike isn't the cheapest way to carry stuff, but it can be the most elegant way to go traveling on two wheels. You don't have to do any adjusting to make sure everything fits, and you'll probably end up with more carrying capacity.

But before you plunk down your money on a big tourer, consider whether it's really the right answer for you. Touring bikes are great on the open road, but they can be a handful in city traffic, to say nothing of the occasional dirt road.

If cross-country touring is really what you're buying a bike for, then a full-dress tourer can be the perfect solution. But if you spend 50 weeks a year riding to work, and two weeks on the open road, you may want to consider one of the other options.

Tips for Street Survival

By the staff of American Motorcyclist

THERE ARE 3.9 million miles of roads in the United States. How many have you seen lately? We want to make sure you ride your share, so we've pulled together information that will help you ride smarter—and farther.

In this chapter, you'll find real-world tips for becoming a safer rider, whether you're commuting to work or heading across the country. You'll also discover how to get un-stranded if the worst happens a long way from home.

So charge up the battery, pull out the road atlas, and start making plans. You've got 3.9 million possibilities to choose from.

STREET SURVIVAL 101

Want to stay alive on the road? Hey, who doesn't? That's why we've put together a list of 32 tips that will help you ride smarter this season, culled from the experienced riders and motorcycle safety instructors on the AMA staff.

Some of what you find here is right out of the rider-training manual. Some of it comes from combined riding experience that amounts to centuries. Either way, we think you'll find plenty of practical tips you can use.

1. Every time you ride, give your motorcycle a quick visual inspection for things like loose parts, leaking fluids, or obviously low tire pressures. Regularly, give it a more complete check, using all the necessary tools.

2. Clear your mind before you even start your bike. We all get preoccupied by work, issues at home, even the outcome of a basketball game. But when you're on the bike, you have to focus on riding. Each time you switch on the ignition key, switch on your brain, too.

3. From the moment you get on the road, train yourself to use the Motorcycle Safety Foundation's SIPDE method for staying out of trouble: **S**can all around you. **I**dentify potential hazards. **P**redict what will happen. **D**ecide how to avoid problems. And **E**xecute your plan. Do it all the time, and you'll drastically reduce the number of dangerous situations you face.

4. Another exceptionally valuable technique is also one of the simplest: Look where you want to go, because the bike will go where you look. Don't stare at that upcoming pothole—instead, look at the clear pavement next to it. Don't fixate on the car turning left in front of you—instead, focus on the opening being created as it moves past, since that's your escape route. At times, it may take a real mental effort to pull your eyes away from an obstacle, but if you can see your way through trouble, chances are you can ride there.

5. It should go without saying, but don't get on your bike if you've been drinking. Your odds of being involved in an accident go up enormously.

6. If you're on a bike that's new to you, or you're riding under unfamiliar conditions (mountain roads, rain, etc.), you're statistically more likely to crash. Slow down, focus, and take extra care.

■ If you're traveling east or west, schedule your breakfast or dinner times near sunrise or sunset so you don't have to stare into the sun when it is low on the horizon.

7. Need to tune up your skills after a winter layoff or to get more comfortable on a new bike? Find a deserted parking lot and do some tight figure-eights and brake tests before you face the real world. Keep at it until you feel truly in control of the machine.

8. Be aware that nailing the brakes isn't the only way to avoid a crash. Sometimes, swerving, or even speeding up, will get you out of trouble more easily.

9. Remember that in the famous Hurt Study in 1981, the most common accident situations involved a car violating a motorcyclist's right of way. Things have changed a lot in the years since, but cars turning left in front of you or pulling into your path from a parking lot or side street remain particularly common hazards. Ride like drivers don't see you in those circumstances, because they may not.

10. With those kinds of hazards in mind, play the "what-if" game as you ride. What if the car you're following slams on its brakes? What if the car on the cross street doesn't stop for the stop sign? What if the truck on your right suddenly swerves into your lane? Could you avoid it?

■ *Especially if you're riding alone, wear a dog tag with your name and contact information. You can get them in a lot of places, including from most pet stores.*

11. What's the best lane position for riding? The left tire track? The right tire track? The center? You can get all kinds of answers, but your real priority shouldn't be lane positioning at all. It should be "traffic

Check your brakes and suspension before every ride.

positioning." Try to create a bubble of space around you. If there's a car exiting a parking lot on your right, move to the left. If there's an oncoming car that could turn left, move right. If there's traffic around you, position yourself so you have the maximum cushion on all sides.

12. On crowded freeways, the most dangerous place to be is often the right lane, where cars are constantly merging in and out. If you don't need to exit anytime soon, traffic positioning tells you that you're probably better off in the left lane, away from all the merging action. But don't get over there unless you're comfortable with the speed of traffic in the left lane—you don't want to trade the hazards of merging cars for the hazards of faster cars closing in on your tailpipe.

13. Most traffic tends to move in clumps, separated by open spaces. Instead of rolling along in the middle of a clump, speed up or slow down to get yourself into one of the open spaces.

Riding in foul weather presents additional challenges. Be prepared.

■ *You've heard it a million times: look over your bike carefully every morning on the road. Checking simple stuff—air pressure, oil level, loose or missing fasteners—can save you from big trouble.*

14. You can use traffic positioning in other ways as well. On crowded roads, don't just stare at the back of the car in front of you. Put yourself in a position where you can look through its windshield at cars farther ahead. Or move to a spot that lets you see around a truck or car that blocks your vision.

15. Changing lanes? Always use your head. Swivel your neck to check your blind spot so you don't change lanes into someone else.

16. In general, it's easier to change lanes into a spot that's in front of you, rather than behind you. See your spot, flip on your turn signal, do your head check, and accelerate into it.

Even a basic knowledge of your bike's mechanics will serve you well on the road. Make sure you know how to properly maintain your motorcycle before you embark on any trip.

■ *Owning good motorcycle gear is worth the expense. Waterproof, breathable linings in boots and jackets will transform the way you think about bad weather. A number of companies offer materials that work well, but always test your gear on a rainy day at home before facing a storm on the road.*

17. Remember that all other vehicles have blind spots, too. This is a particular problem around semi-trailers. As a demonstration, organizers at a recent rally placed four police cruisers and 28 motorcycles behind and to both sides of a parked semi. Not one could be seen from the driver's seat. If you can't see the driver's rearview mirrors, the driver can't see you.

18. Want to improve the odds that other drivers will see you? Don't wear black. Bright-colored riding clothes can make you more visible anytime, while a yellow or orange rainsuit, with reflective stripes, will help you stand out when visibility is at its poorest.

19. Be aware of seasonal hazards. In winter, ice and snow are the obvious problems, but salt can also reduce your traction long after the snow is gone. In spring, road conditions are at their worst—watch for cars swerving to avoid potholes. In summer heat, highway crack sealer creates "tar snakes" that can be very slippery. And in fall, wet leaves are among the slickest surfaces known to man.

20. Construction zones are another hazard associated with summer. If you find yourself on a multi-lane road that's being paved, and one lane is an inch or so higher than the other, try to ride in the higher lane. It's easier to move from high to low than the other way around.

21. Be equally aware of hazards associated with different times of day. In the early morning, watch for dew and frost on roads. Through the daylight hours, you have to contend with sun glare and the highest traffic loads of the day. Sunset is the time when animals are more active, while evening and overnight hours bring the greatest risk of drunk drivers. You can probably add hazards of your own. For instance, it seems the closer you get to quitting time on Friday, the more self-absorbed and rushed the drivers of other vehicles get.

■ *On a long tour, plan for at least one day of doing nothing. Time is the ultimate luxury, and can mean the difference between a vacation and an endurance run. Also, be realistic about your daily mileage. In really scenic areas, 150 miles may make a very full day. Don't assume you can achieve highway mileage on good back roads.*

In autumn, fallen leaves across the roadway are not only extremely slick when wet, but they can also hide other dangerous obstacles. Use caution.

22. Sunset and sunrise can create severe visibility problems. If you can see your own shadow ahead of you, the drivers of oncoming cars will be staring right into the sun. Anticipate that they can't see you.

At intersections, oncoming, left-turning, motorists are your worst enemy. Beware.

23. Of course, rain is a hazard anytime. Be aware that roads will be slickest shortly after it starts raining as the water combines with oil on the road surface. Especially slick are lane markers and other lines painted on the road.

24. Riding with a group of motorcyclists can be fun, but remember to ride your own ride. If you're not comfortable with the pace, slow down. Don't rely on anyone else to make safety decisions for you.

25. Alone or in a group, if you're doing something on your motorcycle that makes you feel like you're in over your head, you probably are. Back off.

26. What's the most dangerous animal in America? Bears? Wolves? Sharks? Not even close. More people are killed in collisions with deer than in all types of animal attacks. Remember that if you see one deer cross the road, chances are good there are more where that one came from. Slow down and look for the second, third, and fourth members of the group.

27. The most dangerous places on surface streets are intersections. As you approach an intersection, scan in all directions so you know what's likely to happen. But before you slow down, also check your mirrors to see what's coming up behind you.

28. Be especially careful when you come up behind a car that's turning left at an intersection. Oncoming cars may not see you, and they're more likely to turn left in front of you.

29. When you stop at an intersection, leave enough room between you and the car in front of you so that you can pull to the left or right in an emergency. Keep your bike in first gear, so you're ready to take evasive action if a car behind you isn't going to stop in time.

30. Parking garages and toll booths have a different hazard—those automatic traffic-control arms. They can be notorious for not going up quickly enough or dropping too soon. One solution is to look for a lane with a human being who will take your money and actuate the gate.

31. Get additional training. Even the best riders can benefit from enrolling in formal rider education programs. Contact the Motorcycle Safety Foundation at (800) 446-9227 or www.msf-usa.org for more information or to find the class nearest you.

32. Finally, if you're feeling tired during a long day on the road and can't decide whether you should stop and take a break, that's a sure sign that you should stop and take a break.

STRANDED? NOW WHAT?

Maybe the bike just quit running. Maybe there was an accident and your motorcycle is no longer capable of going anywhere under its own power. Maybe

> ■ *Do routine maintenance at home with your bike's toolkit, so you're sure you have everything you need along the side of the road. If your bike's toolkit is hard to work with, upgrade it!*

The most important tool you can carry if you get stranded? It could be a cellphone.

Riding with a partner is a great way to make sure you don't get stranded out along the middle of a beautiful, but lonely, mountain road. (Photo courtesy of Toby Ballentine)

you became ill, and you're not capable of riding any more.

There are dozens of such "maybe" scenarios, but they all add up to one thing: You're stranded far from home, and you need help. Fortunately, there are more ways to get "unstranded" these days than ever, especially if you put a little extra planning into your trip.

One of the best pieces of emergency equipment you can carry is a cellphone. Service may be spotty in mountainous areas, but if you can't get a signal in a valley, try climbing to the nearest high point.

If you have an emergency, just dial 911 to get a dispatcher. Be aware, though, that they'll need to know where you are. This can be a real problem for emergency crews trying to respond to cellphone calls. Always know the route number of the road you're on, and look for those little mileage posts along the way. At the very least, remember the last town you passed through and how far back it was.

If you're not facing an emergency situation, a good way to get rescued is with a roadside-assistance service, like AMA MoTow (800-AMA-JOIN). For $25 a year, this plan guarantees you'll get towed up to 35 miles, no matter which of your motorcycles you're riding. Plus, if you're in an accident,

MoTow will reimburse you up to $25 a day for five days of car rental and up to $100 a day for three days for lodging and meals.

MoTow isn't the only service available, but be aware that many road-side-assistance programs for cars specifically exclude motorcycles.

One smart precaution to take before you hit the road is to write the national dealer-locator number for your brand of bike in your owners manual. That way you won't have to rely on the tow truck driver knowing where to take your bike. Here are the phone numbers for several major brands: BMW, (201) 307-4000; Ducati, (408) 253-0499; Harley-Davidson, (414) 343-4056; Honda, (310) 783-2000; Kawasaki, (949) 770-0400; Suzuki, (714) 996-7040; Triumph, (678) 854-2010; Yamaha, (714) 761-7300.

Another step you can take is to join AMA International Help 'N Hands, a network of more than 8,500 individuals and businesses that have signed up to offer advice or help to other members in need. Donations are encouraged, but the program is free, as long as you agree to become a part of that help network yourself. Then you'll get a toll-free number to call that will put you in touch with Help 'N Hands members where you are. To sign up, call AMA Membership Services at (800) AMA-JOIN.

What if you need to ship your motorcycle home instead of getting it fixed on the road? The Federal Companies, an agent for Allied Worldwide, offers special shipping deals for AMA members. Call (800) 747-4100, ext. 217.

Another option is to rent a truck and haul your own bike home. Not all rental companies offer one-way rentals in all locations, but here are some possibilities: Budget Truck Rental, (800) 467-9337; Penske Truck Rental, (888) 996-5415; Ryder, (800) 297-9337 (no one-way rentals); and U-Haul, (800) 468-4285.

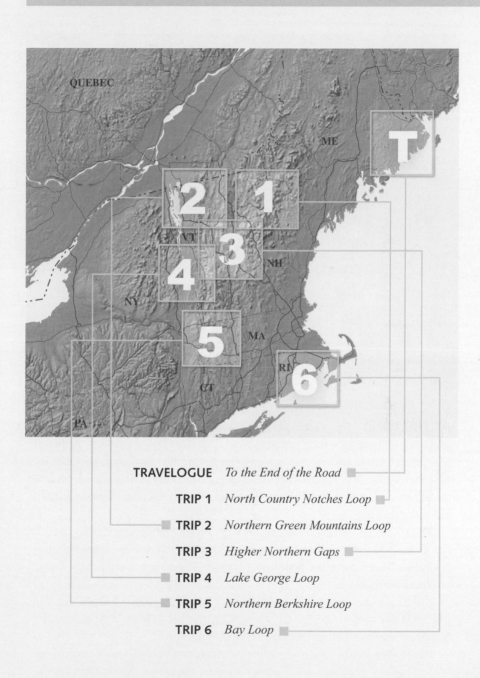

To the End of the Road

Text and photos by Lance Oliver

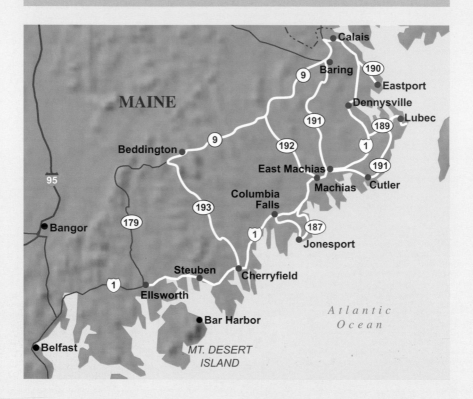

AT THE EDGE of Ellsworth, Maine, I approach the stoplight where U.S. 1 and Maine Route 3 go their separate ways. Ahead, there's a choice. A line of overladen camper trailers and minivans stuffed to the roofline with suitcases fills the two lanes of Route 3 that lead to Bar Harbor, the natural splendor of Acadia National Park, and all the accompanying ice-cream-shop-enhanced tourism opportunities.

The sole left-turn lane leads east on U.S. 1 into Washington County, which has a mere 32,000 residents squeezed into 1.68 million acres. That lane has no traffic. This is what the Wall Street types call a contrarian indicator. I love contrarian indicators.

I pull into the empty left-turn lane, and when the light changes, the big blue BMW's torque sweeps me up U.S. 1 into the "Down East" corner of Maine, a term that defines both a direction and a spirit.

Bar Harbor marks the dividing line between two very different parts of the Maine coast. From here west, stately homes, mansions, and even a former president's retreat dot the coastline. East, or Down East as Maine residents call this stretch of the coast, you're more likely to find modest houses with a pile of lobster traps in the yard.

It's a place where the tides can rise an inch a minute, and water can flow uphill. It's also the first place in the continental U.S. that the sun's rays strike each morning, which is why Washington County sometimes goes by the alias of the Sunrise County.

And it's one of those places that has an end-of-the-Earth feel to it, at least for those traveling within the United States. Despite the fact that there's an expanse of Canada's New Brunswick ahead of you, the map indicates you can find plenty of spots where you can gaze out over the North Atlantic and know that the next bit of land in that direction was once considered a whole world away.

That's what I'm looking for in this trip, that feeling of being at land's end, standing on the edge of the firmament and looking into the unknown.

Nine miles after my left turn onto U.S. 1, I cross a bridge over the back-waters of Frenchman Bay and spot a lonely lighthouse tucked among the evergreens. I think I'm on the right track.

In Eastport, there's no mistaking the meaning of the town monument. Here, they've lived for centuries by pulling fish from the sea.

U.S. 1 parallels the Maine coast, but doesn't follow it. The shoreline is ragged, with craggy peninsulas jutting into the Atlantic, while Route 1 aims generally northeast and varies from that course as little as possible.

But every so often, I have the option of jumping onto a loop road to the end of one of these outcroppings. These detours are where the real face of Down East is found.

Take state Route 191, for example. Just past the town of Machias, home to a small branch of the University of Maine and as close to a bustling town as you'll find in this part of the state, Route 191 wanders for miles along the coast.

At the tiny village of Cutler, I find fishing boats sheltered in a cove and thick morning fog that has settled on the evergreens blanketing the slopes above the water. It seems as though the only thing moving is me.

These traps are empty because my stomach is full. (Photo courtesy of Marty Berke)

The tools of the trade pile up on the docks of Down East Maine, just as they have for centuries. (Photo courtesy of Marty Berke)

I park the bike to soak up the scene. Dominating the shoreline is a stately house where a flag barely stirs in the stillness.

While I watch, a bald eagle circles into view, fishing the clear waters. For a moment, the eagle perches on the topmost branch of a tall pine next to the flagpole. It's a perfect photo-op, but much too far away for my camera and lens. And before I can even think about trying to get closer, he lifts his broad wings effortlessly and soars off.

I wonder if such sights still move those who live here and see them daily. Surely, they must.

Back on the bike, I decide that BMW's big K1200GT is a good choice for these loop roads. Here, the tight turns of the mountains farther west in New England are replaced by bluffs and gentle hills as North America settles into the Atlantic.

The Beemer's Telelever front suspension soaks up the ripples and cracks you'd expect to find on roads that suffer through harsh northern winters. Through chilly fog (raise the electrically adjustable windscreen) and warm

In some parts of the country a dinner of Maine lobsters will leave you without money to get home. By comparison, the prices here are quite reasonable. So eat up. (Photo courtesy of Marty Berke)

sunshine (lower the windscreen on the fly), the GT keeps me comfortable and lets me skim the pavement for hours.

It's high noon when I arrive at West Quoddy Head, the easternmost point in the continental United States, but the fog is still as thick as New England clam chowder.

"It's been this way every morning for the past two weeks," says the woman working at the visitors center for the Quoddy Light, the red-and-white striped lighthouse at the tip of the Maine coast.

"But," she adds, "if you go to the lighthouse on Campobello Island, it's clear."

Perfect. That's my next stop.

Checking my map beforehand, I'd traced out a route up the coast to the Canadian island of Campobello. And three questions immediately came to mind:

What was the word "west" doing in the name of the easternmost point in the United States?

You can hike to the lighthouse at the tip of Campobello Island, but only at low tide. (Photo courtesy of Marty Berke)

How did Campobello Island, on the border between the U.S., where English is the predominant language, and eastern Canada, where French and English are spoken, end up with a Spanish name?

And why is it that this and several other islands hugging the U.S. shore ended up belonging to Canada?

The answers lie right in front of me.

First of all, West Quoddy Head is the easternmost spot in Maine because its counterpart, East Quoddy Head, lies just within Canada, on the tip of Campobello Island.

As for the name, Campobello Island was granted to William Owen, a captain in the British Royal Navy, in 1770, and he gave it the name it has had ever since. Campobello was intended as a compliment to Lord William Campbell, the governor of the province at the time. But Owen, a well-traveled Navy man, also drew on his knowledge of Spanish and Italian. In those languages, Campobello means "beautiful country," which this certainly is.

Then there's the question of why I see a Canadian customs office as I approach the island. This seems odd because the only road connection to Campobello Island is a short bridge from the U.S. side, while it's separated from the Canadian mainland by the entire width of Passamaquoddy Bay.

According to legend, the answer is that Daniel Webster, the U.S. representative when the boundaries were being negotiated, enjoyed a few too many toasts in the interests of diplomatic protocol. So when he went out sailing with a survey party to settle the final boundary, he wasn't too concerned with which islands were becoming part of the United States and which were to remain part of the British Empire.

The Canadian customs officer waves me through the border checkpoint, and after a quick stop at the Campobello Visitor Center for a map, I cruise toward the north end of the island.

Campobello was the favorite summer retreat of Franklin D. Roosevelt, who spent long summer vacations here hiking, sailing, birdwatching, and playing sports. Sadly, it was during a vacation here in 1921 that Roosevelt was stricken with polio. He rarely visited the island after that.

The Roosevelt Campobello International Park, jointly run by the U.S. and Canada, preserves the Roosevelt Cottage where the family spent the summers. Of course, this isn't exactly what you might think of as a cottage, since it has 34 rooms and a view to kill for, but then the rich are different from you and me. If you'd like to get a glimpse of how different, the Roosevelt Cottage is open for tours in summer months.

On a dual-sport bike, I'd wander down some of Campobello's unpaved roads, but instead, the GT and I travel the 10 paved miles to East Quoddy Head. As I pull into the parking area where the road ends, I'm not disappointed.

This has to be one of the world's beautiful spots, at least on a day like today. Just as the woman at West Quoddy predicted, not a wisp of fog blunts a brilliant sun. The white lighthouse, posted on a point of land separate from the rocky bluff where I'm parked, is framed by dark green pines and the glowing blue of Passamaquoddy Bay.

With a little caution and agility, you can walk to the rocky outcropping where the lighthouse sits. But you'd better have good timing and go with grippy shoes. Why? Because of the other thing this area is famous for: its tides.

They're the most extreme you'll find anywhere in the world, with the waters of the Atlantic regularly rising and falling 20 feet or more twice every day in Passamaquoddy Bay, and 50 feet in some nearby backwaters in New Brunswick. At the peak of the incoming tide, the water level can rise an inch a minute.

Sometimes it's nice to know that someone is standing guard at the end of the world. (Photo courtesy of Marty Berke)

Blueberries are a major export from this region. They're also good roadside treats. (Photo courtesy of Marty Berke)

I climb down a steep metal stairway that's bolted to the rocks and pick my way along the one dry pathway across boulders that are otherwise covered with thick seaweed. Then I cross a small gravel beach and boost myself up to another metal stairway that climbs the rocks to the promontory where the lighthouse sits.

This works only because the tide is low, so the gravel beach is dry. At high tide, this "beach" is a channel. And if you cross at exactly the wrong time, when the tide is just about to come in, then dawdle an hour, you can return to find it beneath five feet of water. At that point, the warning signs advise, you'll be waiting eight hours for the tide to go out so you can walk back to the mainland.

East Quoddy Head is certainly as striking as I imagined the end of the Earth to be, and its "you're on your own" warning signs definitely give it a sense of remoteness. But there are a few more tourists debating whether they should try to make it down the stairs than I expected to find at the end of the Earth.

Still, it's the kind of place where I could be tempted to spend a lifetime. Instead, I settle for an hour, then fire up the K-bike to resume rambling.

Wandering the side roads of Washington County gives me a good look at the major local export.

No, not lobsters. Blueberries.

The little village of Cherryfield calls itself the "Blueberry Capital of the World," and as I roll north on Maine Route 193, that looks like no idle claim. Visibility through the curves is unlimited, because the rolling hills on both sides of the road are covered with the splotchy green fuzz of low-bush blueberries, which grow no more than half a foot tall.

By some estimates, 85 percent of the blueberry crop grown in the United States each year comes from this part of Maine.

After several miles of this, I'm developing a serious hankering for a slice of blueberry pie. There's good news and bad news in that. At the end of Route 193, I have the option of turning east or west on Maine Route 9. Neither option leads me toward a lot of population or traffic (good) or restaurant-heavy zones (in this case, bad).

Maine Route 9 is a lot like U.S. 1, only without the lobster traps stacked in the front yards. But the views of lakes and wooded hillsides each time I cross another crest are as soul-soothing as the coastal landscapes are dramatic.

When my wanderings bring me back to Machias, I follow another narrow road that dead-ends at the sea after winding past weathered wooden buildings perched along a bay.

Just before the road ends, I turn left on a dirt lane marked with a large sign that says "Jasper Beach." Here, the sea has built a curving wall of stones six feet high.

The name's a misnomer. These volcanic stones, in purples, grays, and deep reds, aren't really jasper, but they have been polished like gems by the waves.

Aside from watching the tides, there's another form of entertainment at Jasper Beach. Locals arrive in pickup trucks and get a good running start on the narrow dirt lane, then plow into the wall of stones the size of golf and tennis balls. With proper momentum, they can climb high enough to gain a view of the ocean from the comfort of their truck cabs, which is apparently the goal of this exercise.

Jasper Beach is unlike any other beach I've visited, but I figure any place with pickup-truck ruts can't be the end of the Earth, so the K-bike and I roll on.

Trees, rocks, water, road: All the ingredients of a great ride.

A still and foggy morning in Cutler, Maine. Life's different Down East.

There are a few more must-see sights and must-ride roads on my Down East ramble, so I aim the BMW back inland, pausing momentarily at the spectacularly bucolic and impeccably named Meddybemps Lake. Then, just before the Canadian border, I swing right onto a small side road that splits the Moosehorn National Wildlife Refuge.

The refuge is a welcome stop for migrating birds and a nesting ground for bald eagles, which is why I'm here. Along the road, pairs of eagles have built their aeries on man-made wooden platforms perched atop tall poles. One pair has been nesting here annually since 1991.

South of Moosehorn, at the little crossroads of Pembroke, I begin searching for the strangest stop on this tour.

You know all those tourist-trap "mystery spots" where water allegedly runs uphill? Forget them. Right here in Maine is the real thing. It's called Reversing Falls. But be warned: It's not easy to find, and you can't get there on pavement.

After a few wrong turns, I spot a tiny sign pointing down Clarkside Road and carefully maneuver the big BMW along a mile and a half of dirt road. Eventually, I reach a park that's little more than a few waterside trails.

Here, in the shallows between Mahar's Point and Falls Island, you can actually see the tide rushing down over the rocks in one direction as it goes out, and then up over the same rocks when it comes back in.

It's not easy to find Reversing Falls, but if you do, you can honestly say you've seen water flow uphill.

East of Pembroke, I turn south onto Maine Route 190, a dead-end road that leads to the waterfront town of Eastport. Here, storefronts from the 1800s line the wharf at the center of town, which is also the edge of town, come to think of it.

Sardine canning was invented here in 1875, and spread up and down the coast. At one time, Eastport had 18 canneries running. Now, there's one.

Salmon farming in huge pens built in the bay has taken up some of the slack. Like other towns on the Maine coast, Eastport is also a popular spot for whale watching or viewing puffins. These birds, looking a little like tiny penguins wearing clown makeup, gather on offshore islands by the thousands to nest.

Despite these new sources of income, Eastport still has the feel of a town that's idling, not booming. Its population today is less than half what it was a century ago. There are plenty of free parking spaces for the BMW on the waterfront.

But there is activity here. It's just that most of it's on the water.

I find a perfect place to watch it by claiming an outdoor table at the waterfront WaCo Diner, where the fresh breeze off the bay and the beaming sun compete to cool and warm me.

Ferries ply Cobscook and Passamaquoddy Bays, connecting Eastport, Campobello, the New Brunswick mainland, and other points. Cars line up for the ferries on one side of the pier, while fishermen wrestle their catches from the water on the other side. Nothing moves too quickly.

Maybe, I think as I watch the ferries and fishermen, the feeling of being at the end of the Earth comes not from the place, but from the pace.

If I had the time, how long would I spend at East Quoddy Head, watching the tide cover and uncover my path back to the mainland? How many mornings would I reserve for watching eagles circle over the cove at Cutler? How many times would I watch Reversing Falls reverse?

These are the sorts of things I think about while sitting at a diner on the waterfront in Eastport, waiting without hurry for dinner.

This may not be the end of the Earth, but it is the end of the road, right there a few feet from my table. And right now, that feels just as good.

1 North Country Notches Loop

Text and photos by Marty Berke

DISTANCE *253 miles without side trips*

HIGHLIGHTS *Gentle hills of central New Hampshire, the highest point in the northeastern United States, the 45th parallel, and "Moose Alley"*

0.0 From White Lake State Park, in Tamworth, New Hampshire, turn left onto Route 16 north

15.0 In Conway, turn left to stay on Route 16 north

26.1 In Glen, bear right to stay on Route 16 north

28.4 At Jackson, turn right onto Route 16A (Jackson covered bridge)

29.0 Bear right onto Route 16B

30.6 Turn left to stay on Route 16B

32.2 Turn left to stay on Route 16B (Carter Notch Road)

34.3 Turn right onto Route 16A

34.7 Turn right onto Route 16 north

46.6 Mt. Washington Auto Road side trip or proceed on Route 16 north

54.4 In Gorham, turn left onto Route 16 north/Route 2

55.8 Turn left onto Route 2 west

72.8 Near Jefferson, turn right onto the North Road

79.9 In Lancaster, turn right onto Route 3 north

80.6 Bear right to stay on Route 3 north

129.3 In Pittsburg, turn right onto Route 145 south

147.4 In Colebrook, turn left onto Route 26 east

169.0 In Errol, turn right onto Route 16 south

204.8 In Gorham, turn right to stay on Route 16 south

253.3 Turn right into White Lake State Park

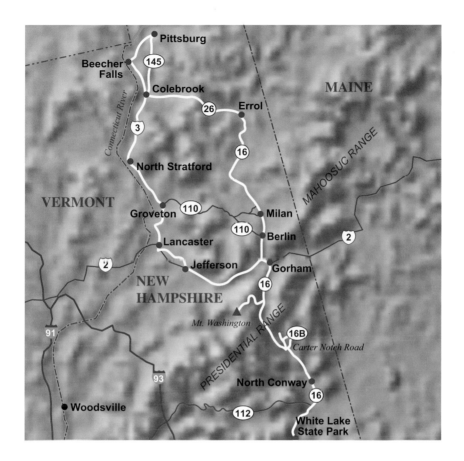

START OUT FROM White Lake State Park in Tamworth, New Hampshire, and head through North Conway on Route 16. In Glen, 26 miles north of base camp, turn right at the traffic light to remain on Route 16. Here you start to feel, not just see, the high country. Only 2.4 miles farther, turn right over the picturesque covered bridge to Jackson village. One-half mile beyond the bridge is the intersection of Routes 16A and 16B. Bear right onto Route 16B and ride up the steep hill following the Route 16B loop. You are heading into your first notch of the day, Carter Notch. The road climbs higher and higher past meadows and mountain views. Just before the Black Mountain ski area, turn sharply left to remain on Route 16B and begin your descent on the second half of the Carter Notch loop. After crossing a river at the intersection with the Carter Notch Road, turn left and return to your loop's start, the intersection of Routes 16A and 16B. You'll pass historic inns and scenic Jackson Falls as you complete the Carter Notch loop.

Turn right on Route 16A, returning to Route 16 and turn right, heading north. This section of road sweeps from side to side and climbs steadily into

MT. WASHINGTON AUTO ROAD

If you'd like to ride to the top of New England, the 16-mile round trip on the **Mt. Washington Auto Road** will set you back $8. (Passengers are extra.) I approached the toll booth with a mixture of apprehension and excitement. The ranger was just changing the weather board to up the wind gust velocity to 60 mph. I asked him what the story was. He said "Motorcycles are allowed up as long as the wind gusts stay below 65 mph."

It's only gusting to 60, averaging 35," said the ranger as I paid the toll, and received my THIS BIKE CLIMBED MT. WASHINGTON bike-sized bumper sticker. This was a good omen and confidence builder. The ranger thought I'd be successful!

The beginning of the route is simple enough: the road is paved, wooded on both sides, and immediately starts a steep climb. The signs on the descent

Your next stop is the home of the "world's worst weather:" Mount Washington. If it's doable (and they will tell you), go for it.

side of the road before each pulloff state "cool brakes frequently." The degree of climb will make you understand why 4-wheeled vehicles need to make frequent stops on the descent. The steed felt comfortable in second gear until I broke the tree line.

The road alternates between roadbed and pavement from the tree line to the summit. The switchbacks and vistas caused me to alternate between first and second gears for the second four miles of the eight-mile climb. It's probably better to do your rubbernecking on the way down with the views and road in front of you. I had a car a few hundred yards ahead of me and wanted to keep that buffer, not only for safety reasons, but to make my ride steadier for not having to adjust to the pace of the car.

When I reached the summit, I pulled up next to five more steeds. They seemed to stake out a comfortable parking zone. Everywhere I turned was a photo opportunity, and this was just the parking lot!

Climb the stairs to "Tip Top Hill." The structure on it, the "Tip Top House," was a hotel in 1853 when you could only get to the summit by climbing. The hotel failed, though, and the Tip Top House became the publishing offices of the *Among The Clouds* newspaper until 1915. The carriage road was completed in 1861 and the Mt. Washington Cog Railroad was completed in 1869. The railroad's

Ride to the Sky is a popular annual motorcycling event held at the Mt. Washington Auto Road. (Photo courtesy of the Mt. Washington Observatory)

coal-fired steam engine still climbs its 37-percent grade—the second steepest in the world—on daily trips out of Bretton Woods. Most of the track is laid on wooden trestles.

The descent was all I anticipated. First gear the whole way down; I hardly had to apply the brakes. You'll genuinely appreciate the ability to do the same. The air is often heavy with the stinging odor of cooking car brakes. The view is unrivaled and the ride deliciously slow. I recommend the trip if the weather cooperates, which happens only a few precious days a year.

the White Mountain National Forest. The Presidential Range, sometimes referred to as the "Ridgepole of New England," starts to loom larger and larger off to the west.

The drama builds as you enter Pinkham Notch (add it to your collection); the full mountain range is at your feet. Mt. Washington, the highest peak in the Northeast (elevation 6,288 feet), has some of the harshest weather in North America. In fact, the highest wind ever recorded was measured at 237 mph on the summit in the 1938 hurricane. There is plant life at the summit that only thrives in arctic conditions. And . . . you can get to the summit via the Mt. Washington Auto Road.

(See Side Trip to Mt. Washington Auto Road, page 44.)

Rejoining Route 16 north in your invigorated state, head for the northern reaches of the White Mountains. Because of its proximity to the Appalachian Trail and the Presidential Range, Gorham, at the junction of Routes 2 and 16, is popular with hikers, bikers, and outdoor sports people. Just eight miles north of the Mt. Washington Auto Road, you can choose from a variety of motels, campgrounds, small inns, and restaurants if you want to move home base farther north.

The Blessing of the Bikes at Colebrook is a yearly event in mid-June that draws a big cross-section of motorcyclists.

Turn left at the intersection by the Gorham village green where Route 2 joins Route 16. At the far end of the Gorham business district, turn left or west, staying on Route 2. Just ahead on the right is Jimtown Road to **Moose Brook State Park.** Open mid-May to mid-October, Moose Brook offers camping, fishing, hiking, swimming, and showers. If you do choose to move your base camp farther north, this would be a good choice. Route 2 heading west to Jefferson, is a wide, smooth two-laner with easy passing. Seventeen miles from Gorham, turn right, on the North Road. This is the first right turn after the junction of Route 116 and Route 2 on your left. This alternative to staying on Route 2 to Lancaster is more rural with less traffic and more twisties.

Relax to the sounds of Beaver Brook Falls. It's open to the public, and a good place to set up a picnic.

After seven miles on North Road, you will arrive in the town of Lancaster. This is home to the largest public event in the Great North Woods region of New Hampshire, the Lancaster Fair. Each Labor Day weekend for more than 130 years, folks have turned out at the Lancaster Fairgrounds for 65 acres of fun and food. If you timed it right, don't miss this classic New England fair. Turn right on Route 3 heading north. Route 3 is a truck route until you get above Colebrook; however, it does parallel the Connecticut River from Lancaster to its headwaters in West Stewartstown, providing valley scenery.

On Route 3, 35 miles north of Lancaster, is the **Shrine of Our Lady of Grace.** This is a large shrine depicting the birth of Christ. It is also the site of an annual blessing of motorcycle riders. Thousands of bikes gather here each year in the middle of June to be blessed. The White Mountain Riders Motorcycle Club is host to the annual gathering. This may be the only memorial to two-wheelers. It's the only one I've seen.

Return to Route 3 north after the shrine, and roll into beautiful downtown Colebrook. Eight miles north of town on Route 3, in the town of West Stewartstown, you'll find the **Spa Restaurant.** In continuous operation since 1927, this landmark has been serving excellent steaks and seafood to tourists and residents alike. Just north of the Spa is a steep hill. The top of this hill is marked as the 45th parallel (halfway between the North Pole and the equator.) You are really way up north now! Just nine miles more and you are in Pittsburg, the northernmost point on your ride. At 360 square miles, Pittsburg has the distinction of being the biggest town east of the Mississippi. If you haven't seen Bullwinkle or any of his brethren yet and want to, continue on Route 3 north past First Connecticut Lake. Locals call this road, **"Moose Alley."** Watch the marshy areas for moose, especially very early in the morning or at dusk. If you see parked cars, they are probably watching moose, or, as the locals say, "swamp donkeys."

Take a hard right on Route 145 south back to Colebrook. Route 145 is one of the top roller-coaster roads in New England. The first part of this 18-mile run back to Colebrook rises and falls so quickly in places that you'll feel like a fighter pilot fighting G forces! After that section, Route 145 settles into some fine twisties. Three miles before Route 145 ends back in Colebrook, it passes Beaver Brook Falls on your left. This gorgeous spot is open to the public for viewing the impressive falls, picnicking, and general relaxing. Once back in Colebrook, turn left onto Main Street (Route 3) for 150 yards then turn left onto Route 26 heading east. Get ready for Dixville Notch and The Balsams.

Route 26 climbs east, out of Colebrook. As it does, it begins to twist, following and sometimes crossing the Mohawk River. In sharp contrast to the natural beauty, you'll soon come upon a massive collection of used heavy equipment. This is Nash Equipment Sales. Fine pre-owned bulldozers, graders, tree harvesters—you name it, you can get one here. A bit under 12 miles down Route 26, you'll come to **The Balsams.**

The Balsams formal garden. (Photo courtesy of The Balsams Grand Resort Hotel)

This grand old New Hampshire resort is similar to the Mt. Washington Hotel and billed as the Switzerland of the U.S. Turn left just past Lake Gloriette and views of the tile-roofed resort to take the half-mile-long driveway to the hotel. I always pull in for something cold to drink, and a rest. I'd suggest it to be the final stop but $200 to $300 a day is as steep as Dixville Notch Road. The guests here are usually three generations deep; whole families come for a week at a time. The surroundings and environment are

The Great White Albino Moose at L.L. Cote Hardware.

something to relish. It is wonderful to stroll the grounds overlooking the lake and the Notch.

Late afternoon on the veranda (in season) can bring sumptuous hors d'oeuvres, like fresh strawberries and chocolate for dipping—no charge for guests, of course. The Balsams is a legend, which you can enjoy today.

When you hear the national election returns with reports that Dixville Notch has completed its voting ahead of the rest of the nation, this is where it has taken place. There's a special room in the hotel where the ballots are cast. It's worth a visit, as there are many interesting photos of political dignitaries.

Back out on Route 26, turn left to climb through Dixville Notch and ride the 12 miles to Errol. Just before town, check out Errol International Airport, with its tiny hangar. A solitary Cessna sat on the tarmac when I went by! The junction of Route 26 and Route 16 in Errol is a major crossroads for motorcyclists and outdoor enthusiasts of all kinds. In these parts, there aren't many places to buy fuel and food, so just about everyone stops in Errol. In summer, the **Northern Exposure Restaurant** is jammed with motorcyclists and hikers. In winter, packs of snowmobiles take over the entire town. Don't pass up your chance to see the stuffed albino moose and other fascinating taxidermy in the **L.L. Cote Hardware** store on Main Street. Turn right heading south on Route 16 from Errol. Here the road follows about every single bend in the

Androscoggin River, exposing pristine land, marsh, and riverbank. The only interruption is an occasional canoe or angler or moose in the river.

The 13 Mile Woods scenic area is a favorite with local bikers because of the turns, isolation, and remoteness. I chose to incorporate this run into the Northeast Loop. You are hardly disturbed traveling this 30-mile stretch of road from Errol except by your own imagination . . . until you reach Berlin (pronounced BER-lin). Just north of Berlin, is the town of Milan (pronounced MY-lun). As you approach the town line between these two northern hamlets, look to a steep hill on your right. The 170-foot steel frame of the Nansen Ski Jump looms high above the horizon. It hasn't been used in ages, but more than 40 years ago, stalwart ski jumpers soared high above the Androscoggin Valley on giant wooden skis!

Across the road from the jump is the **Nansen Wayside Park.** This 14-acre state park on the river is a great place to picnic, view the river, go fishing, or just relax. If you do stop at the park, be careful. The long gravel driveway can sometimes be a bit bumpy. Just in case you are ready to eat again, or maybe you'd like some ice cream, the **Northland Restaurant and Dairy Bar** is just three miles south of the ski jump and park. This eatery is very popular with the locals. It features a huge menu including their famous haddock dinners (poached or fried), buffalo burgers, a wide sandwich selection, six different

These signs are no joke. Moose are not quick animals, physically nor mentally.

soups each day, homemade desserts, and great ice cream creations, to boot! In summer months you'll often see many motorcycles sporting Canadian license plates parked out front.

Berlin is dominated physically, economically, and socially by its paper mill. The physical presence is awesome, yet incongruous with the mountains in the background. I saw the paper mill from Mt. Washington, although at the time I didn't realize what it was; it dominated the valley even from that perspective. It's the only work in town. Stay upwind if you can! Route 16 back to home base is a straight shot.

For more trips in this region see *Motorcycle Journeys Through New England* by Marty Berke, available from Whitehorse Press.

2 Northern Green Mountains Loop

Text and photos by Marty Berke

- **DISTANCE** *213 miles with options to shorten the distance*
- **HIGHLIGHTS** *Twisty roads, the most beautiful notch roads in the state, scenic vistas, and leisurely touring at its best*

0.0 Turn left onto Route 12 north when leaving Elmore State Park, in Lake Elmore, Vermont

2.6 Turn left onto Mt. Elmore Road and immediately turn right onto Washington Highway (Street)

4.2 In Morrisville, turn left onto Randolph Street

7.1 Continue straight across Childress Village Road

7.8 At intersection, turn right onto Randolph Road

10.6 Proceed to Route 100 south

13.6 At Stowe, turn right onto Route 108 north (Mountain Road)

30.8 At Jeffersonville, bear right at the traffic island onto Main Street to stay on Route 108 north

31.1 Proceed across Route 15. Stay on Route 108 north

31.5 Turn right onto Route 109 north

46.5 Turn right onto Route 118 south

53.1 At Eden, turn left onto Route 100 north

62.4 At Lowell, turn left onto Route 58 west

72.8 Turn right and then, across the bridge, immediately turn right again onto Route 242 east

84.4 At Jay, turn left onto Cross Road

85.9 Bear left onto Route 105 west

104.7 Bear right onto Berkshire Center Road (Route 118 north)

111.4 Proceed straight on Route 108 north

112.1 At East Franklin, turn left onto Route 120 west

112.7 Turn left to continue on Route 120 west

112.9 Where Routes 120 and 236 split, bear right to stay on Route 120 west

122.6 Proceed straight across Route 105 onto North Sheldon Road

123.6 Turn right onto Sheldon Road

126.1 Turn left onto Main Street; it becomes North Road

131.7 At Fairfield, proceed across Route 36 onto South Road; it becomes Fairfield Road, then becomes Cambridge Road, and then becomes Pumpkin Harbor Road

145.8 Near Cambridge, turn left onto Route 15 east

148.3 Turn left onto Route 108 north

167.5 At Enosburg Falls, turn right onto Route 105 east

173.6 At East Berkshire, turn right onto Route 118 south; the road passes through Montgomery Center and Belvedere Corners; stay on Route 118 south

195.6 At Eden, turn right onto Route 100 south

204.9 At Hyde Park, turn left onto Routes 100 south/15 east

208.0 Turn right to stay on Route 100 south

209.2 In Morrisville, turn left onto Route 12 south

212.9 Turn right into Elmore State Park

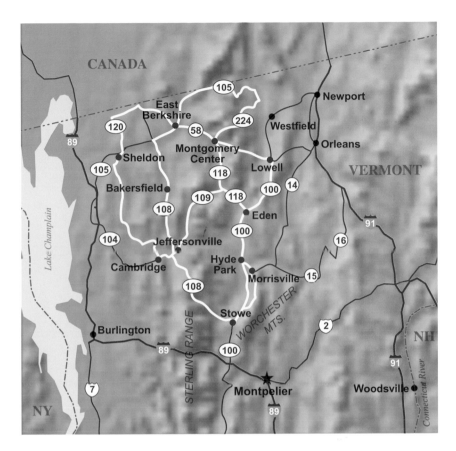

THIS VERMONT RIDE begins at **Elmore State Park** in Lake Elmore, Vermont, and heads north and around Mt. Elmore to Stowe by the back roads. Route 100 quickly brings you into the center of Stowe village and then up the Mountain Road where all the services one could expect of a town that advertises itself as the "Ski Capitol of the East" are to be found. Some of the best gourmet and specialty restaurants in Vermont will be found on Route 108 between the center of town and the ski slopes.

The riding fun begins once you pass the ski area and enter the Mt. Mansfield State Forest and begin to climb into **Smugglers Notch,** so named from the popular trail used to smuggle goods and livestock to Canada in defiance of Thomas Jefferson's Embargo Act of 1807. The road snakes around massive boulders that have fallen from the cliffs above and no matter how good a rider you might be, when you exit that last severely banked curve and reach the top of the Notch, you want to be in first or second gear and going about 10 mph. Pedestrians, hikers, and drivers rubbernecking at climbers scaling the cliffs, combined with blind corners flanked by solid rock and the narrowest paved highway in the state, make this a place to ride defensively.

Large boulders form part of the scenic landscape in Smugglers Notch and the road is forced to weave around and between them.

As you begin your descent on a hot summer day, slow down and stay to the right side of the road to catch a cold shower from the waterfall as you pass; conversely, on a freezing autumn morning stay close to the center lane to avoid black ice. The rest of the way to Jeffersonville is an easy and quick descent.

Route 109 is one of those highways the local riders try to keep secret. It's almost all curves and corners and if you don't get stuck behind a school bus or farm tractor it can be an exciting stretch of road. When you reach Route 118 you have two options: the most scenic is a 26-mile loop of which about 10 are gravel road; the other option is a quick eight-mile run on Route 118 north to Montgomery Center. If you're riding as a group this option allows anyone who doesn't wish to tackle the gravel road through Hazens Notch to wait for the rest over a cup of coffee and breakfast in Montgomery Center.

For the bold souls, it's a quick, scenic, and rather fun trip down Route 118 south to Route 100 north, then to the turn onto Route 58 west by the little green gazebo in the village of Lowell. Not as stupendous as Smugglers Notch and not as challenging a ride as the Appalachian Gap, Hazens Notch is the most northern, and perhaps the most scenic, road through the Green Mountains.

Besides, if you're going to boast about riding Vermont's famous gaps you don't want to answer no to the question, "Oh yeah, have you ridden over Hazens Notch?"

Now back down to Route 118 in Montgomery Center and at the southern end of Route 242 you're about to be let into another secret. The following—Routes 242 east, 105 west, and 118 south—form a loop around Jay Peak where Vermont and Quebec riders test their new Hayabusas, Ducatis, and Bahn-burners. This route offers some incredible views into Canada, but I suggest you either slow down and sightsee or keep your eyes to the pavement and boogie within the limit, of course. What an exciting run it is down the backside of Jay to Stevens Mill without a single house, driveway, or joining road to consider!

Instead of taking Route 118 south, bear left onto Berkshire Center Road (Route 118 north) and enjoy the narrow roads that interconnect these tiny rural villages. This agricultural area is just a couple miles from Canada; farm roads cross the border like it does not officially exist. After rounding the northern end of Lake Carmi, it's time to head south through the rolling countryside that lies between the Champlain Valley and the western edge of the Green Mountains.

The tiny village of Sheldon has the distinction of being part of the northernmost action of the Civil War. On October 19, 1864, a small group of 22 Confederate soldiers led by Bennett Young infiltrated St. Albans, robbed the bank of more than $200,000, shot and killed a local bystander, and torched the covered bridge in Sheldon to

A scenic view looking northeast toward Canada from Route 242.

This round barn on Route 12 in Elmore is one of only a handful surviving in Vermont. Vermont's unique 19th century barns are rapidly disappearing from the landscape.

cover their retreat. They escaped to Canada where they found official sanctuary.

The section of this tour from Fairfield to Cambridge on narrow, twisting town roads with almost no traffic offers the kind of touring I like best. This ends when reaching Route 15 in Cambridge. The modern bridge over the Lamoille River replaced the magnificent covered bridge that now graces the entrance to the Shelburne Museum on Route 7. But head east because **Jana's Cupboard** is only a couple of miles away.

Pristine lakes fill the valleys of the region and provide ample opportunities to clear your mind.

After picking up something to eat at Jana's Cupboard deli—and some pastries for a midnight snack—head west to the intersection of Routes 15 and 108. Those who feel that they've done enough riding for today can either head back through Smugglers Notch on Route 108 east or continue on Route 15 west to Morrisville (15.6 miles). But . . . if you want to add a

Watch out for moose in the Northeast Kingdom. Some of the townships in this region have more moose than people.

few more choice miles to your day, head north on Route 108. From Jeffersonville to Enosburg Falls is one of the best routes for viewing fall foliage in the northern part of the state. There are only a handful of round barns that have survived and you pass two of them: one on Route 108 and one on Route 12. Old-timers tell you that they were built round "so that the devil couldn't corner ya," but actually they were part of the great agricultural experimentation that occurred at the end of the 19th century. The circular shape was meant to be more efficient for milking and feeding the cows, but this design proved to be far more costly and much more difficult to heat than conventional rectangular barns.

Route 15 east brings you to Route 118, where riding south will let you experience the last of the Jay Peak loop. Retracing your path to Route 100, turn right and continue south to Morrisville. The **Charlmont Restaurant** is a good place for supper before logging the last five miles home to Elmore State Park.

Cliffs and curves make Route 108 through Smugglers Notch one of the most popular motorcycle roads in Vermont.

■ For more trips in this region see *Motorcycle Journeys Through New England* by Marty Berke, available from Whitehorse Press.

3 Higher Northern Gaps

Text and photos by Marty Berke

■ **DISTANCE** *199 miles*

■ **HIGHLIGHTS** *Hairpin corners, mountain passages on gravel roads, scenic vistas, and beautiful valley roads*

0.0 Turn left onto Route 53 south from Branbury State Park, in Salisbury, Vermont

5.8 Turn left onto Route 73 east

19.3 Turn left onto Route 100 north

20.5 At Rochester, turn right onto Bethel Mountain Road

30.9 Turn left onto Route 12 north

36.3 At Randolph, turn left onto Route 12A north

51.0 At Roxbury, turn left onto Warren Road

56.7 Turn left onto Plunkton Road, which becomes Brook Road; proceed into Warren

59.6 In Warren, turn right onto Main Street

59.9 Turn left onto Route 100, then . . .

60.7 Immediately turn right onto Lincoln Gap Road

71.9 At Rocky Dale, turn right onto combined Routes 116 north and 17 east

73.6 Turn right onto 17 east

89.3 In Irasville (Waitsfield), turn right onto 100 south

109.2 In Hancock, turn right onto Route 125 west

125.2 At East Middlebury, turn right onto Route 7 north

137.2 At New Haven Junction, turn right onto Route 17 east

145.3 At Rocky Dale, turn right onto Lincoln Gap Road

157.3 At Warren, turn left onto Route 100 north

162.8 At Irasville, turn left onto Route 17 west

178.5 Turn left onto combined Routes 17 west/116 south

181.2 Turn left onto Route 116 south

192.4 At East Middlebury, turn left onto Route 7 south

195.2 Turn left onto Route 53

198.7 Turn left into Branbury State Park

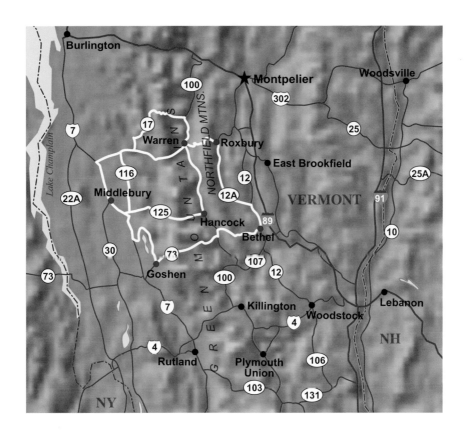

START OUT FROM the campground at Branbury State Park in Salisbury, Vermont, taking the 25-mile stretch of road east to Route 12. From Forest Dale, Route 73 climbs along the edge of the gorge formed by the Neshobe River to reach the top of Brandon Gap at 2,170 feet. On the eastern side of the gap, just below the crest, there's a turnoff facing the sheer cliffs on the south side of Mt. Horrid. In the early morning and late evening, you'll probably spot moose in the mud wallows of the pond, while during summer days you might catch a glimpse of peregrine falcons returning to their nesting sites on the cliff face. At the foot of the mountain, the highway makes a 90-degree turn; gravel on the road and an old concrete bridge should make one cautious of this corner.

After crossing the iron bridge over the Second Branch of the White River, turn left and ride into Rochester. Mountain Road begins at the northern end of the bucolic village green and the gas station on the corner would be a good place to top off your fuel tank.

Just a mile and a quarter up Rochester Mountain the road makes a 90-degree turn to the right and continues to climb. The east side, now called Camp Brook Road, is filled with twisty corners until it ends at Route 12.

The road over the Lincoln Gap is very much like roads found in the Apennine Mountains of Italy: narrow, steep, and beautiful.

Follow Route 12 into the village of Randolph, then onto Route 12A, which follows the Third Branch White River, to the small village of Roxbury. Roxbury Gap is one of the prettiest of the Green Mountain gaps, but it's used mostly by locals. These rural roads often change names depending on your direction. In that style, this road is known as Warren Mountain Road on the east side (because it runs west to Warren) and as the Roxbury Gap Road on the west side of the mountain. About a mile and a half from Roxbury it turns to packed gravel that tends to be washboarded in the corners. Just below the crest of the gap on the west side there's a narrow turnoff and a magnificent view of "The Valley." The Appalachian Gap (the lowest point in the range) can be easily identified by its communications tower. Short stretches of the road are paved to prevent it from being washed out, but be careful of gravel in the corners!

At the four-way intersection, take a left and follow Brook Road down to the village of Warren. Either bear left onto Flat Iron Road (it's a street) or turn left at the tiny traffic island in the center of the village. Turn right, dip down, and cross the recently restored covered bridge and up to Route 100. Diagonally across the main highway is the road that goes over Lincoln Gap to Lincoln and Bristol.

In the next 12 miles the road changes to packed gravel twice: a mile-long segment on the east side, and a mile-and-three-quarters section on the west. It reminds me of mountain roads in Europe. At the top of the gap I stopped at the parking area and hiked a portion of the Long Trail, the path that follows the spine of the Green Mountains for the entire length of the state. This is one of the most popular trailheads for weekend hikers; the long expanse to the multiple peaks within the Green Mountains is awesome.

After a long, beautiful descent, much of it along the New Haven River, the road junctions at combined Routes 116 and 17. The last three-tenths of a mile have been along the New Haven Gorge; the New Haven Falls (which swimmers can walk behind) is a popular swimming hole. Turning right, the highway, which runs on top of the Champlain Fault, marks the western boundary of the Green Mountain Range. The wistful feeling brought about by Lincoln Gap lingers until you make a right turn off Route 116 and continue on Route 17 on what is known as the McCullough Turnpike.

Route 17 is the most challenging 16-mile stretch of road in Vermont. Hairpin (and double hairpin) turns come up without signage—90-degree stuff without warning. The road climbs with alpine dexterity to and through the Appalachian Gap at 2,356 feet. More than a few bikes run the McCullough Turnpike on weekends. Using extreme caution, cross the road and park in the trailhead pulloff to enjoy the views to the west and perhaps to talk with other riders doing the same. The road down the eastern side also has dangerous S turns before *and* after passing the ski area. It's a road you will refer to whenever you play "Oh yeah, well have you ridden …"

(Note: Local riders make cautious inspection runs before aggressively tackling these corners. Later, this tour will bring you over the gap from east to west, so memorize the banking and placement of these corners.)

Route 100 at Irasville is just the road you need after the McCullough Turnpike's challenges. Like a racehorse cooling down after the run, it follows the Mad River to its source in the Granville Reservation, then along Alder Meadow Brook to Route 125. Be looking for a paved pulloff on the right as you begin your descent; park and walk past the first waterfall to the beautiful Moss Glen Falls.

Looking west from the crest of the Appalachian Gap with Route 17 visible below.

At the junction of Route 125 is located the **Old Hancock Hotel,** in which resides the **Vermont Home Bakery.** Three miles up Route 125 is a right-hand turn leading to Texas Falls, should you be inclined to take a break. The climb through this gap is leisurely with just a short stretch of twisting highway on the west side between Ripton and East Middlebury.

In East Middlebury, Route 125 merges with Route 7 north until reaching downtown Middlebury, where it divides and continues west to Crown Point. (See the Lake George Loop.) Route 7 takes you north to New Haven Junction, where a right turn onto 17 east and five miles of undulating highway lead into Bristol.

The view on Route 116 along the base of Lincoln Mountain seen while riding north toward Bristol.

The quaint appearance of Bristol might be recognized from the 1989 film *The Wizard of Loneliness,* which was set here in "Stebbinsville." It also has a legend of lost treasure said to be buried south of town on a mountainside known as Hell's Half Acre. According to the "Ballad of Old Pocock,"

The Appalachian Gap is plainly visible as the low point on the horizon as seen from the top of Roxbury Gap. In between lies what locals call simply "The Valley."

THE NORTHEAST

Bristol's original name, Simeon Coreser raised a large sum of money to finance his lost treasure diggings. His chief surveyor was his private occultist. His partners, it is told, actually found treasure but Coreser ripped them off with a "field of schemes." The legend of buried treasure lives on, but has yet to be found in Hell's Half Acre.

The Squirrel's Nest Restaurant, on Route 116/17 less than a mile outside of town, is a family-style restaurant where quantity is never debated. Try the sesame chicken or the Big Barrel Breakfast, depending on the time of day and your appetite.

Only four-tenths of a mile beyond the Squirrel's Nest is a right turn onto the road leading through Lincoln Gap, only this time you'll run the gaps in reverse, going west to east through Lincoln to Route 100 in Warren and east to west over the Appalachian

An honest road sign on the eastern side of Lincoln Gap.

Gap. After completing this 35-mile loop you'll ride past the Squirrel's Nest, through the village of Bristol, and to the four-way intersection on the west side of town. Bristol sits on what was the delta of the New Haven River where it entered the Champlain Sea a mere 10,000 years ago. As you ride down the hill you might catch a glimpse of the now distant Lake Champlain.

At the intersection, turn left and follow Route 116 south along the very edge of the Green Mountains to East Middlebury and, just over a half-mile farther, Route 7. This time, take Route 7 south, then Route 53 back to base.

■ For more trips in this region see *Motorcycle Journeys Through New England* by Marty Berke, available from Whitehorse Press.

4 Lake George Loop

Text and photos by Marty Berke

- **DISTANCE** *156 miles without side trips*
- **HIGHLIGHTS** *Scenic lake and mountain views, points of historic interest, nice stretches of highway for pure motorcycle riding pleasure*

0.0 Turn left exiting the Crown Point Campground, in Crown Point, New York

3.6 Turn left onto Routes 9N south/22 south

7.2 In Crown Point, bear to the left

14.9 Proceed straight on Route 9N south. (For a side trip to Fort Ticonderoga, turn left here onto Routes 74 east/22 south)

15.7 Bear to the right to proceed on Route 9N south. Proceed around the rotary, then turn right onto Montcalm west for side trip to Mt. Defiance and Fort Ticonderoga

52.7 In Lake George, bear left onto Canada Street (combined Routes 9N south and 9 south)

53.4 Proceed on combined Routes 9N and 9. (For an alternate route along the east side of Lake George, turn left here onto Lake Street toward the steamship docks and Route 9L)

54.6 Where Routes 9 and 9N split, proceed straight on Route 9 south

57.2 Turn left onto Route 149 east

64.7 Proceed straight through the intersection of Route 9L

72.0 In Fort Ann, turn right onto Routes 149 east/4 south

73.9 Where Routes 4 and 149 split, bear left and proceed on Route 149; *caution advised*

82.0 At Hartford, turn left onto Routes 149 east and 40 west

82.4 Turn right on Route 149 east

88.1 At South Granville, bear left to stay on Route 149 east

90.0 In Granville, turn left onto Routes 149 east/22 north. *Immediately* bear right to stay on Route 149 east

90.8 Bear right to stay on Route 149

92.9 Turn left onto Route 30

102.7 In Poultney, observe *caution* for a dangerous 90-degree left turn

102.9 Turn right and proceed on Route 30

138.9 At Middlebury, turn left onto Route 125 west

147.3 At Bridport, turn right onto Routes 125 west and 22A north

147.7 Turn left on Route 125 west

155.3 Proceed straight when Route 125 junctions at Route 17

156.2 Turn left into the Crown Point campground

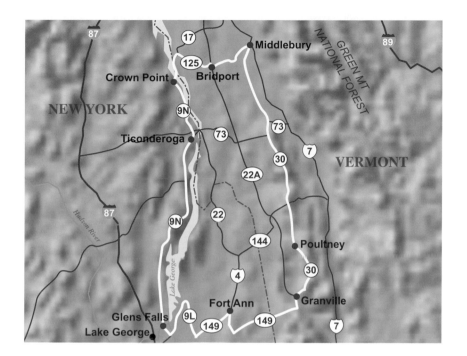

THE RUN FROM the site of the Crown Point fortifications, in Crown Point, New York, to that of the more famous **Fort Ticonderoga** is a quick 15-mile ride south on Routes 9N and 22. "Fort Ti" is a must for all Revolutionary War buffs and offers expansive views of Lake Champlain. The easiest way to reach the fort is by turning left at the intersection of Route 74 and following it west; the entrance is well marked. But to truly understand its strategic importance one must first visit Mt. Defiance. At the small rotary, make a 180-degree turn and follow Montcalm west into the center of downtown Ticonderoga, then a right onto Champlain Street and the next left (well marked) leading to the Mt. Defiance Toll Road. From the summit at 853 feet you can look down on the fortifications and enjoy spectacular views of the lakes. With its guns facing down on Fort Ticonderoga, you get a feeling for the historic battles that took place here.

South of Ticonderoga the road gets a little twisty as you approach Hague and receive your first views of Lake George. The road dips down to some vicious curves on the very edge of the lake as you enter the village proper. Exactly six miles beyond the junction of Route 8 in Hague are two turnoffs along the lake. *Stop.* These are the best vantage points for photo ops on this loop.

Immediately beyond the turnoffs the road heads away from the lake and twists and turns as it climbs into the Tongue Mountain Range. For the next nine miles Route 9N becomes motorcycle heaven as it runs through the wilderness, offering one of the best rides in the region.

Bolton Landing can be a busy little town during the height of the tourist season, but because of this it offers a wide variety of places to eat. Try a late morning breakfast at **Bolton Beans** or **Frank's Breakfast and Lunch** or wait until reaching Lake George. There are plenty of places to eat in the next 11 miles and your choice may be dictated as much by traffic as any other factor.

The village of Lake George is touristy with all the trappings, not that you mind getting trapped now and then. In early June the **Americade** touring rally draws 50,000 motorcyclists to a village that has a winter population of less than 500 residents and you really have to experience it to visualize this village packed with bikes of all descriptions. A different mode of seeing the town and lakeshore is by steamship out of the harbor. Opposite the steamship docks is Fort Henry which protected the southern end of the lake.

On the southern end of the village Route 9N heads west, but you want to continue straight on Route 9 for another 2.5 miles to the junction of Route 149. **The Great Escape Fun Park** is the largest amusement park in New York, with more than 100 rides and attractions. Although this park is listed as being in Lake George, you actually have to continue south on Route 9 almost to Glens Falls to find it. Once on Route 149, you'll be happy to bring your steed up to a comfortable 55 mph once again.

South of the village of Fort Ann, Route 149 crosses the Champlain Canal and the open landscape with undulating hills becomes an enjoyable ride with plenty of tight corners lurking just behind the next slight rise. Beyond Fort Ann, where Routes 4 and 149 split, exercise great caution as you make the left onto Route 149, since northbound traffic on Route 4 is fast and your visibility to that traffic is poor. In Granville you might notice that almost every building has a slate shingled roof. This is the heart of the "slate belt" where quarries produce the gray, green, purple, and red sedimentary stone that was traditionally used for roofing slate, but which now finds more use as floor and patio tiles. You'll notice piles of waste rock and the giant boom cranes of Douglas fir positioned over active quarries from here to Castleton, Vermont.

Riding north on Route 30, the highway gets squeezed between Lake St. Catherine and St. Catherine Mountain—the western edge of the Taconic Mountains—before winding into the town of Poultney. Then it's a straight

Old forts can be fascinating to explore and watch come back to life. (Photo courtesy of Fort Ticonderoga Museum)

Bolton Beans restaurant is popular among riders cruising through Bolton Landing.

shot north along the shore of Lake Bomoseen and then along the Champlain Valley, which offers dramatic views of the Adirondacks on your left and the Green Mountains on your right. Rubbernecking is allowed because Route 30 is a smooth and easy ride the rest of the way to Middlebury.

Most places have their own local lore and Lake Bomoseen is no exception. In the middle of the lake you might notice a small island, Neshobe, which used to be a popular summer retreat for Hollywood celebrities during the 1930s and 1940s. Legend has it that one of these residents finally got tired of the auto-graph seekers trespassing on the island and one day when a boat load of these tourists disembarked Harpo Marx was lying in ambush. When they were close enough he charged from the underbrush screaming, naked, and painted blue from head to toe. This solved the problem for the rest of the season.

Middlebury is a college town with all the associated food, drink, and rest-ing places. **Woody's** is a place to get some good food and see a lively cross-section of the town's residents. If you're into live steeds (if you brought this book I assume you are already into the iron variety), the University of Ver-mont's famous Morgan Horse farm is just five miles north of Middlebury in Weybridge. (If you take Route 23 to Weybridge, just continue to Route 17 and then turn west to return to the Crown Point campsite.) Route 125 heads west across the undulating Champlain Valley, briefly joining Route 22A, be-fore bringing you back to the Champlain Bridge and hence to home base on the other side.

■ For more trips in this region see *Motorcycle Journeys Through New England* by Marty Berke, available from Whitehorse Press.

5 Northern Berkshire Loop

Text and photos by Marty Berke

- **DISTANCE** *182 miles*
- **HIGHLIGHTS** *Plenty of tight curves, a climb to the summit of the highest mountain in Massachusetts, and a Bridge of Flowers*

0.0 From the intersection of Main Street (Route 7A) and Walker Street (Route 183) in Lee, Massachusetts, proceed east on Walker Street

0.2 Bear left to stay on Route 183 east

1.0 Bear right onto Lee Road

1.2 Turn right onto Route 7 south and immediately bear left onto Route 20 east

17.6 Near Becket Center, turn left onto Route 8 north

36.5 At Dalton, turn right onto Route 9 east

59.4 At Goshen, turn left onto Route 112 north

92.8 At Jacksonville, Vermont, bear right onto Route 100 north

99.5 Near Wilmington, bear left to continue on Route 9 west

129.1 Beyond Hoosick, New York, turn left onto Route 22 south

136.7 At Petersburg, New York, turn left onto Route 2 east

146.3 Near Williamstown, turn left onto Routes 2 east/7 north

148.5 In Williamstown, bear right and continue on Route 2 east

152.8 Near North Adams, turn right onto Notch Road

160.6 Turn right onto Rockwell Road, OR turn left to proceed to the summit parking lots

168.2 In Lanesborough, bear right onto Greylock Road

168.6 Turn left onto North Main Street

169.4 Turn right onto Route 7 south

181.5 Bear right onto Route 7A south

182.8 End loop in downtown Lenox

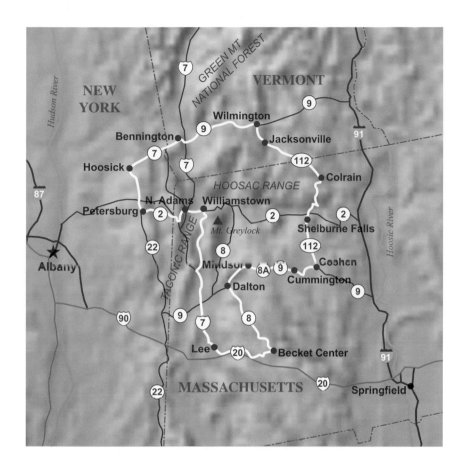

THE BEGINNING OF this loop goes through the busy town of Lee, Massachusetts, then Route 20 loops back and forth across I-90 (Mass Pike) four times before reaching Bonny Rigg Corners. Route 8 north follows the west branch of the Westfield River and has lots of enjoyable twists and turns. If you aren't awake by now, these roads are eye-openers.

In the village of Dalton, just past Center Pond, the right turn is marked as Route 8A and Route 9. This is one of the major roads in the region (leading west to Pittsfield) and traffic can be heavy at times. Routes 8A and 9 divide in Windsor and in just a few miles, Route 9 becomes an enjoyable ride with plenty of swooping turns.

Route 112 is a pleasant but tame road all the way to Shelburne Falls. The center of this old mill town can be circumvented by way of a loop onto Route 2 and back onto the old Route 112 on the north edge of the village. The **Bridge of Flowers,** the old concrete railway bridge over the Deerfield River, is a unique garden spanning the river that attracts tens of thousands of visitors each year. The easiest way to reach it is to follow the bypass loop, but upon

The Bridge of Flowers is a good example of what happens when you leave your bridge lying around in Shelburne Falls. Keep 'em close. The florists are ruthless. (Matthew Cavanaugh photo courtesy of Shelburne Falls Area Business Association)

reaching Route 112 again, turn left. You can either turn right onto Cross Street (you'll see signs) or onto Main Street. On Main Street you'll see the Bridge of Flowers on your right as you cross the steel suspension bridge and can easily find parking on this side of the river. There are several restaurants in the downtown area, so, depending upon timing you might wish to enjoy an early lunch or snack here, or you could wait until you reach Wilmington or Bennington.

North of Shelburne Falls, Route 112 turns into one of the most popular motorcycling roads in New England. Since it connects with the famous Route 100 in Vermont, you'll have plenty of two-wheeled company on weekends. There are two steel suspension bridges with open-grate flooring that cross the East Branch North River on this route. The first is just north of Colrain and the second six-and-a-half miles farther; caution is advised for both of them. Route 112 passes by the North River Winery, then, four-tenths of a mile farther, junctions at Route 100 in the tiny village of Jacksonville.

The next five-and-a-half miles is a delight as the highway twists and turns through mostly forest as it climbs to Wilmington. If you are riding on a weekend be especially careful of traffic due to the large flea market located where Route 100 merges with Route 9 just east of Wilmington.

Wilmington is a popular village and with the local ski areas—Haystack, Mt. Snow, and even Stratton—offering summer events like world championship mountain biking competition and major concert series featuring top names, it can be a very busy place. **Dot's Restaurant,** adjacent to the small concrete bridge, is the place to stop for a late breakfast or gooood four-alarm chili (five alarms being the max). The chef has won a couple of Vermont state ribbons.

Bennington boasts a bountiful history. (Nicholas Whitman photo courtesy of the Bennington Museum)

Route 9 still offers a few sections filled with exciting curves, especially just west of Wilmington, but since it is a major commercial highway, each year it seems that another corner gets straightened and there are miles of road where you can make very good time. Panoramic vistas and lower gear riding await you on the west side of the mountain range as you drop over 1,400 feet in elevation in the 10 miles from Woodward to Bennington, including a three-mile stretch where signs recommend a truck speed of five mph.

Who says you can't find sophisticated culture north of Boston? (Photo courtesy of the Clark Art Institute)

Bennington is the second-oldest settled township in Vermont, famous for its red clay pottery and Bennington College. The Sunoco gas station on Main Street is owned by **Hemmings Motor News** and you'll find some very interesting items for sale in its double bays; the musuem is located next door. The famous **Bennington Museum** is only four-tenths of a mile beyond the Sunoco gas station. A major collection of Grandma Moses paintings, Bennington pottery, and one of the major genealogical archives in the East are located here. Two-tenths

Hemmings Sunoco is a pit stop to linger at. Check out the motorcycle and automotive memorabilia, books, and gifts. The museum next door is a recommended tour.

The summit of Mount Greylock is a popular motorcycle destination. The ride up to the summit proves the adage that it's the journey, not just the destination, that counts.

The Memorial Tower on the summit of Mount Greylock, the highest mountain in Massachusetts. (Kindra Clineff photo courtesy of the Berkshire Visitors Bureau, DEM)

of a mile farther is the right turn leading up to the Bennington Battle Monument. Although this battle, which was the turning point in the Revolutionary War, was actually fought in Hoosick, New York, the 306-foot tall monument was erected at the site of the storehouse that the British sought to capture. Most of the buildings in Old Bennington date to the end of the 18th century, and while George Washington never slept here, Thomas Jefferson and James Madison are among the notables who frequented the Walloomsac Inn (now a private residence). Behind the Old First Church, a well-marked path leads through the Old Burying Grounds to the gravesite of poet laureate Robert Frost.

Vermont Route 9 turns into New York Route 7, then Route 22 follows the western side of the Hoosac Range to Route 2. When the traffic isn't heavy on this road, the six-mile climb through the pass and the 3.8-mile twisting descent into Massachusetts is a delight.

Route 7 north leads to the intersection of Route 2 at the **Clark Art Institute** in beautiful Williamstown. The small downtown area has become completely encircled by the ever-expanding campus of Williams College. I suggest checking your fuel levels while on Route 2 and consider topping off your tank before continuing through the wilderness area of **Mt. Greylock.**

After crossing the Hoosic River for the second time, you'll want to take your second right turn. This is a residential street leading to Notch Road. The terrible condition of Notch Road is notorious, but local residents prefer to leave it neglected to reduce traffic speed. Upon entering the reservation,

It's like riding through a calendar. Foliage in New England can be breathtaking. (Kindra Clineff photo courtesy of the Berkshire Visitors Bureau)

the road narrows and resembles those in European alpine regions. It's first and second gear as you twist through the forest, climbing the shoulder of Mt. Greylock; beware of the deep trenches designed to channel water across the pavement! The top of the mountain at 3,491 feet is the highest peak in Massachusetts. Park and climb to the top of Memorial Tower for a spectacular 360-degree panoramic view. If you need to stretch your legs I suggest a stroll along a portion of the Appalachian Trail, which passes within a few yards of the tower. Despite the rough roads, this is one of the most popular motorcycle destinations in western Massachusetts, so expect plenty of company on any fine touring day, especially during the descent on Rockwell Road. (Note: Don't bear right on the first Greylock Road you encounter; wait until Rockwell Road ends at the second intersection of the same name.)

The farther south you go on Route 7, the straighter and more commercial the road gets. Once you pass through the town of Pittsfield, after running along the shore of Pontoosuc Lake, it's a short run into the village of Lenox.

■ For more trips in this region see *Motorcycle Journeys Through New England* by Marty Berke, available from Whitehorse Press.

6 Bay Loop

Text and photos by Marty Berke

■ **DISTANCE** *174 miles*

■ **HIGHLIGHTS** *Hundreds of miles of scenic coastline, great beaches, famous fishing ports, museums at every turn, and fabulous Newport*

0.0 Exit Burlingame State Park, in Charlestown, RI, on the access road and turn left on R.I. Route 1 north

14.1 Exit "Narragansett/Point Judith" and turn right on Route 108 south to Point Judith

18.3 Turn left on Route 108 north to Ocean Road, Narragansett

23.2 Bear right as Ocean Road merges with Route 1A north at Narragansett

30.5 Turn *left* onto entrance ramp to Route 138 east to cross bridges at Newport

37.5 Take first exit after Newport Bridge at SCENIC NEWPORT sign

37.6 Bear right onto Thames Street when the sign for Memorial Boulevard and Route 138 indicates a left

40.4 Turn left onto Ocean Drive until it connects with Bellevue Ave at Bailey's Beach

41.2 Turn left onto Bellevue Avenue

43.1 Turn right onto Memorial Boulevard

44.5 Bear left onto Route 138A north which merges with Route 138 north/138 east (signs inconsistent)

58.5 Bear left on Route 24 north

62.5 Exit NORTH TIVERTON and turn left onto Route 138 north

68.8 Exit right at DAVOL STREET and double-back on water side to Battleship Cove

69.8 Exit Battleship Cove, turn left onto Route 138 north, right onto I-195 east

82.9 Take Exit 15 DOWNTOWN NEW BEDFORD onto Route 18 south and follow brown signs to parking for the Whaling Museum at Elm Street Garage

84.4 Exit right from garage on Elm Street for 2 ½ blocks, turn right on Pleasant Street to rotary and exit west on Mill Street which is Route 6 west

90.7 Turn left on Route 177 west

92.6 Turn left on Route 88 south to Horseneck Beach

101.2 Turn left at water and follow shore road to South Westport

108.9 Turn left on Hixbridge Road, cross Route 88, right at T, left at Westport Lobster Co. to Adamsville

113.6 Turn right onto Route 179 west

117.1 Turn right onto Route 77 north

124.6 Turn left onto Route 24 south/138 south which becomes Route 114 south

129.1 Continue on Route 114 south which becomes Route 138 west

145.8 Exit right from Route 138 west after bridge onto Route 1A south

157.0 At light at Narragansett, turn right on Narragansett Ave to Route 1 south

158.4 Turn left onto Route 1 south

174.2 Exit Burlingame State Park Campground to home base

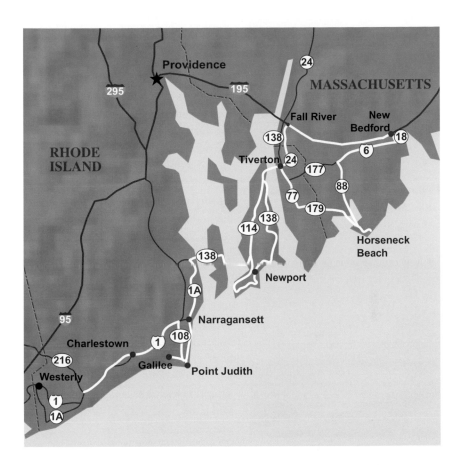

THIS LOOP THROUGH Rhode Island and Massachusetts can easily take two to three days depending on how much beach, culture, and sightseeing you want to do. This is an extensive trip, although the mileage is short. The Bay Loop passes the most beautiful beaches and breathtaking shoreline in New England. Many of the oldest shipping ports in the nation are along the way.

From the late 1800s to the mid-1900s, some of the wealthiest people in the world chose Newport and its surroundings to live in. They built mansions on the cliffs above the sea that rival the palaces of European royalty, and many are open to tour and enjoy.

Narragansett Bay is still the summer playground for the rich, but more modest folk can play here, too. And you will want to get off the bike and explore the many unique attractions this area has to offer. Water sports abound and this may be the perfect time to take a whale watch cruise or a hike on the famous Cliff Walk. Parking is plentiful and on average, safe.

The first things you notice while riding on Route 1 east and north from the home base at Burlingame State Park, in Charlestown, Rhode Island, (the

This is the Casino Arch on Ocean Road in Narragansett, Rhode Island.

Want lunch with a view? Try the Coast Guard Restaurant on Ocean Road in Narragansett.

highway department is inconsistent in their signage) are the exit signs on the way to Narragansett. Every one of the signs names a beach: Charlestown Beach Road, Moonstruck Beach Road, Matunuck Beach Road, and just for variety, a sign for the Theater by the Sea. All within 10 miles of where you first got on the road.

Route 108 south, off of Route 1, is a four-lane undivided highway. If you have the time and decide to go to **Block Island,** take Galilee Road just beyond Fisherman's Memorial State Park. This takes you into Galilee, where the Block Island Ferry docks. Just 12 miles off the coast and called by some "one of the last great places on earth," it's very much worth the brief ride. There is a bustling harbor with shops and beautifully restored Victorian-era inns and houses, a bird sanctuary, and acres of beautiful pristine open space to enjoy. You can take your motorcycle on the ferry if you want, but you may prefer a break from the saddle. Bicycles are for rent on the island and the walking is superb.

Continuing south on Route 108, you arrive at **Point Judith Light.** The lighthouse itself is a mile down the road to the right after you see the water and is now a Coast Guard station not accessible to the public. The last German U-Boat sunk in World War II was two miles off this point.

When you retrace your steps from the lighthouse, continue straight on Ocean Road rather than turning left onto Route 108. Over the next eight miles of winding road hugging the sea, you'll pass eight beaches and some wonderful early summer houses. Scarborough State Beach is a surfing beach, so there's plenty of action at the sea and on the shore for us buoys and gulls who are young or young at heart.

Farther up the road is the town of Narragansett and its even more active beaches. If you're interested, check to see if they still give free surfing lessons on Wednesdays at noon. But watch the conditions. The last time I was through, a Nor'easter was on its way and the surf was blowing over the seawall leaving the road covered in a foot of foam. For me, the best features of Narragansett town beach are the so-close-at-hand establishments serving cold refreshments. **The Coast Guard Restaurant** has a nice observation deck for the scenery.

Narragansett was (and is) an elegant summer resort. In the late 1800s, rich Newporters would ferry across the bay to partake of the entertainment offered by the Narragansett Casino, a country club by today's definition. A fire destroyed the casino in 1900. All that's left is the dramatic stone arch and towers over Ocean Road.

Route 1A north intersects with Route 138 about eight miles up. Follow signs east to Newport and Jamestown Bridge. The Jamestown Bridge and the Newport Bridge on the other side of Conanicut Island offer spectacular views of Narragansett Bay.

Back on Route 138 east, cross the Newport Bridge ($2 toll) from Jamestown to Newport. Keep one eye on the bridge traffic, but check out the harbor and the yachts as you cross. Welcome to the land of the rich and the tourists!

Mansions of yesterday dot the Newport, Rhode Island, coastline. Many are available for tours. (Photo courtesy of the Newport, RI Convention & Vistors Bureau)

Despite the huge estates and quaint shops, Newport is still a working harbor. (Photo courtesy of the Newport, RI Convention & Vistors Bureau)

Newport's grand history makes for a grand visit. (Andrea Carneiro photo courtesy of The Preservation Society of Newport County)

Just one of the many homes that will blow your mind. (Richard Cheek photo courtesy of The Preservation Society of Newport County)

You will have to put up with traffic in the town of Newport as it is a popular destination resort, especially in the warm months.

Just as you enter the wharf area, you'll spot the **Newport Transportation and Visitors Center** that will be on your right, an invaluable resource for accommodations, sightseeing, and events if you plan to stay a day or two. Downtown hotels, inns, and B&Bs are pricey but if you want to treat yourself, this may be the time to splurge.

The **Newport Harbor Hotel and Marina** will cost you close to $200 per night, but the rooms are first class and overlook the boats in the beautiful harbor. The hotel even provides binoculars on your window sill for a close-up look.

If you're watching your budget but still want to stay overnight, head for one of the more modest motels on the outskirts of town, or ask for a recommendation in your price range at the Visitors Center. There's something for every pocketbook here.

Fine eating places abound but you might want to try the **Red Parrot Restaurant** on the corner of Thames Street and Memorial Boulevard and a short walk from The Newport Harbor Hotel and Marina. They advertise "hot" desserts and "cool" jazz, along with fresh seafood, creative pasta, and unique appetizers. Get a window seat and you can check out the passing sidewalk scene, which is always pretty colorful on busy Thames Street. For breakfast, the locals go to **Franklin Spa,** a short walk up the hill on Spring Street for grease and gab.

CONANICUT ISLAND

The Jamestown Bridge deposits you onto Conanicut Island, as serene and sophisticated as its more famous neighbor, Newport. If you stay straight on East Shore Road, rather than following Route 138, you will arrive in the village of Jamestown. Park in the lot at the harbor and have a cup of award-winning coffee and pastry at **East Ferry Market & Deli** out on the patio overlooking the bay.

Facing the water from your patio perch, take the road in front of you to the right, following the shoreline to Fort Wetherill State Park, once a shore artillery battery. Picnic tables and the usual day-tripper facilities are available from Memorial Day to Labor Day. The park itself remains open all year. This is a favorite spot among scuba divers.

Exiting the park, take your first paved left, Hamilton St., which is flanked by some pretty spectacular new homes. At the next intersection, go straight ahead; a small town beach will be on your left. Go across the isthmus. On the right, just at the end of the isthmus, is the entrance to Fort Getty State Park, a seaside campground sitting on a small knoll, with a magnificent view, overlooking the mouth of Narragansett Bay. Even though it is usually full during camping season, it's worth a drive through.

Bear left onto Beaver Tail Road just after the Fort Getty entrance to get to **Beavertail Lighthouse State Park.** The lighthouse is the third oldest in the country, built in 1749 after the Boston Light (1716) and the Brant Point Light (1746) on Nantucket. The museum inside commemorates the lighthouses of Rhode Island and their keepers.

You can either retrace your trip back to Route 138 or take Southwest Avenue to North Main Street to the bridge. The latter route lets you check out the **Jamestown Windmill,** which is right beside the road just before you reach Route 138. It's interesting to see anytime but you can learn how it works when the windmill itself is open to visitors on Saturdays and Sundays, 1 p.m. to 4 p.m., from mid-June to mid-September.

The Jamestown windmill can be toured on summer weekends.

It's hard to miss George's Family Restaurant and his great homemade root beer in Fall River, Massachusetts.

For a quick coffee stop and some local chatter, try the Sip-N-Dip Donuts Drive Thru in Fall River, Massachusetts.

To get to the famous **Ten Mile Drive,** take a right onto Wellington Avenue as you circumnavigate the harbor. This is a spectacular scenic ride along the coast, past all the humble abodes of the more fortunate. Two outstanding examples are the Hammersmith Farm and the Inn at Castle Hill.

The Hammersmith Farm, also known as "the Summer White House," was Jackie Kennedy Onassis' mother's (Mrs. Hugh Auchincloss) summer home. Jackie had her debut and her wedding reception with JFK here. The 50 acres of farmland by the sea make up the only working farm in Newport. Scenes from *The Great Gatsby,* with Robert Redford, were filmed here.

The **Inn at Castle Hill** just down the road (watch for signs since you can't see it from the road) offers a panoramic view of the bay. Watch the great ships entering and leaving the harbor while you sit on the patio enjoying something cold to drink, then walk to the cliff's edge to see Castle Hill Light.

Back on the Ten Mile Drive, you will shadow the ocean's edge until you reach Bellevue Avenue. This is where the **Great Mansions of Newport** were (Vander)built in pre-income-tax America. You can tour them (it takes a good day or two to do all 10 properties that are now open to the public). If your schedule is tight, choose just one, and make it **The Breakers,** Cornelius Vanderbilt II's opulent 70-room Italian Renaissance palace where balconies and terraces overlook a spectacular view of the Atlantic Ocean. The furnishings, most made expressly for the house, are all original. The tour takes about an hour and tickets ($15 for adults) can be purchased at the gatehouse.

If you are just passing through, take a minute to drive into a few of the entrances (I hesitate to call them driveways) and get a feel for the grandeur of these elegant "summer homes." It's amazing to think that some of them were used by their owners for only a few weeks of the year. Others, like the Vanderbilt family, stayed all summer with Cornelius commuting on weekends by steamer from New York City. Imagine your arrival as a guest, then play it out: at the Astor's Beechwood Mansion, the Beechwood Theatrical Group welcomes your arrival as if you were one of the original "Newport 400" arriving for the season in the 1890s.

Once your "coming out" party is over, rejoin Memorial Boulevard and merge with Route 138 north. Pass through Tiverton, Rhode Island, and head straight for Fall River, Massachusetts, on Route 24 north. Just after the Rhode Island border, on Route 138 in Massachusetts and on the left, is the un-miss-able **George's Root Beer,** a

PT 796 is a Higgins-class PT boat, and a National Historic Landmark. (Photo courtesy of Battleship Cove)

white and blue building with bright yellow sandwich boards out front advertising $2–$4 dinners. George makes his own root beer, and it is delicious.

If it's too early for a cold one, three blocks farther on is the **Sip-N-Dip Donuts Drive Thru,** another not-to-be-missed "original," with homemade donuts and the owner's daughter-in-law, Lucy, at the window. They open at 4:30 a.m. and don't close until 11:00 p.m. I can't guarantee that Lucy works 24/7, although she is the type who just might!

Follow the road signs to **Battleship Cove,** "the world's largest collection of historic naval ships," and Fall River Heritage State Park. You will see the battleships in the cove to your left just after Route 138 north goes under I-195. Route 138 north is elevated at this point so it's quite a view. Exit

An aerial shot of the USS Kennedy and her berthmates. (Photo courtesy of Battleship Cove)

right at Davol Street and double back on the water side to park for free and walk around the cove to the ships. The USS Massachusetts, affectionately called "Big Mamie" by her crew, is more than 200 yards long. You can tour the entire ship, climb inside the turrets, and aim the anti-aircraft guns on the main deck. You can also patrol a PT boat, a destroyer, a submarine, and the Hiddensee, the only Russian missile corvette on display in the world.

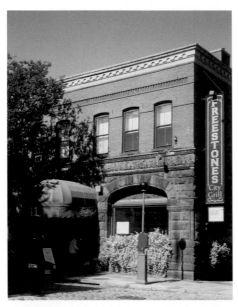

New Bedford's Historic District has cobblestone streets and gorgeous architecture.

The **Marine Museum** down the street has an excellent exhibition focused on the Titanic, including a video of her rediscovery and a 28-foot replica. There's also a Railroad Museum and the magnificent old wooden carousel from the Lincoln Amusement Park to explore, so leave a good part of the day free to do it all. The **Waterstreet Café** is just across the street and a good choice for a light snack or a full meal.

Before exiting **Fall River Heritage State Park,** check out the little museum there too. It has a small theater and rotating exhibits depicting the rich ethnic history of the people who came to Fall River and made it their home. From the 1840s to the 1920s, waves of immigrants predominantly from England, Ireland, Canada, Portugal, and Poland came to work in the textile mills and the shipping yards. The city was believed to have the largest percentage of foreign-born people of any major American population center, and their cultural pride still exists today.

Follow signs to Interstate Route 195 and go east to Exit 15, DOWNTOWN NEW BEDFORD, and Route 18 south. Watch for the brown whale signs to the NEW BEDFORD WHALING NATIONAL HISTORIC PARK, which will

At the New Bedford Whaling Museum you'll have a chance to see the big ones that didn't get away.

The widows watch on this typical shore home lets you see over the high dunes and out to the sea.

direct you to exit onto Elm Street. Because New Bedford still has cobblestone streets in the Historic District, which does nothing for traction, especially if wet, I recommend you park in the Elm Street garage ($3–$4) and walk the three blocks to the museum itself.

The **New Bedford Whaling Museum** is devoted to American whaling, with a multi-media approach to this period of history. There are paintings, artifacts, harpoons, whale skeletons, murals, and an 85-foot exact half-scale model built in 1916 of the whaling ship *Lagoda*. You can shiver your own timbers onboard—it's as though you climbed into one of those "ship in the bottle" models!

On my last trip through, the theater was showing a fascinating movie on the

Seamen's Bethel was an inspiration for Herman Melville and his classic Moby Dick.

Small is large and large is humongous at Brickley's where they make the ice cream in back, so you can drop it down your front.

It looks like you can do pretty much whatever you want between November and April at the Westport Town Beach.

rich history of the area called *The City That Lit the World,* which among other things, included a re-enactment of a whaling expedition. For the real thing, check out the TV monitor near the *Lagoda* replica for another film made in 1922 in New Bedford on board an actual whaling ship. An actor portrays Charles W. Morgan, the boat's owner and namesake of the Charles W. Morgan Whaleship moored in Mystic Seaport, Connecticut, and built in New Bedford.

Across the street is the **Seamen's Bethel.** Built in 1832, it provided inspiration for Herman Melville's whaling classic, *Moby Dick.* Melville's sister, whom he came to visit often, lived in New Bedford. The cenotaphs (memorial stones on the walls) commemorate sailors who sailed out of New Bedford and never returned. The plaque at the entrance reads from the novel, "In the same New Bedford there stands a whalesman's chapel and few are the moody fishermen shortly bound for the Indian or Pacific Oceans who failed to make a Sunday visit to this spot."

Time to head for home, so pick up Route 6 west, which is commercial and congested but a means to an end, and follow it to Route 177 west.

Stay on Route 177 if you want to shorten the loop, or shoot down Route 88 (watch your speed on this 55 mph runway) for more beaches and more

Burlingame State Park offers tall pines, comfortable camp sites, and a nice pond for swimming and fishing.

coast to explore. **Horseneck Beach** is a Massachusetts state park with day parking, camping, and a whole bunch of diverse people. During the good weather, the RVs are lined up right at the water's edge and it's easy to see why the spot is so popular, but as the "no" sign on the Westport Town Beach section says, there's to be "no horse play" from April 1st to November 1st.

After you've had your fill of sea air, work your way back up on the country lanes to Tiverton and the crossing to the Newport peninsula and then onto the bridges into Rhode Island proper.

No matter which option you choose, however, watch for **Brickley's Homemade Ice Cream** on the left of Route 1A south (about four miles after you exit Route 138 west at the end of the Jamestown Bridge) and just past the idyllic Casey Farm which will be on your right. As I often find with places like this, small is large and large is humongous and unliftable, so watch what you order. But the cones are scrumptious, and they make the ice cream right in the back.

At the light at Narragansett, cut over to Route 1 and head for your little home among the pines at **Burlingame State Park Camping Area** in Charlestown.

■ For more trips in this region see *Motorcycle Journeys Through New England* by Marty Berke, available from Whitehorse Press.

THE MID-ATLANTIC

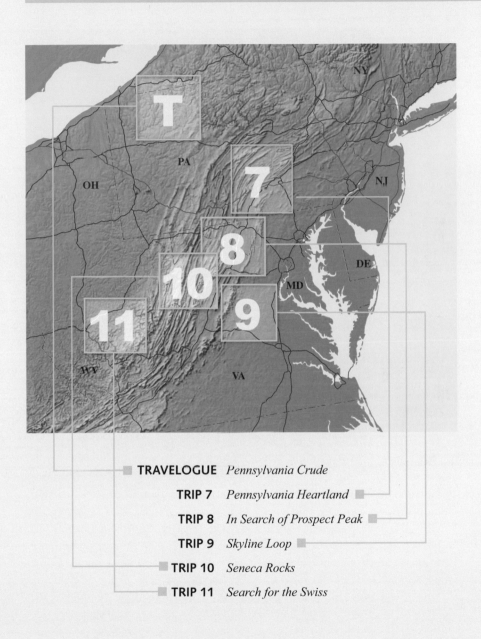

Pennsylvania Crude

Text and photos by Bill Kresnack

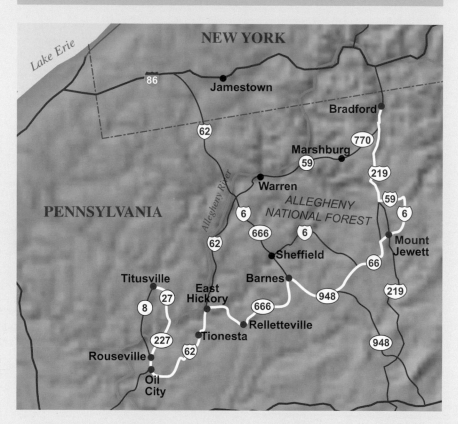

I EASE THE Triumph off the road to check the map and get my bearings.

Let's see—Oil City, Burning Well, Derrick City, Petroleum Center—yep, I must be right in the heart of oil country. But we're not talking Texas or Oklahoma or California here. This is America's original oil country, located in northwestern Pennsylvania.

It was here that native Americans skimmed the fluid off the surface of oil pits for ceremonial purposes. Later, after the arrival of European settlers, salesmen known as "snakes" would sell vials of the stuff from the backs of their wagons. It was guaranteed to "cure what ails ya."

But it was also here that in the late 1850s, a former train conductor and jack-of-all-trades by the name of Col. Edwin L. Drake changed the world.

You could think of Col. Drake as the great-great grandfather of all motorized transportation. No, he didn't invent the motorcycle or the automobile. He discovered the fuel that made all that possible. Right here.

No wait. Right there—about a mile up the road. I click the Triumph into first and aim for the northern end of Oil Creek State Park, near Titusville, Pennsylvania.

Moments later, I idle slowly into a shaded parking area and plant the bike on its sidestand. To my right is a clue that this land still has untapped stores of petroleum: A small pond glistens in the late-morning sunlight. On the water's surface is the slight rainbow sheen of oil.

All around, the air is filled with the thick and pungent aroma of petroleum. And ahead of me I can see the **Drake Well Museum**, the place where the oil revolution got started. To the faithful followers of the Church of Internal Combustion, this is hallowed ground.

Oil wasn't an unknown commodity when Drake came here. Early explorers passing through the region noted that Indians were collecting oil from ponds and natural seeps. The substance became well known among settlers for a variety of medicinal purposes, including its laxative effect.

But a fuel? Hardly. At least not then.

In the 1820s, a well had been sunk in New York to tap underground stores of natural gas, which could be readily burned to provide light. But it wasn't until 1850 that someone found a way to refine crude oil (in a whiskey still), making kerosene, an attractive source of fuel for lighting.

However, there was still a problem. Skimming oil off the surface of ponds or collecting it in seeps was hardly the most efficient way to harvest this resource. So a group of speculators in Connecticut formed the Seneca Oil Company and sent Drake, who wasn't

Ah, mother's milk—the Triumph nuzzles up to a derrick in the Pennsylvania oil country.

A replica of Pennsylvania's (and the world's) first successful oil well at the Drake Well Museum in Titusville.

really a colonel, to Titusville to experiment with a new method of extracting black gold from the ground.

On August 27, 1859, Drake drilled down 69½ feet into the Pennsylvania dirt and struck oil. Soon he was pumping more than 400 gallons a day from his well.

With reliable ways to get and refine oil, production skyrocketed. Within two years, over 2½ million barrels of oil had been pumped out of the ground in this part of Pennsylvania, known as the Venango District. And within a decade, more than 5,000 wells had been sunk. Ironically, that drove the price of oil down so far that Drake and his partners went out of business.

After 140 years, the McClintock No. 1 well still pumps oil.

The problem was that no one had yet come up with ways to use all that oil. The first uses were for lighting, heat, and lubrication. But then, in the 1870s, a German by the name of Nikolaus August Otto built the first practical internal-combustion engine. And the rest is history.

Today, the Drake Well Museum features a replica of the world's first successful oil well. Get there at the right time and you can even see exactly how oil was brought to the surface in those days, with a wood-fired boiler providing steam to work the pump.

Nearby is a display of state-of-the art oil-pumping equipment from the early years of the 20th century.

There's a central engine house surrounding one of those early gasoline powerplants, the kind with the exposed crankshaft and connecting rod working away right in front of your eyes. That engine operates an incredibly complex system of actuating rods that snake all over the park to operate various well pumps. Picture the way

The Penn-Brad Oil Museum tells the story of oil in Pennsylvania.

you would work a rowing machine if your only connection to it was through a 10-foot pole and you're pretty close. You can even walk right under some of the operating rods, rocking back and forth on hinged supports.

The collection of mechanisms adds up to a huge Rube Goldberg device. But with the engine going through its "bang, chuff, chuff, chuff" cycle dictated by a governor, the actuating rods creaking at every antique hinge and the pumps themselves slowly drawing crude out of the ground, the whole thing has a wonderfully purposeful and mechanical sense to it, even if it's hard to sort out what all the pieces are doing.

After wandering through the displays in the museum, I stand and soak up the atmosphere of it for a while. Then, before setting off, I pull the Triumph upright and check the oil level sight glass, appreciating the amber liquid in there more than ever.

This is a motorcycle, this is a sign. Put the two together and you get big fun on the road to Kinzua Bridge. (Photo courtesy of Matt Benson)

The oil trail continues as I head south on state Route 227. This road takes you past the location of Pithole City, America's first oil boomtown. In January 1865, when the Frazier well came in at 250 barrels a day, get-rich dreamers came from far and wide to get in on the opportunity of a lifetime.

More wells were sunk, more oil was pumped, and by September, there was a town of 15,000 in what had been an open field. A reservoir was created. Water pipes were laid. A railroad and an oil pipeline connected the new town to the rest of the world. And when a bank opened, it took only three weeks for deposits to surpass a quarter-million dollars.

But as quickly as it sprang up, Pithole City started to collapse. In 1866, oil well fires started and burned out of control. During August alone, there were 27 well fires. By the end of the year, the population was down to 2,000 and dwindling fast.

Today, not a single building remains. The site is preserved as a historic location where you can make out the foundations of the old structures, but Pithole City has been wiped off the map.

The same can't be said about the McClintock No. 1 well along state Route 8 between Rouseville and Oil City. Of all the slowly nodding pumpers you pass in the area, this one has seniority. A sign along the highway indicates that it is the oldest producing oil well in the world, having pumped continuously since August 1861.

That's 140 years of production from the same well. Oil producers picked a good spot on Mr. McClintock's farm all those decades ago.

Oil City marks the transition point in a tour through this area. The name and the pervasive scent of refineries tell you this is still oil country. But it's also a stop along the scenic Allegheny River, which is just a great place to ride a motorcycle.

I turn onto U.S. Route 62, heading northeast through a series of gentle uphill and downhill sweepers. The road slices through heavy forest, but occasionally, the trees part and you can look down on the river far below.

The highlight is up ahead, though, when you reach the 500,000-acre Allegheny National Forest. It's here that you can find an exceptional road with an unusual name. It's a 30-mile stretch of pavement into the heart of the forest that carries the designation state Route 666.

Dense forest, smooth pavement, no traffic. It doesn't get any better. (Photo courtesy of Matt Benson)

The 2,053-foot-long Kinzua Bridge.

The Devil's Highway? Not on your life. This recently paved two-lane might even be sportbike heaven, as long as you give yourself enough of a cushion to ensure you don't become a fallen angel.

The road starts innocently enough along the banks of the Allegheny at the little town of East Hickory. Leaving the houses behind, you ride into a mixture of woodland and farms that eventually turns to deep forest.

By the time you reach the Tionesta River near the town of Kellettville, you'll be leaning through a fair number of tight twisties mixed in with the gentle sweepers.

But then things start to get really interesting.

I hit a twisting downhill section with forest on the left and the river far below on the right. At the bottom is a tight right-hander, and if you blow it, you're in the trees. No room for mistakes here.

More tight turns follow, with a switchback thrown in to keep you alert. All in all, it's a thorough workout for your cornering skills.

But then, having turned you every which way but loose, 666 calms down again. In the final miles before the road essentially ends at the town of Barnes, it goes from a narrow two-lane to something approaching a freeway, giving you a chance to wind down before returning to civilization.

So take my advice: If you get to this area of Pennsylvania, ignore the satanic number and get your kicks on Route 666. It's a great ride.

Oil may have been the reason I came to this area of Pennsylvania, but as I continue east, I can't resist an attraction from the Age of Steam. It's Kinzua Bridge, a bona fide national engineering landmark.

What has a 250-horsepower motor and two lighters bigger than you are? Zippo's 1947 promotional car.

The National Lighter Museum in Bradford, Pennsylvania. (Photo courtesy of Zippo)

I jog south on state Route 948, then turn north on state Route 66 and then onto U.S. Route 6 to the small town of Mount Jewett. Just north of here you'll find Kinzua Bridge State Park. A short walk through the trees from the parking area brings you to a clearing, and a view of the bridge that takes your breath away.

This railroad viaduct, originally constructed in the year 1882, is 2,053 feet long and, at its center, stands 301 feet above the valley floor. At the time it was completed, it was the world's highest and longest railroad bridge.

For years, Kinzua Bridge was an important link in the state's rail system. But then it fell out of use for decades. Recently, though, a sightseeing train started service from the nearby town of Kane, so you can still ride an authentic steam train to the park and across this historic bridge.

But for me, Kinzua Bridge is a side trip on my way to the location of Pennsylvania's second oil boom—the area around Bradford, still promoted by the local newspaper as: "The High Grade Oil Metropolis of the World."

There was a time when that statement was literally true. In 1881, the oil field in and around Bradford pumped 77 percent of all the oil produced in the world!

It's not hard to find evidence of those days. Just head to the McDonald's restaurant on Main Street, which was built around the Cline Oil No. 1 well, drilled in the early 1870s to a depth of 1,125 feet. Almost 130 years later, it continues to pump 31½ gallons a day.

As in the Titusville area, the oil boom had a huge impact on Bradford. In 1863, before oil fever struck, reports indicated that land around here was selling for six cents an acre. Then, in 1871, the first successful oil well was drilled. By 1875, with more oil being found nearly every day, land prices had jumped to $1,000 an acre.

The Bradford oil field doesn't play such a big role in the world oil market today, but you can find out about its impressive history at the Penn-Brad Oil Museum, just a few miles south of Bradford on U.S. Route 219.

On the way there, though, I visit the town's other historic museum, at the home of Zippo lighters.

Did you know that Zippo, founded in Bradford in 1932, has made some 300 million lighters in the 68 years since? Or that 300 million lighters, laid side by side, would be enough to pave the streets of Bradford, Pennsylvania, 1.8 times?

See, you travel, you find out stuff.

The main thing I find out at the Penn-Brad Oil Museum is that working in the oil fields was a difficult, dangerous way to make a living. This message comes to me from Joe Shurilla, born and raised in the Bradford area, who worked as an oil well tooldresser for 34 years.

Shurilla declines to reveal his age, but he notes that when he was growing up, all the equipment for the wells—including the nitroglycerine used to break up sandstone deep underground where the oil was trapped—came in by horse and wagon.

Shurilla says that one day, a nitroglycerine wagon blew up, killing both the driver and the horse. He was a kid at the time, but he remembers it quite clearly, because he earned a quarter for helping pick up "meat" scattered around the blast site.

"That nitroglycerine," he says. "It's funny stuff."

Putting that image out of my mind, I start the Triumph again and turn toward home. And it strikes me that in a couple of days of riding through Pennsylvania's oil country, I've yet to pick up a single souvenir—not even a postcard.

Then I notice that the low fuel warning signal has just come on. I pull in at an old gas station and fill 'er up. It is, I decide, the perfect remembrance of the trip—a tankful of Col. Drake's magic elixir.

7 Pennsylvania Heartland

Text and photos by Dale Coyner

■ **DISTANCE** *191 miles*

■ **HIGHLIGHTS** *Scenic overlooks, covered bridge hunt, East Broadtop railroad, fall foliage, Appalachian Trail, gossiping at Path Valley Restaurant*

0.0 Begin at intersection of PA 116 and US 15 in downtown Gettysburg, Pennsylvania	**80.2** Left onto Red Rock Road
	81.7 Left onto Adams Grove Road
5.9 Right on Cold Springs Road	**82.5** Right onto T311
14.7 Cold Springs becomes South Mountain Road	**82.6** Right onto SR 3006
	83.5 Left onto PA 274
17.0 Right on SR 233	**98.5** Left onto SR 75 Path Valley Road
62.9 Right on Carlisle Street in Landisburg	**105.5** Right onto PA 641, Spring Run Road
63.0 Right onto Kennedy Valley Road	**114.0** Right onto US 522
63.4 Arrive at Rice Bridge, turn around	**119.4** Left onto PA 994, Meadow Street
63.9 Left onto Carlisle Street	**119.8** Arrive Shade Gap Railroad
64.0 Straight on SR 233/SR 850	**120.2** Right onto US 522
66.9 SR 274 joins SR 850	**147.3** Left onto PA 16, Lincoln Way when you arrive in McConnelsburg
75.3 Left onto Couchtown Road SR 3008	**179.3** Left onto PA 116
79.3 Right onto SR 3005	**191.3** Arrive in Gettysburg via PA 116

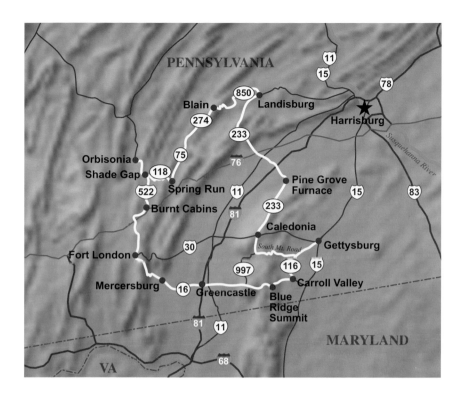

IF TIME IS short and you have the chance to try just one route through Pennsylvania, make it this one. This route features more varied terrain, sights, smells, and sounds than any other I've found yet. Go in early October when the trees are heavy with apples and the leaves are at their peak. It will be chilly when you begin, but you'll soon forget about that, I assure you. The route begins by following Route 116 west out of Gettysburg, the Confederate Army's trail of retreat from the Battle of Gettysburg. The retreating train stretched out 17 miles along this road. At the time it was so bumpy that many of the wounded who were able walked the route rather than endure the hardship of riding in wagons without springs. About five miles outside town, look for Cold Springs Road on your right.

Cold Springs Road is a direct route to nowhere, but runs through some beautiful orchard country. When the trees are loaded with fruit, the air is fragrant with the smell of ripening apples. It isn't the smoothest road; an easy pace will be comfortable. You're not in a hurry anyway, right? Just keep plugging away until you reach Route 233 north.

A good portion of time spent on Route 233 will be through state forest land, first Michaux State Forest and then Tuscarora (www.dcnr.state.pa.us). Along the way, our path will cross that of the **Appalachian Trail** (www.nps.gov/appa/) for the first of many times throughout our travels. The

Pennsylvania has more covered bridges than any other state—more than 200.

trail, which stretches 2,144 miles along Appalachian ridges from northern Maine to Georgia, is managed and maintained by a coalition of public and private interests and has often been called "a gift of nature Americans give themselves." By early October, the foliage in central Pennsylvania has turned and your route is lined with a fantastic assortment of fall colors. Your encounters with several major thoroughfares that cross your path are blessedly uneventful. As you ride under Interstate 81 and hear the traffic thunder overhead, you can't help but wonder where all those people are going. They seem to be in such a hurry to get there, and it makes your 40 mph pace feel even more comfortable.

As Route 233 passes through McCrea, the front of Blue Mountain looms in front of you. It doesn't look like there is much place for a road to go unless it tunnels under the mountain, but it craftily follows a narrow valley through Doubling Gap and into another small valley. Just ahead at Landisburg, you can take a brief detour to Rice's Bridge, a long covered bridge still in use over Sherman Creek. At the intersection with Route 850, make a right. Turn right on Kennedy Valley Road and follow it for a few tenths of a mile.

There are more covered bridges in the United States than anywhere else in the world, and more in Pennsylvania than any other state. At one time, there were more than 1,500, but that number has now dropped to 221. (Next in line

THE MID-ATLANTIC

is Ohio, 140; Vermont, 99; and Indiana, 93. Iowa, the setting for the best-seller *The Bridges of Madison County,* has 12.)

Wooden bridges became popular in the mid-1800s with the development of a support system called the triangular truss. This allowed bridges of substantial length to be built at a lower cost than ones using stone or iron. They were covered to shelter them from the elements and preserve their longevity. Many of the spans in Pennsylvania were built in the 19th century, with some of those built near the end of the era still in use today, like the bridge here at Landisburg.

If you are interested in finding more bridges, they are near the main route and easy to find. Follow Route 850 west out of Landisburg until it joins Route 274 near Fort Robinson, then follow Route 274 to the left when it splits from Route 850. All of these roads are wide open with gentle sweeping curves and made for power road sofas like my Honda Gold Wing. However, any bike will enjoy tracing a smooth line through the curves, taking in rural Pennsylvania framed on either side by gentle ridges of the Alleghenies.

Just past Centre, make a left turn on Couchtown Road, SR 3008. The bridge along this route is to your left off the main traffic route. Make a right on SR 3005 and follow it over the covered bridge, then turn left on Red Rock Road, and make a left on Adams Road to the Enslow Bridge. This is a particularly pretty bridge, framed by trees. To the right of the bridge down the creek is a bench perfect for a brief stop to soak in the atmosphere of the countryside. Follow SR 3005 until it ends on SR 3006. Turn right on SR 3006 and follow it through Blain, returning to Route 274 where you resume your westward trek. Two other bridges are close to the road along your way, though neither was open to traffic when I passed by. Along 274, look for bridges down Mount Pleasant Road and New Germantown Road, both on your left.

Backroads like these offer a lesson in never knowing what to expect around the next bend. Just after entering Red Rock Road I rounded a corner to find a young Amish boy on an old scooter trundling rapidly downhill toward me. Surprised by the encounter, both of us shifted paths to avoid a collision, but he still managed to give me a friendly wave as we passed. Not half a mile later, I rounded a bend to find a pickup truck parked dead smack in the middle of the road. More unusual was the sight of a pair of legs sticking out from under the truck across the road. No reason to call a tow truck when you can fix your vehicle on the spot.

Future apples in progress along Cold Springs Road near Gettysburg.

Engineers ready the trolley at East Broadtop for another ride into the past.

An engineer explains the unique features of this trolley built and used in Brazil.

After New Germantown, the route enters the **Tuscarora State Forest** again and **Big Spring State Park.** There are some quick switchbacks in this section, so don't let the relatively easy ascent fool you. Descending rapidly, you'll meet wide-open Route 75. Turn left and follow it south to Path Valley.

There isn't much in the way of food service along the route, but if your timing puts you in the area of Spring Run, Pennsylvania, near mealtime, make a point to stop by the **Path Valley Family Restaurant** (717-349-2900). Last time through the area, I dropped in on a Sunday afternoon well past the usual dinner hour. I squeezed the bike into the last remaining spot of available pavement near the edge of the lot. Inside, the place was packed and my only option was the seat at the counter nearest the cash register. It turns out that was just the place to be.

When I visit places like Path Valley, my favorite pastime is enjoying the conversations around me about local people and events. Oh sure, some might call that eavesdropping. I tend to think of it more as cultural study. At the end of the counter, the waitresses assembled their orders, and it was the perfect spot to engage in a little of that study. Most of the banter was the usual friendly chit-chat that helps pass time at the workplace.

At some point I happened to hear one girl ask, "Honey, did you see your 'ex' at the dance Friday night?"

"Yeah, I sure did," replied the other. "I was so surprised. I turned around and walked right smack into him. And I said to myself 'Lord have mercy, I didn't know he was out of jail yet!'"

Check please.

When you've, er, done your time at the Path Valley, hop back on the bike for the rest of this run. The restaurant is right at the intersection where you'll want to turn. Head west on Route 641. This is a fun road that jumps over Tuscarora Mountain with pretty vistas along the upper ridges. To the west, you can see the Shade Mountain Gap. That's where we're headed. Route 641 meets US Route 522 at Shade Gap. Follow Route 522 north to Orbisonia and the **East Broad Top Railroad** (EBT) (www.ebtrr.com).

The EBT began operating in 1872 to connect the isolated southwestern coal and iron fields of the state with iron furnaces and the Pennsylvania Railroad. In the fall, the railroad hosts a weekend special when they draw out nearly their whole line of rolling stock. If you're anywhere near the railroad, you'll hear another tradition: the annual whistle salute. Not only does each train have a distinctive whistle, each conductor has his own unique way of using it. The EBT offers rides to passengers from June to October. If you're interested in a ride, call ahead for an exact schedule.

Another attraction located near the EBT is the **Rockhill Trolley Museum** (www.rockhilltrolley.org). This working museum has a collection of 18 trolley cars and operates on a schedule in conjunction with the EBT. One car in particular is made of Brazilian hardwoods that look as rich and beautiful as the day the trolley started service.

As I stood in front of the railroad taking pictures, a few folks stopped to take a look at the Gold Wing and comment on its enormous size and array of gadgetry. One older gent and his wife stopped for a look. "Nice bike," he said. "What is that, an Indian?" I guess it had been a while since he was part of the motorcycling scene. A few minutes later, an Amish family strolled by, mother and father and two young children in tow. Mother and the children passed by with a polite nod, but the father paused just a moment and glanced at the bike. "Nice Wing," he said and shot me a grin. Now do you suppose he is a closet . . . ? Naah.

Your chance to "catch the first thing smokin'" at East Broadtop Railroad. 'Course it only goes about a mile.

The return route passes by another covered bridge near Saint Mary's Catholic Church near Shade Gap and then enters open farmland, much of which is maintained by Amish farmers. You will often see them working the land with a harnessed mule team, or traversing the highway in their familiar black buggies. This setting, quiet and isolated, seems more suited to the Amish than the much-hyped Pennsylvania Dutch country. In Penn Dutch country, the Amish are like a novelty attraction that you pay to view; here they blend into the countryside. But I'll bet that if one particular Amish farmer had his way, his buggy would have a flat-six, reverse gear, and two wheels. Ahead of you is a

long stretch of US 522 heading south toward McConnelsburg. Like PA 274, your bike seems to find a naturally soothing touring pace on this road. Perhaps it's because you don't pass through many small towns on this stretch. One in particular though rates a mention.

The grand Gettysburg Hotel offers accommodations for the discriminating rider.

Today when a developer builds a town, the marketing department will twist itself into knots trying to find a name that strikes just the right chord. Reston, Virginia and Celebration, Florida, come to mind. But out here in

Two Harleys pose in Gettysburg Square.

the backwoods of Colonial Pennsylvania, marketing types were hard to find, so folks just called things as they saw them. And that's how Burnt Cabins (www.burntcabinsmill.com) came to be.

What happened was simple. Settlers moving west in the 1740s had invaded land that was occupied by the Native Americans in that region. When the settlers scared off the game, the chief complained to the governor who had the illegal squatters packed

Downtown Gettysburg is great for strolling and browsing.

up and their cabins torched. That's the kind of direct action you could count on from a governor back in those days.

US 522 intersects with PA 16 in McConnelsburg, and at this point, it's time to head east for the return trip. On your way back via PA 16, you'll pass through several towns that, like Gettysburg, feature a large town square. Each square is filled with unique shops that you won't find in any strip mall. These squares (sometimes referred to as "diamonds") are actually the result of the influence of Scots-Irish settlers who patterned them after the cities and towns of Ulster.

After passing through Waynesboro, you'll soon run upon PA 116, the route that began our journey. You'll pass **Ski Liberty** (www.skiliberty.com) on your right as you make the return trip. The hills around Ski Liberty won't impress hard core winter sports enthusiasts. If you're like me and you just want to slide downhill on a tube and enjoy the benefit of riding a ski lift back uphill, it's a great cold season venue.

Before you know it, you've passed Cold Springs Road and are within striking distance of Gettysburg. You've had a good day's ride, so park the bike and take one last stretch on Gettysburg's town square before rustling up some grub. Just be careful who you run into. You never know who's just finished doing their time.

■ For more trips in this region see *Motorcycle Journeys Through the Appalachians* by Dale Coyner, available from Whitehorse Press.

8 In Search of Prospect Peak

Text and photos by Dale Coyner

■ **DISTANCE** *136 miles*

■ **HIGHLIGHTS** *The National Road, Sideling Hill, Park-N-Dine, C&O Canal, Fort Frederick, Berkeley Springs, Prospect Peak, and the Paw Paw Tunnel*

0.0 Begin MD 144 (Baltimore Pike) at Pleasant Valley Road (Rocky Gap Camp) in Cumberland, Maryland	**41.7** Right on Fort Frederick Road
	43.2 Arrive Fort Frederick
	44.7 Right onto MD 144 east
17.4 Right onto Orleans Road	**51.4** Right onto MD 68 south
17.9 Left onto I-68 East ramp	**55.9** Right onto US 11 West
23.9 Arrive Sideling Hill Visitors Center, then continue straight	**62.3** Right onto WV 901 west
	67.7 Right onto WV 9
26.9 Right onto MD 144	**110.8** Arrive Paw Paw, West Virginia, WV 9 becomes MD 51
31.7 Arrive Park-N-Dine	
32.1 Join I-70 East toward Hagerstown	**136.0** Arrive Cumberland, Maryland
40.4 Right on MD 56 at Big Pool	

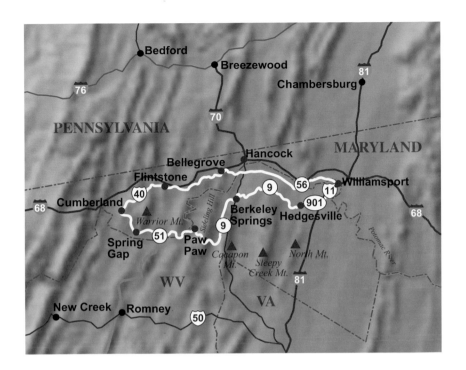

BEGIN YOUR SEARCH for Prospect Peak by following the older alignments of the National Road, out of Cumberland, Maryland. These alternate routes are either labeled US 40 or MD 144 and are sometimes referred to as National Road, National Pike, or the Baltimore Pike. Whatever. The point is, all these old alignments parallel I-68 between Cumberland and Hancock.

There are some special sections of highway waiting for your personal discovery along Scenic 40, graceful curves that lead you into a turn at a quick pace and set you up perfectly for the next. They beg to be ridden on two wheels. Thank the interstate highway system for taking most of the traffic off this road and opening it up for pleasure riding.

Topping out at Town Hill, you can see Sideling Hill in the distance, identified by the big notch carved into the mountain, marking the point where I-68 passes through. The **Town Hill Hotel** (www.townhillbnb.com) is perched atop the ridge, looking neat and trim. This would be a great place to stay on a warm summer evening, enjoying great views and refreshing breezes. A few miles past Town Hill, Scenic 40 intersects with I-68. Jump back on the Interstate to catch the **Sideling Hill** exhibit just ahead.

Sideling Hill is a western Maryland landmark. In order to straighten a challenging section of the roadway, engineers blasted down a few hundred feet through the middle of the mountain to a point where a straight section of road could be made. During construction they found that during the time the

The Park-N-Dine is a favorite of riders around the region.

Beautifully situated atop a ridge crest, Town Hill Hotel started life as a fruit stand.

Appalachians were being formed the mountain had sagged in the middle like a fallen layer cake. Perhaps it should have been baked another million years or so. The state built a bridge for pedestrians across the highway to give you the best opportunity to view this natural wonder without the risk of parking on the side of the road. A visitor center is accessible from the walkway with more information and displays explaining how the mountain was formed, plus general travel information.

The ride into Hancock is short, eight or 10 miles. If you wait on breakfast until you get to Hancock, I promise you will not go unrewarded. Hancock is home to the **Park-N-Dine** (301-678-5242), one of those places where the cooking is good, the plates are loaded, and the price is laughably low. When you order a $3 breakfast, you'd better be ready to let out your suspenders and pop the top button on your trousers. Riders of all brands flock to the Park-N-Dine, especially on the weekends.

Directly behind the restaurant is the Potomac River and the **C&O Canal National Park** (www.nps.gov/choh). In the early 1800s speculators and politicians were all afire about finding new ways to move goods between the East

THE MID-ATLANTIC

Coast colonies and the newly opened Midwest. The ridges of the Appalachians made that no ordinary task. Some people thought roads were the answer, some gambled on the canal, and others built railroads. Canal construction began in 1828 in Washington, D.C., and crawled into Cumberland some 22 years later, but was made obsolete by speedier railroad service almost as soon as it was opened. The towpath along the canal is now a trail for hiking and biking and is a good place to walk off that third stack of pancakes you polished off. Also in Hancock is the **C&O Canal Museum,** which features a slide show, artifacts, and photos. Maybe after a short hike to the canal and museum you can swing your leg over the bike again. Then again, maybe you'll need a hoist.

The route out of Hancock follows Interstate 70 for a brief period, making an exit at Big Pool. Turn right and follow Route 56 east. **Fort Frederick State Park** (www.dnr.state.md.us/publiclands/western/fortfrederick.html) is just about one mile down the road. Fort Frederick is the only remaining original fort from the French and Indian War (1754-1763, for those who snoozed in history class). You can tour the fort and visit the barracks, which have been restored to show you what a soldier's life was like. Be glad you live in the 21st century, friend. You can have equal fun touring the well-appointed museum or just strolling around the large open grounds. The quiet, green lawns would make a great place to spread out a blanket for a picnic lunch.

Resume the tour on Route 56 east and take advantage of the whoop-de-doos—those sections of the road that lift you out of your seat and cause your co-rider to hold on tighter. Route 56 ends on Route 68, turn right. Route 68 starts wide then narrows and remains a straight shot into Williamsport, a small blue-collar city on the West Virginia border that was once considered for the federal capital. Your best bet is to follow Route 68 into town where it intersects with U.S. Route 11. Route 11 passes through a small section of suburbia, then Route 901 appears on your right. Follow Route 901 west and get set for some good riding.

It's too bad Route 901 is only a few miles long, because it winds through beautiful countryside. Side roads in this area are bound to reward you with more good riding. The route ends all too quickly on Route 9 at Hedgesville. Turn right on Route 9.

Between Hedgesville and Paw Paw, some 42 miles distant, there are far more good riding miles than there are

Fort Frederick was erected by Governor Horatio Sharpe in 1756 to protect English settlers from the French and their Indian allies. (Photo courtesy the Hagerstown-Washington County CVB)

Down the hill into downtown Berkeley Springs. (David Fattaleh photo, courtesy of West Virginia Tourism)

bad. The initial traffic you encounter in Hedgesville quickly fades as you head deeper into the country. Soon the entire roadway is yours. Entering the town of Berkeley Springs and seeing all of that traffic is really quite a bit of a culture shock. **Berkeley Springs State Park** is the site of a watering hole that has been popular since colonial times. Imagine soaking your tootsies in the same refreshing waters as our founding fathers did! Okay, maybe that image doesn't capture your imagination, but these springs have long been known for their restorative powers. West of Berkeley Springs, the road winds slowly up Cacapon Mountain on a steep incline, testing the bottom end of your bike's power curve.

I remember the first time I toured this area a few years ago, my wife clinging to me on the back of a little 600cc sport bike. We were searching for a spot called **Prospect Peak** (www.panoramawv.com/prospect.htm). The peak has been named by the National Geographic Society as one of the 10 prettiest spots in America. (Road trip!) As you reach the summit of Cacapon (KAK-upon or CAKE-upon) Mountain you'll find an overlook for the peak on your right. In the valley below, the Potomac looks like a thin silver ribbon draped over the landscape. Sideling Hill starts here and runs from left to right into Maryland. To the far right lies Pennsylvania and to the left, the small village of Great Cacapon slumbers. These are the Appalachians as few people see them.

When you descend the ridge and ride through the country you've seen from above, it's like stepping through the frame and into the painting. Route 9 follows the contours of the Cacapon River in places accounting for some of the curves. Other times it takes a turn seemingly for the fun of it. Forest lines the road on both sides so thick it looks as though you are flying through a long green waterslide.

Your entry into Paw Paw is likely to go completely unnoticed. The road enters the edge of town and quietly exits on the north side. Just over the line in Maryland, look for the sign designating the **C&O Canal Paw Paw Tunnel** (www.berkeleysprings.com/tunnel.htm). The town and the tunnel took their name from the Paw Paw, a fruit-bearing tree that grows wild along the ridges in this area.

For more than two centuries, visitors have traveled to Berkeley Springs to soak up its warm mineral waters. (David Fattaleh photo, courtesy of West Virginia Tourism)

Tunnel construction began in 1836 and cut through 3,118 feet of rock to avoid a six-mile stretch of the Potomac River—a major engineering feat in its time. You can walk through the tunnel now, but bring a flashlight. There is also a hiking trail that crosses over the top of the tunnel.

It took 14 years to build the tunnel instead of the two years originally planned and when completed, it was just wide enough for one boat at a time. This usually didn't cause problems, but occasionally two boats entered from opposite ends and met somewhere in the tunnel. On one occasion, a standoff ensued between a couple of captains, neither of which would agree to back out of the tunnel. After a couple of days, the tunnel superintendent was finished with such nonsense, so he built a smoky bonfire of green cornstalks on the upwind side of the tunnel. It didn't take long for both boats to make their way out of the tunnel. There's no record of which of the boats backed out first, but the winner of this standoff was the superintendent.

When you cross over the river, Route 9 becomes Route 51 in Maryland. In addition to the tunnel, there are a number of spots along the route marked to indicate the remains of locks along the canal. They represent a good chance to hop off the bike for a quick stroll. Dual-sport fans will find a plethora of side roads leading over the ridges and into the arms of the mountains. When you're ready to wrap up the loop, just follow MD 51 west to return to Cumberland.

■ For more trips in this region see *Motorcycle Journeys Through the Appalachians* by Dale Coyner, available from Whitehorse Press.

9 Skyline Loop

Text and photos by Dale Coyner

- **DISTANCE** *135 miles*
- **HIGHLIGHTS** *Skyline Drive, Shenandoah National Park, hiking trails with remnants of old homesteads, Sperryville Emporium, Misty Mountain Vineyard*

0.0 Start at entrance to Skyline Drive on US 340 in Front Royal, Virginia

30.7 Left on US 211 East at Thornton Gap

37.7 Right on US 522 in Sperryville

38.5 Right on VA 231

59.0 Right on US 29 Business South in Madison

60.3 Join US 29 South toward Charlottesville

62.1 Right on VA 230 North

72.9 Right on US 33 West

87.4 Right on US 340 North at Elkton

135.0 Arrive Front Royal via US 340

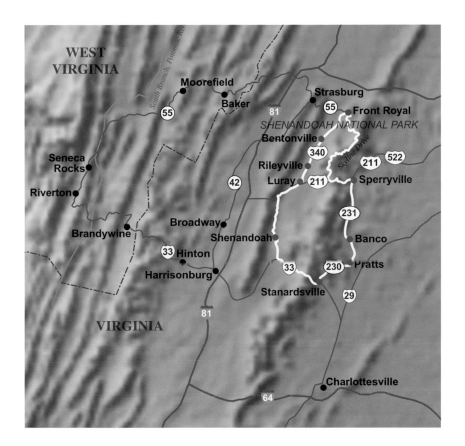

THIS VIRGINIA TOUR is best suited for a day when you have ridden a lot in days past and want to take a break. There are ample opportunities to get off your bike and explore the dozens of hiking trails along **Skyline Drive.** We will also pay a visit to a couple of quaint mountain towns and stop off at a vineyard for a personal tour—perhaps by the owner himself. We will then return over the **Blue Ridge** via Route 33, a popular run for riders.

The tour begins at the north entrance to Skyline Drive in Front Royal, about two miles south of town on Route 340. Admission to Skyline depends somewhat on how the ranger views your mode of transportation. There are different rates for cars and bicycles, and I have been charged both at different times. I think the bigger your smile, the better your chances of getting the bicycle rate!

Be sure to keep your speed at or near the posted limit of 35 mph. Motorcyclists have a mixed reputation on this road, so we should do our best to improve it. It may be tempting to lean into some of the curves, but considering the hiking trails that cross the road and curves you can't see around, 35 is the speed to go. Besides, the purpose of this drive is to relax and enjoy the view.

This trip takes you bouncing along the mountain tops. (Photo courtesy of the National Park Service)

Skyline Drive is a thin ribbon that traces the length of the 200,000 acres comprising **Shenandoah National Park** (www.nps.gov/shen). Each year the park attracts hundreds of thousands of visitors, many of whom ride from one end to the other and pronounce themselves satisfied, riders included. Too bad. In addition to the 75 overlooks along the way, there are about 500 miles of hiking trails, waterfalls, black bear, ancient hemlock forests, fern-shrouded pools, and the ruins of pioneer homesteads awaiting your discovery.

Trails range from a few tenths of a mile to dozens. The terrain is gentle so you can hike with a minimum of equipment; sturdy shoes, clothing to suit the season, and a supply of water are adequate for a few hours. Bring lunch or a snack to boost your energy along the trail and you're set for a full day.

If you get an early start, watch out for deer. An estimated 6,000 deer live in the 400 square miles of Shenandoah National Park, so the question is not whether you will see deer, but rather how many. The first few miles of the park climb to the crest of the Blue Ridge. The first pullover looks down on the Front Royal area and will give you a hint of what is to come. Next is the **Dickey Ridge Visitor Center,** where the 1.2-mile Fox Hollow Trail begins.

The trail passes through part of the 450 acres once owned by the Fox family. Along the trail are large rock piles, now covered with gray-green moss that makes them look like burial mounds. These stones came out of the fields under cultivation. You will also see the Fox family cemetery, and a low stone wall that ran along the property line between the Foxes and their neighbors, the Merchants.

The Merchants and the Foxes weren't the first to settle this area. It had been a prime hunting ground for Native Americans as far back as 1000 B.C. The first few waves of European settlers washed ashore in the 1600s and used the seemingly limitless supply of wood to build their homes and villages. By the early 20th century, the entire area was a wasteland, stripped of all its resources. Congress designated the area a park in 1924 but didn't authorize any money to be spent. For 12 years the state of Virginia slowly bought land and accepted donations from private individuals until the park was finally established on the day after Christmas 1933. When you gaze up the trunk of a mighty oak, hickory, or black locust that grow here so thick, it is hard to imagine that these trees are only between 50 and 70 years old.

Before you leave the visitor center, be sure to go inside and collect your National Parks Passport stamp.

The rolling contours of the gentle Blue Ridge are the perfect setting for building a world-class scenic parkway, and a heck of a fun motorcycle ride! The Drive itself weaves along the crest of the Blue Ridge joining its kin, the Blue Ridge Parkway, 105 miles south at Afton Mountain.

Autumn is a beautiful time to ride if you can brave the chill. (Photo courtesy of the National Park Service)

The Civilian Conservation Corps did most of the work, with much of the stonework done by expert Spanish and Italian stoneworkers who had just arrived in the United States. The result is an unforgettable mix of flora, fauna, and twisty pavement.

As you sweep through the curves, be sure to stop occasionally at the overlooks to enjoy the view. You can see farthest during the late fall, winter, and early spring when weather patterns move clear

A Pipevine Swallowtail butterfly seeks out an afternoon's meal.

Riders often gather at the Sperryville Emporium after conquering US 211. It's a kitsch collector's paradise.

northern air through the Shenandoah Valley. On a good day, you can easily see 60 or 70 miles across the valley to the Shenandoah and Allegheny Mountains on the other side. To the east, the Piedmont region is clearly visible, gradually giving way to the coastal plain. Small towns and villages dot the landscape on both sides; those little specks you see moving through the fields are probably tractors.

Motorcycle campers will find campgrounds at Matthews Arm, Lewis Mountain, Loft Mountain, and Big Meadows, the latter available by reservation. There are also lodge and cabin rooms available. To camp in the backcountry, you'll need to get a permit at any entrance to the park. If you want a campsite, my advice is to set up camp early and then go exploring, especially during the summer season. These campgrounds fill up fast. For a room reservation, call well ahead. Many months ahead.

On our tour, exit from Skyline at the Thornton Gap exit. Turn left on Route 211 toward Sperryville. This is a fast five-mile descent with hairpin turns sharp enough that you can really grind the floorboards. Your arrival into the hamlet of Sperryville begins with a collection of roadside stands selling a wide variety of "must haves," including apples, peaches, and cider; lawn ornaments of distinction; furniture; fajitas; "I Love Virginia" toothpick holders; and Elvis commemorative hand towel and bed linen sets.

You can have a fun time just stopping at different stands and looking over the goods. The most impressive collection is at the **Sperryville Emporium** (540-987-8235). It is packed from floor to ceiling with furniture, fruit, a vast array of concrete lawn ornaments, and decorative cedar plaques with moving quotes for those times when a "thank you" card just isn't enough. A seasonal flea market operates along the perimeter, and a local barbecue joint operates a stand. In the early fall during apple season, the place is so packed it takes on a carnival atmosphere. You'll often run into other riders here who are passing through on their way to the Drive, and many of the local riders will offer tips on other roads to try.

Modest old homes line the street that is downtown Sperryville, each with its own picket fence and front porch. Some have been converted into shops that sell locally made crafts, antiques, even Native American jewelry. There are plenty of surprises to be found in the antique shops, including pieces and parts of old motorcycles. A rider friend told me he entered a shop one day just as a fellow wheeled an old Indian out the door with a smile on his face as wide as Texas. "Four hundred dollars," the proud new owner told my friend before the question could form in his mouth.

When you've done all the wandering you want, it's time to suit up and head out. Follow Route 522 south out of Sperryville toward Culpeper and into the lush Piedmont. The right turn for Route 231 comes up just on the outskirts of town. Turn right and follow it. Route 231 is designated as a Virginia Byway, and we know just what that means—more great riding!

Route 231 isn't as curvy as it is scenic. I discovered this road one day by accident, being lost and simply looking for a way to get from one point to another. I quickly discovered that getting lost out here is a good thing. The smooth pavement tempts you to slip into top gear and tilt your head back to smell the air. It's so fresh and sweet you can almost taste it. There's nothing to hear but the drone of your motor and the rushing wind. Just make sure you don't relax so much you miss that next curve!

It's easy to find the road less taken in Shenandoah National Park.

On your right **Old Rag Mountain** appears from behind the trees, with its bald, rocky top looking somewhat out of place among the tree-covered hills beside it. Old Rag is a little different because geologists say it is an extinct volcano. Old Rag is a popular day trip for weekend warriors who want to test their mettle in the outdoors (and want to be assured a victory). If you decide to conquer it, be sure to bring along the essential gear, plus a little extra food and water. To get to the parking area, turn right on Route 646 and follow this bumpy little cowpath to the foot of the mountain and Route 717, the road which leads to a parking area. Don't park along the side of the road at the trailhead as it'll rile the neighbors. You don't want to rile the neighbors in these parts.

Finishing out the first leg of Route 231 brings you into the town of Madison. Here the homes are more stately, and the folks are more likely to give you a second look than they would in Sperryville. Don't worry, they don't mean anything by it, they just don't see too many dashing leather-clad figures like yourself darting through town.

Madison is another appropriate place to climb off the bike for a look-see. Whether it be this journey or another through the Appalachians, you're always passing some kind of craft shop of one kind or another, and after awhile they all begin to look alike. If you want to purchase a genuine hand-made souvenir without wondering if it was really "made in the far, far east," check

Darting in and out of forests and pastures is an excellent pastime.

THE MID-ATLANTIC

out Madison's own **Little Shop** (540-948-4147). You won't find any Elvis towel sets here, just some of the best handiwork anywhere in the region, and at affordable prices.

To depart Madison, continue to follow US Business 29/VA 231 west toward Charlottesville. A few miles west of Madison, make a right turn on Route 230 west. Here the straights are long and the view of the Blue Ridge rising in front of you invites your imagination to speculate what it will be like to attack the ridge. Entering the town of Stanardsville, turn right on Route 33. Your answer will come quickly.

If you need a break from the saddle, these trails will offer you a chance to stretch your legs in the peace and quiet. (Photo courtesy of the National Park Service)

First you enter a series of warm-up curves to get your tires scuffed. Then the road suddenly turns tame and the immediate fun seems over. This doesn't last long; the more serious curves are just ahead. The road widens, giving you two lanes to set up your curves, and you can really give your cornering a good workout. If you have anything left of your footpegs from Route 211, you're liable to wear them out on this stretch. Your ascent is smooth, like you're gliding on some of the low hanging clouds that brush the ridge when they pass. Tight curves, wide pavement, and little traffic offer you the opportunity to set up wide and lean hard into the curves.

Follow Route 33 down the mountain and pick up US 340 north at Elkton. This is an easy return ride offering clear views of the Blue Ridge to your right and Massanutten Mountain on your left. You'll also see several long steel truss railroad bridges, some of them a few hundred feet long. The ride is pretty similar to what you experienced on Route 231 and 230, with long straights and an occasional town.

◼ For more trips in this region see *Motorcycle Journeys Through the Appalachians* by Dale Coyner, available from Whitehorse Press.

10 Seneca Rocks

Text and photos by Dale Coyner

- **DISTANCE** *224 miles*
- **HIGHLIGHTS** *Seneca Rocks, Germany Valley, Southern Kitchen Restaurant, and curves, curves, curves*

0.0 Begin at point where VA 55 departs US 340/522 north of Front Royal, Virginia toward Strasburg. Follow VA 55/WV 55 to US 33 at Seneca Rocks

94.1 Left on US 33 East at Seneca Rocks

158.2 Left on VA 42 in Harrisonburg

201.7 Left on US 11 in Woodstock

214.3 In Strasburg, continue straight to rejoin VA 55 east toward Front Royal

224.4 Arrive in Front Royal, Virginia, at US 340/US 522 via VA 55

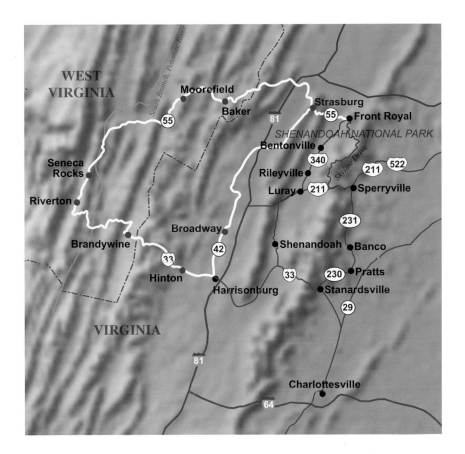

YOU'VE GOT TO promise you'll keep this one a secret. Well, okay, you can share it with your riding friends, but please don't tell any car drivers about this route through Virginia and West Virginia. Of all the roads I've traveled throughout the Appalachians, this route covers two of my all-time favorites. This is the one route I would recommend to even the most jaded *I've-ridden-'em-all* rider as a showcase of the best riding the Appalachians have to offer. Let's get to it.

From Front Royal, Virginia, pick up Route 55 west and make your way through Strasburg and over the Interstate. From this point, Route 55 becomes a pleasure to navigate, with virtually no traffic and perfectly banked curves that come rapid-fire, over and around the contours of the Shenandoah and Allegheny Mountains. Just before you enter Wardensville, there's a sign along the road indicating the point which was at one time during the mid-1800s the geographic population center of the United States.

First stop on the tour is the **Kac-ka-pon Restaurant** in Wardensville. The Kac-ka-pon offers a great value for any meal, and the prices are as down home as the cooking. If you stop in time for lunch, be sure to save room for a slice from one of their homemade pies.

Out of Wardensville you'll find another 25 to 30 miles of even better riding, crossing numerous mountain ridges and following rivers. Route 55 joins U.S. Route 220 at Moorefield and follows it south for a few miles before returning on its westerly course at Petersburg. Route 220 is a good road itself, following narrow valleys through West Virginia and well into Virginia. It is often named as one of the best unknown roads in America, but Route 55 is even better.

Starting somewhere before Petersburg and with increasing frequency you'll notice signs for the Smoke Hole Caverns, Crystal Grottoes, Seneca Caverns, etc., etc. There are probably more attractions of this type in this region than any other because many of the ridges in this area bear limestone caves. Spelunking is a popular pastime. It's not unusual to see a couple of parties of cavers parked by the roadside, headlamps in position, ready to venture into the subterranean passages of the Appalachians.

After Petersburg, Route 55 spends its remaining time chasing a series of rivers before intersecting with US Route 33 at **Seneca Rocks National Recreation Area** (www.wvweb.com/www/nra). This is a popular destination for day-trippers who come to climb the rocks. Seneca Rocks's ragged edges stand out from the smooth ridge lines of the hills that surround them. Often in cases like this, the rock that remains was molten rock that was pushed to the

Seneca Rocks was once believed to hold mystical powers. When viewing the site at sunset, it isn't hard to imagine why. (David Fattaleh photo courtesy of West Virginia Tourism)

THE MID-ATLANTIC

surface by geologic forces below. The heat and pressure made it harder than the surface it pushed through and when that surface wore away, the harder rock was exposed.

Next is a great section of Route 33 between Seneca Rocks and Harrisonburg, Virginia. The first ascent you'll make is long by East Coast standards. It will bring you to a fantastic panorama of the **Germany Valley.** If you are tempted to pull off for a picture, wait until you get to a spot along the road that has a "Germany Valley" marker. It's near the top and offers the best view. This view is a good candidate for your widest lens or a recyclable panoramic camera. To the left and

Old fences and high meadows enhance the beauty of Appalachian highways.

right are the high, imposing ridges of the Alleghenies, while in the valley below, a series of small, uniform ridges punctuate the valley floor.

From Franklin, the route settles for a minute and then makes another ascent before dropping into Brandywine. Brandywine is home to a popular recreation area that offers secluded primitive campsites and a lake for swimming and fishing. From here, the last great ascent is soon upon you as you trek up the Shenandoah Mountains. After a few miles of switchbacks you can pull off to the side of the road and retrace your path, finding Brandywine in the valley below. Once over the hills, it's another 20 miles or so to Harrisonburg. To avoid the traffic, make a left on Route 42 and head out of town.

When you reach Broadway you face a decision. If you're hungry, follow Route 259 to US 11. On US 11 north at New Market you'll run across the **Southern Kitchen Restaurant,** which is the best place in the area to eat, bar none. You can also continue to follow Route 42 north through Woodstock where you will eventually catch up to Route 11 as well. Route 42 is a more scenic rural ride.

Route 11 crosses paths with Route 55 in Strasburg. If you're inclined, Strasburg is a good place to hop off and walk around for browsing. There are dozens of small shops willing to accept your credit card and to ship. (No space on your bike? Not a problem!) Return to Front Royal on Route 55 east to complete the Seneca Rocks tour.

■ For more trips in this region see *Motorcycle Journeys Through the Appalachians* by Dale Coyner, available from Whitehorse Press.

11 Search for the Swiss

Text and photos by Dale Coyner

- **DISTANCE** *214 miles*
- **HIGHLIGHTS** *Helvetia Historic District, West Virginia State Wildlife Center, Monongahela National Forest*

0.0 Depart US 19 from Summersville, West Virginia, at junction with WV 41

1.3 Left on CR 43/2 also listed as Old US 19

2.9 Left on CR 19/8 (Peach Orchard Road)

11.0 Bear left on CR 15 (Swandale Road)

24.2 Right on WV 16

25.4 Right on WV 4

72.4 Right on WV 15

81.5 Left on CR-22 (Corley Caress Road)

82.4 Straight on CR-23 (Vernon Road)

99.7 Left on WV 20 North at Hacker Valley

100.3 Right on CR-3 (Left Fork Holly Creek Road) **Significant portions of this road are broken pavement and gravel. See text for description of alternate route.*

112.0 Left on CR-47 in Pickens

113.0 Left on CR-45 toward Helvetia

117.5 Left on CR-46 in Helvetia (becomes CR-11)

137.5 Left on WV 20 South

201.7 Straight on WV 55 at WV 20/WV 55 split in Craigsville

207.4 Straight on WV 41 where WV 41/WV 55 split

213.9 Arrive Summersville on WV 41 West

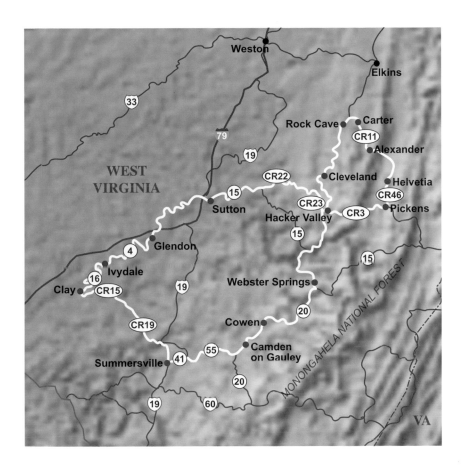

CREDIT GOES TO my e-mail pen pal Steve Fowler for introducing me to this section of West Virginia and the hamlet of Helvetia. I only wish I had quizzed Steve more about his preferred route before I set out on my own. I offer you now the opportunity to profit from my misadventures.

Start your search for the Swiss out of Summersville northbound on US 19. Just 1.3 miles north of the intersection with WV 41, make a left turn on CR 43-2, also designated as Old US 19. Again, a short distance up the road, turn left on CR 19-8, Peach Orchard Road.

Peach Orchard Road gives you the impression that a road engineer once handed a crayon to his 2-year-old and said, "Draw me a line between Summersville and Clay and use your imagination." However it came to be, you'll enjoy the ups and downs and arounds this road offers. After crossing a few ridges, you'll enter high farming country for a stretch, then revert to forest-lined roads. Route 19-8 becomes CR-15 in Clay County and ends on CR-11. Turn left and you'll come out at Clay. Make a right turn on WV 16, then another right shortly thereafter on WV 4.

The view to the south from the top of Seneca Rocks in the Monongahela National Forest would make even the steadiest among us dizzy. (Photo courtesy of the USDA Forest Service)

I made three notes on my run up Route 4—flat, fast, and fun. After feathering the throttle for 20 miles on the backroads, it's fun to open up the bike a little across this great stretch of road. Route 4 follows every contour of the Elk River between Clay and Sutton. Route 4 makes a sharp turn to the left out of Sutton and continues north. Follow it just to Laurel Fork and turn left on WV 15.

Route 15 is suitable for a sedate touring pace or a faster, sporting ride, depending entirely on your preference. After getting jazzed up by Route 4, I was running an assertive pace when I whizzed right by my scheduled turn-off on CR-22, Corley Caress Road. That was a sign I should have interpreted as "stay on WV 15," but having carefully planned out a particular route, I felt obligated to turn back. CR-22/CR-26 leads off from WV-15 and cuts through Replete and Wheeler becoming CR-3 as the road passes into Webster County. There is nothing smooth about this section of road, but at a reasonable pace, it's an enjoyable ride nonetheless. CR-3 then intersects WV 20 at Hacker Valley.

It all seemed so simple when I was mapping out this route. According to the map, CR-3 was a road that would allow me to trace a path into Helvetia from a southern approach. As I turned left on WV 20, CR-3 appeared again on the right at the bridge over the Left Fork of the Holly River. What I found was more of the same. Pavement, rough in spots, but the isolation and scenery made up for the quality of the pavement.

Soon, however, I noticed a trend. A stretch of gravel appeared and I thought, if this is going to turn to gravel, I'll turn around. Pavement reappeared. Okay, a short stretch of gravel, that's not bad, I'll keep going. Gravel, then pavement, then more gravel. Well, you know what happened next. It wasn't long before the brief stretches of gravel were replaced by brief stretches of pavement, then no pavement at all.

Now I don't mind running on gravel, even on a heavy bike. But after a while, this gravel got deep, really deep. What's more, I was running along a ledge overlooking a drop of a hundred feet or so in some places. The slow pace and the toil of pulling through gravel a few inches deep was driving up the temperature gauge on the Wing, so I pulled over at a wide spot in the road and stopped to let it cool down while I considered my options. This would have been a useful place for a GPS, for all I could do was guess at my location on the map. I hadn't passed any cross roads, fire roads, or trails for what seemed like an eternity, so there was nothing to match up on the map. Either I was lost (gulp), or I had a long way yet to go (gulp, gulp).

The idea of turning around appalled me more than the thought that I might never come out at the other end, so I swung a leg back over the bike and soldiered on, riding slowly, carefully, and looking straight ahead. About a mile farther along, I passed a side road and then knew a) I wasn't turned around and b) I had about five miles to go. It wasn't long after that a

Gravel road, switchbacks, 800-pound bike. Yeah, that could be a good time.

stretch of pavement appeared, then gravel, then pavement. The pattern appeared to be reversing itself on this end of the road, so I returned to a faster pace on the pavement as the bike climbed a steep hill. As I popped over the top and started down the other side, you guessed it, nothing but gravel. Using up the last quarter ounce of good fortune in my luck account, I let the bike coast down the hill. I gradually brought my speed back down to

Hey Midge, you smell something?

a rate suitable for any condition. This is a road I do not recommend to the touring bike riders. Dual-sports will have a blast. I'll lay out an optional route for the rest of us momentarily.

Thankfully, the road from Pickens to Helvetia (www.helvetiawv.com) was paved and pleasant and my entry into the village was uneventful. **Helvetia** (pronounced Hel-VAY-sha) is a curiosity in a state that already abounds with the unexpected and unusual. Swiss immigrants from Brooklyn, New York, sought out this place in the mountains in 1869, looking for a landscape more familiar to them. At its height, Helvetia's population topped 400. Many of the few dozen people who live here now are direct descendants of the original founders. **The Hulle Restaurant** (304-924-6435) serves many Swiss specialties and the **Beekeeper Inn** (same owner, same phone) offers accommodations. No phone, no TV, and breakfast around the pot-bellied stove in the kitchen. Getting away from it all is the only option here in Helvetia.

Out of Helvetia, turn left on CR-46. You'll enjoy miles of clean pavement and curves on the way out to WV 20. Over the county line, CR-46 becomes CR-11 in Randolph County. At the intersection of CR-11 and WV 20, pay a

Monongahela National Forest is a great place to stretch your legs and grab some lunch. Just be sure to take your cupcake wrappers with you when you go. (Photo courtesy of the USDA Forest Service)

THE MID-ATLANTIC

visit to the very interesting **West Virginia State Wildlife Center**. The center began as a resource for restoring wildlife populations in the state, but after a few years in operation, realized its value as a tourist destination. The small entrance fee you pay helps cover the cost of operating the center and its continuing mission. Residents at the center include black bears, bobcats, and elk.

Next, the southbound trek to Summersville follows WV 20 for a little over 60 miles and is my leading candidate for the best route in the state. It delivers mile after mile of sweepers and bends. Passing through Webster Springs, I had to laugh as I passed the hospital (not my normal reaction). You will too when you notice one of the roads leading into the hospital is marked "Dead End."

Seeing that caused me to reflect on the valuable lessons learned on this trip. First, brochures describing Helvetia warn prospective visitors "Don't take any short cuts." I would have done well to heed that advice. Second, next time I will listen (maybe) to that little voice that says "This road is a bad idea."

In Craigsville, WV 20 heads south. Continue to follow WV 55 until it picks up WV 41. Follow WV 41 west to make your return to Summersville.

Given all I know now about the route in and out of Helvetia, the preferred route is obvious. When you join WV 20 at Hacker Valley, head north and follow CR-11/CR-46 into the village, then turn around and retrace the route. It's such a pleasant ride, you won't mind covering this section of road twice. And for goodness sake, keep the rubber side down and the shiny side up!

■ For more trips in this region see *Motorcycle Journeys Through the Appalachians* by Dale Coyner, available from Whitehorse Press.

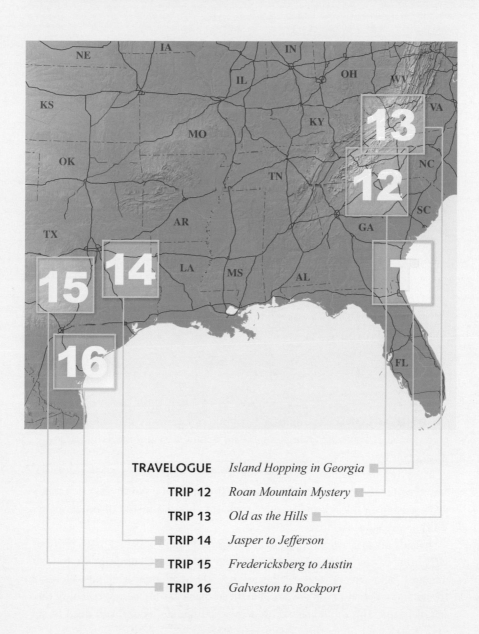

Island Hopping in Georgia

Text and photos by Bill Kresnack

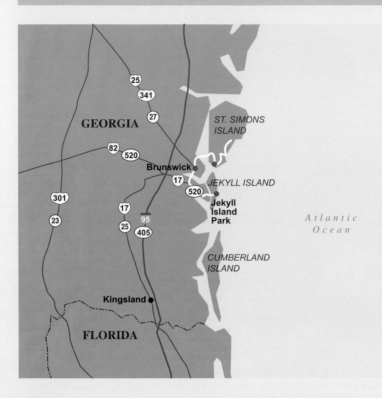

CRUISING ALONG a six-mile black ribbon of causeway that cuts through green marsh, I leave the Georgia mainland behind and aim the Triumph toward open water.

"Leaving the mainland behind." On a sunny, summer morning, I love the sound of those words. Because it isn't just continental North America that's disappearing in the mirrors of the Sprint RS. It's the hustle of modern life. Work. Schedules. All that.

Islands always seem to operate in a different time zone, and that's particularly true of the barrier islands separated from the Georgia coast by salt marshes, tidal rivers, and backwater sounds. The road I'm on—Georgia Route 520—doesn't even get out of sight of the coastline before reaching tiny Jekyll Island. But on the short trip across the marshy water, you need to set your watch back about three centuries.

It was near here that the British, arriving in the 1730s, established the colony of Georgia in the so-called Debatable Land between South Carolina and

Florida. Scanning the miles of waterfront forest, patrolled by snowy egrets and great blue herons, it's possible to believe that little has changed since.

The causeway ends, and I bank the Triumph right, onto South Riverview Drive, which circles the island. The narrow road winds between oak trees draped with Spanish moss. Within minutes, it feels like I've entered a completely different world. The bike, and I, slow down to match its pace.

I appreciate the scale of islands. On the mainland, riding from coast to coast can take several days. Here, it's only a few miles before I emerge on the island's south end, where I get my first glimpse of the fine-sand beaches that surround it. I pull into a sandswept parking lot and find a bench where I can enjoy some shade and a drink.

Model of WWII "Liberty Ship" in Brunswick, Georgia.

It's still early, but the Georgia heat is building, and the humidity warns of a storm on the way. For now, though, it's relaxing to sit and watch Atlantic waves crashing on a beach that's nearly as empty today as it was in the 1700s.

Back on the bike, I turn north, heading for a bit of history: the home of the island's first British settler, Major William Horton. It's near the northern end of the island, but that's only about eight miles away, so the trip takes just minutes.

Horton was one of 650 British troops brought over by Gen. James Oglethorpe when he founded the Georgia colony in 1733. The major established a farm on Jekyll Island that produced crops needed by settlers at the military outpost of Frederica on nearby St. Simons Island. Then, when Oglethorpe returned to England in 1743, Horton took his place as commander of the colony's military forces.

I pull up in front of the Horton home, which was built in about 1742 from "tabby," a combination of sand,

Unspoiled beach at Georgia's Jekyll Island.

lime, oyster shell, and water mixed into a mortar. It's one of the oldest surviving tabby structures in Georgia, having withstood Atlantic storms and hurricanes for more than 250 years.

Nearby stand the remains of Horton's other venture, another tabby structure where he made beer for British troops. It has the distinction of being the first brewery in Georgia. In these warm-weather islands, I imagine business was brisk.

The island had few residents when Horton lived here. And all these years later, it's still pretty empty. But for a time in the late 1800s and early 1900s, this small patch of land became one of the playgrounds of America's richest families.

In 1886, a group of about 50 millionaires, including J.P. Morgan, William Rockefeller, Joseph Pulitzer, Frank H. Goodyear, and plumbing magnate Richard Crane, bought the island. They built themselves a palatial clubhouse surrounded by luxurious "cottages," many of which had dozens of rooms. Appropriately enough, Crane's cottage even had 17 bathrooms!

The millionaires maintained the Jekyll Island Club until 1942. But by then, the rich had found other places to vacation. In 1947, the state purchased the island to preserve both its environment and the remains of that historic era.

The shell of Major Horton's two-story home stands as a reminder of the British hold on Georgia in the 1700s.

The place to learn about that time is the Jekyll Island Club Hotel, which occupies the old clubhouse. This building served as a hunting lodge during the early decades of the 20th century, but it was also an important place to engage in what would now be called networking. In fact, America's Federal Reserve system was conceived in one of these meeting rooms in 1910.

Wandering the manicured grounds and croquet fields, you get a sense of the size of this 100-room, Queen Anne-style structure. Walking inside, you can't help but notice the luxurious details. Extensive verandas, detailed woodwork, bay windows, pine floors, and leaded art glass all take you back in time.

Back on the bike, I finish my lap of Jekyll Island and cross the causeway again. My next destination is St. Simons Island to the north. But first, there's a stop I need to make on the mainland, in the town of Brunswick.

To get away from it all, millionaires in the late 19th century escaped to Georgia's Jekyll Island. You can too. Their clubhouse is now a hotel.

According to local historians, Brunswick, Georgia, is actually named for Braunsweig, Germany, the ancestral home of British King George II, who granted Georgia's original land charter. But I'm not here in search of historical footnotes. I'm here for the Brunswick stew.

There are several places that claim to be the original home of Brunswick stew. In particular, Brunswick County, Virginia, has built its reputation on the claim. But those Virginia boosters will get a serious argument here, because there are many who say that real Brunswick stew comes from Georgia.

I pull up at Spanky's restaurant in Brunswick to consider the evidence from a table overlooking a marsh.

At Spanky's, Brunswick stew is a mix of chicken, beef, pork, onions, corn, peas, potato, beans, and seasonings. Like so much regional fare, though, it originated with whatever ingredients were most available. And in the 1800s, that meant Brunswick stew was usually made with squirrel.

The consistency of the Spanky's recipe is surprising, more like thick soup than stew. But the taste is outstanding, with slow-cooked meat that is tender

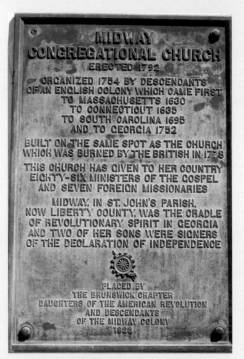

MIDWAY
CONGREGATIONAL CHURCH
ERECTED 1792

ORGANIZED 1754 BY DESCENDANTS
OF AN ENGLISH COLONY WHICH CAME FIRST
TO MASSACHUSETTS 1630
TO CONNECTICUT 1635
TO SOUTH CAROLINA 1695
AND TO GEORGIA 1752

BUILT ON THE SAME SPOT AS THE CHURCH
WHICH WAS BURNED BY THE BRITISH IN 1778

THIS CHURCH HAS GIVEN TO HER COUNTRY
EIGHTY-SIX MINISTERS OF THE GOSPEL
AND SEVEN FOREIGN MISSIONARIES

MIDWAY, IN ST. JOHN'S PARISH,
NOW LIBERTY COUNTY, WAS THE CRADLE
OF REVOLUTIONARY SPIRIT IN GEORGIA
AND TWO OF HER SONS WERE SIGNERS
OF THE DECLARATION OF INDEPENDENCE

PLACED BY
THE BRUNSWICK CHAPTER
DAUGHTERS OF THE AMERICAN REVOLUTION
AND DESCENDANTS
OF THE MIDWAY COLONY
1923

This plaque on the Midway Congregational Church provides a brief history.

and infused with flavor. I can't say whether Georgia's Brunswick stew is better than Virginia's, but it sure is good.

From Spanky's, I ride north just a little way to a toll bridge leading to St. Simons Island, the largest and most populated of what are known as "The Golden Isles" off the Georgia coast.

Of course, that also means St. Simons has the most traffic, which makes it a little like riding on the mainland, at least near the bridge at the southern end.

Fortunately, the crowds thin out once you head north up the center of the island on Frederica Road. Moss-covered live oaks form a canopy over your head along much of the route, making the road feel much more remote than the thriving island really is.

Within minutes, I come across a beautiful, white-painted church set amidst the trees. I pull in, park under a large live oak and walk up the shaded path to the door. This is Christ Church, an Episcopal house of worship that dates from 1884. But this location also has historic significance for the Methodist religion.

When Oglethorpe founded the Georgia colony, he brought with him a number of ministers from the Church of England, including two brothers, Charles and John Wesley.

Charles was appointed as minister to the Frederica settlement on St. Simons Island, while John was rector of Christ Church in Savannah, farther up the coast. By the time they arrived in America, though, both were already involved in a splinter movement within the British church. After their return to England, they were the primary founders of the religion that became known as Methodism.

The first church on this site wasn't built until the early 1800s, long after the Wesley brothers had left Georgia. By that time, the American branch of the Church of England had adopted the Episcopal name. The original Episcopal Christ Church here was destroyed in the Civil War, and it was replaced by the current church in the years after the war.

The inside is peaceful and surprisingly cool, illuminated only by sunlight passing through intricate stained-glass windows.

Behind the church is a small cemetery that, according to legend, contains the remains of a young woman who was terrified of the dark. After she died, her husband would bring a lighted candle each night to her grave. Eventually, he, too, died, but according to the legend, you can sometimes see a flickering candle in the graveyard at night.

The sun is still well up in the sky, but the deep shade and hanging moss give the cemetery a suitably mysterious feel as I walk between the rows of old headstones.

Returning to the Triumph, I take a short hop up the road to Fort Frederica, Georgia's first military base. Established by Oglethorpe in 1736, this outpost would form part of a southern line of defense for the British colonies against the Spanish, based in Florida.

Frederica was a planned community, with the original 116 settlers (44 men and 72 women and children)

It's a small church with a big sign.

This still-active chapel in South Newport, Georgia, is 10 feet by 15 feet in size and claims to be the smallest church in America.

chosen based on the skills the town would require. Today, you can still walk down its old Broad Street and see the remains of buildings and fortifications those colonists created.

The need for this southern fort becomes apparent at the National Park Service's Bloody Marsh battle site nearby. It was here that the British put a stop to Spanish excursions outside of Florida.

In 1742, a fleet of 36 Spanish ships brought 2,000 troops to St. Simons Island with the goal of bringing Georgia under Spanish rule. Oglethorpe, with his 650-man regular regiment, along with some Scot Highlanders, colonial rangers, and native Americans, was equally intent on defending the land.

Some 200 elite Spanish Grenadiers, who served as advance troops, were spotted preparing to cross this open marsh on their way to Fort Frederica. Defenders waited in ambush, firing from the trees at the hapless victims in the marsh.

Even though the Spanish far outnumbered the British defenders, they fled after a two-hour battle, and never again challenged British rule over Georgia. When the battle was done, witnesses said the marsh was red with the blood of the wounded and dead, giving the place its name.

Just one of the many millionaire's "cottages" preserved on Georgia's Jekyll Island.

Travelogue: South

Standing in the forest at the edge of the marsh, I try to picture the scene. But with the sun shining brightly and the marsh alive with green vegetation, it's hard to imagine any place on Earth more peaceful.

Although the Spanish never again attacked St. Simons, the island did play a vital role in a later conflict. In 1794, live oak trees from the island were cut for use in building the U.S.S. Constitution, the pride of the fledgling U.S. Navy in the War of 1812. Those trees helped earn the ship its nickname of "Old Ironsides."

"When live oak dries, and you try to cut it with an axe, the axe just bounces off," a park ranger tells me. "It's like steel."

Of course, by the time Old Ironsides sailed the seas, much had changed in Georgia. Many of the settlers who had helped found that British colony had risen up against the crown and created a new nation.

Georgia's historic St. Simons lighthouse, completed in 1872.

Its accomplishments in the years since have been many and varied, from landing a man on the moon to inventing the Big Mac.

But the bulk of that has taken place over there, on the mainland. Even after all these years, there's not much evidence of it on parts of Georgia's barrier islands.

It's as though the tide of progress washed over these islands generations ago, and never returned, leaving them firmly rooted in another time.

And that's just fine by me.

12 Roan Mountain Mystery

Text and photos by Dale Coyner

■ **DISTANCE** *149 miles*

■ **HIGHLIGHTS** *Brown Mountain "lights," Linville Gorge and Falls, Loafer's Glory, Roan Mountain, and the Linn Cove Viaduct*

0.0 Begin NC 268 out of Ferguson, North Carolina	**82.0** Right on NC 226
15.4 Right on Warrior Road	**84.4** Left on NC 261 (Roan Mountain Road)
16.0 Right on SR 1353 (Setzers Creek Road)	**97.0** Arrive Roan Mountain Summit, continue on TN 143
18.3 Right on NC 90 (Collettsville Road)	**109.4** Right on US 19E South at Roan Mountain, Tennessee
23.5 Left on SR 1337 (Adako Road)	**116.1** Left on NC 194
31.8 Right on NC 181 North	**122.5** Right on NC 184
45.3 Left on NC 183	**127.0** Right on NC 105
49.3 Right on Old NC 105	**131.0** Left on US 221 North
49.8 Right on US 221	**134.0** Left on Blue Ridge Parkway North
51.7 Left on NC 194	**147.3** Right on US 321 at Blowing Rock
55.7 Left on US 19E North	**148.8** Arrive Blowing Rock via Blue Ridge Parkway
69.7 Right on NC 80 North	

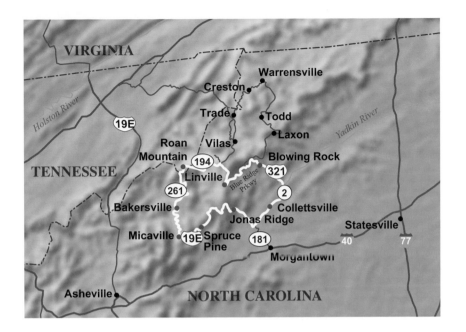

WESTERN NORTH CAROLINA is filled with legends of ghostly figures, strange events, and unexplained phenomena. The strange things which happen in this area aren't as widely known as sightings of the Loch Ness monster or those unexplained crop circles in England, but they remain well documented events which defy scientific explanation to this day.

Our search to uncover these mountain mysteries begins westbound on Route 268 toward Happy Valley. Here the road hugs one side of the valley in places, perhaps to maximize the amount of land available for farming. This makes the road follow a drunken path with an occasional straight followed by a series of curves. It's a good warm up exercise. It's also part of the Overmountain Victory Trail, marking the route that a band of mountaineers marched to fight the British in the battle of King's Mountain, South Carolina. It was a decisive victory for the patriots and a turning point in the Revolutionary War.

Route 268 ends on Route 321. Cross the road and you will be on Warriors Road, a dinky little footpath that could be called paved in the loose sense of the word. This leads through the woods to Setzers Creek Road, a right turn. Setzers Creek Road then ends on Route 90. For a state route, 90 isn't much bigger. The road has stood up well to the beating it has taken from lumber trucks. This area is well-suited to dual-sport bikes. There are dozens of side roads to follow, some leading deep into the hollows that see few outsiders. Route 90 turns northward at Collettsville and passes through some beautiful, remote backcountry, bounded by the Johns River on one side and sheer rock

The award-winning Linn Cove Viaduct crosses the southern slope of Grandfather Mountain. (Hugh Morton photo courtesy of www.grandfather.com)

walls vibrant green with native ferns and mosses on the other. Suddenly the road becomes dirt. Huh? I thought state primary routes were supposed to be paved, but this one isn't. I made a note to myself: "Get knobbies for Wing." Like General MacArthur, I shall return. Retracing my path to Collettsville, I found the turn I had planned to make. Adako Road crosses the Johns and continues to follow the narrow valley around Brown Mountain. It becomes Brown Mountain Beach Road before intersecting with Route 181.

Brown Mountain (www.brownmountainlights.com) has a long history as a source of mysterious lights, reported by Indians well before the first settlers reached the eastern shore. They are seen at night and are reported to roam around the mountain. Dozens of studies and expeditions have been conducted to discover the source of the lights, including some done by departments of the federal gub'ment. Explanations include trains (there are no tracks on the mountain), car headlights (there are no roads on the mountain), swamp gas (no swamps) and a slave searching for his lost master. That one can't be so easily disproved.

Make the right turn on Route 181 to return to the mountains. Soon the road becomes one long, well-banked sweeper after another—a pleasant, fast ride. A left turn on Route 183 will bring you to a parking area for the **Linville Gorge and Falls** (www.nps.gov/blri/linville.htm). You can easily spend an hour or two here hiking the paths that lead to different views of the waterfalls of the Linn River. The gorge, about 2,000 feet deep, was formed when twisting and shearing forces that built up the mountains caused a weak seam to split, kind of like popping a kernel of corn. (Well, that's how my mind pictures it, a geologist would no doubt take issue with that.) You don't have to walk far to see the falls, just a few tenths of a mile for the upper section, another few tenths for the lower.

You can find a good lunch at **Famous Louise's Rockhouse Restaurant** (828-765-2702). Follow Route 183 to Old Route 105, then right on Old 105 to Route 221. You'll find Louise's at the intersection. What's so famous about Famous Louise's? All you have to do is walk inside and look at the ceiling. The restaurant sits on the exact intersection of Avery, Burke, and McDowell counties, and signs along the ceiling indicate which county you are in. Your food is prepared in Avery, eaten in Burke, and paid for in McDowell!

Return to Route 221 and follow it east to the point where Route 194 enters from your left. Turn on Route 194 to cut across to Route 19E, a busy corridor through the upper northwest. Some areas around Spruce Pine are ragged from mining operations. People have been digging holes in the ground around here for a thousand years for minerals. There is a spot somewhere in the hills called Sink Hole Mines, a place where Spanish conquistadors reportedly found silver in great quantities.

Past Spruce Pine is a nice little road, Route 80. The road surface is good in most places, if not smooth, though a few gravel hazards exist at some entrances. The road twists in and out of the North Toe River Valley, making three turns where seemingly one would do. Suits me fine. You'll often find a few other riders out here, as this is a popular spot among locals.

About halfway along your route you pass through Bandana, which got its name when a railroad worker tied a bandana to a tree to indicate where a stop was to be made. When Route 80 arrives at a T intersection, make a left turn. Route 80 ends in Loafer's Glory on Route 226.

There was once a store here which was a popular gathering place for the local men folk to hang around during the day, playing checkers, taking an afternoon snooze, and generally being stinking lazy. Eventually it became known as a "loafer's glory" among the wives of the community and the name stuck.

Linville Falls's rocky river gorge is more easily admired from the trail than from a canoe. (Photo courtesy of NC Division of Tourism, Film, and Sports Development)

Enter the town of Bakersville and make a left on Route 261. This section of road is reminiscent of Route 181 in its sweeping curves and great sightlines. It takes its good ol' time winding up the mountains, eventually reaching Roan Mountain State Park on the Tennessee-North Carolina border.

Roan Mountain is the typical southern Appalachian bald. A bald is a treeless area, usually filled with large rhododendron gardens like Roan, although it can be a large grassy area. None of the Appalachians rise above the treeline. There isn't anything inherently different about the soil. So why haven't they been covered with trees like other areas? No one knows. Another unusual feature of Roan Mountain is occasional strange humming or buzzing noises, as though bees are swarming. Sometimes the sound is described as crackling, like high-tension electrical wires. The most likely source, we are told, is the passing of opposing electrical charges between clouds and the ground. Again, no one knows why.

The view from Roan is nothing short of spectacular. The Blue Ridge fills the southern and eastern horizon while the Great Smokies lie to the north and west. You can almost ride right into the gardens. Across from the visitor center is a trail leading to the peak of Roan, a lofty 6,285 feet.

Route 216 becomes Route 143 in Tennessee, making a graceful descent through Cherokee National Forest and **Roan Mountain State Park** (www.state.tn.us/environment/parks/parks/RoanMtn). The state park would make a nice night's layover. They have cabins and a lodge, trails, and a swimming pool, but most of all they are in a beautiful location with a relaxing atmosphere. The road through the park gets twisty and narrow in places. Look well through your curves before picking an aggressive line. You will encounter

The grassy hilltops around Roan Mountain are great places to stop for a picnic. Just beware of the singing Austrian families. (Photo courtesy of NC Division of Tourism, Film, and Sports Development)

an occasional recreational vehicle on its way to the camping area and you don't want to be so fully committed to a line that you can't make an adjustment.

Route 143 ends on Route 19E. We've caught up to the same road we followed west to get to Spruce Pine, now we'll follow it south to return to Route 194. I found myself checking and rechecking my map at each intersection on routes throughout this area. The confused folds and tucks of the Appalachians have made a mess out of the usual north-south, east-west corridors. A global positioning receiver would be more useful than a map.

Rider's Roost is situated along the Yadkin River in Ferguson, North Carolina. Owners Uncle Roy and BC have a great moto-facility.

You'll find Route 194 at Elk Park (No elk, no park. Hmmm . . .). This brings you back to the Banner Elk area (No banner, no elk. What's going on here?). A right on 184 and another on Route 105 puts you in Linville. This is the fastest way to return to the Parkway. Turn left and follow Route 221 to the Parkway. Just a little way ahead is the **Linn Cove Information Center** (www.blueridgeparkway.org/linncove.htm) at the head of the Linn Cove Viaduct. Since its completion in 1987, the viaduct is probably the most photographed spot on the Parkway.

The Blue Ridge Parkway had been built from both ends until reaching a difficult area at **Grandfather Mountain.** The roadway had to be built without attachment to the mountain, and to preserve the delicate ecosystem, no heavy equipment or traditional techniques could be used. In fact, the means to construct the viaduct had to be invented as there was no precedent anywhere in the world. The resulting bridge uses pre-cast concrete and steel beam construction. The pieces were cast to such tight tolerances there was never more than a .01-inch variance from the specified fit. No piece of the bridge is perfectly straight except for the southernmost link. It's a blast to ride—you feel like you're just hanging in the air as you glide across the face of Grandfather. For an up-close look, there is a 300-yard paved trail from the information center to the underside of the bridge. Your path home can be traced down the Parkway to Blowing Rock. Here you can follow Route 321 south to Route 268 to return to Ferguson.

■ For more trips in this region see *Motorcycle Journeys Through the Appalachians* by Dale Coyner, available from Whitehorse Press.

13 Old as the Hills

Text and photos by Dale Coyner

■ **DISTANCE** *120 miles*

■ **HIGHLIGHTS** *Two unique general stores, Grandfather Mountain, Cone Manor House, the Blue Ridge Parkway*

0.0 Begin Blue Ridge Parkway North out of Blowing Rock, North Carolina	**64.4** Left on US 421 South at Trade, Tennessee
15.2 Left on US 421 North	**65.2** Right on SR 1233 (Old US 421)
17.7 Right on SR 1359 (Brownwood Road)	**73.2** Left on US 321 South
20.4 Left on SR 1100 (Cranberry Springs/Todd Railroad Grade Road)	**74.9** Right on NC 194
25.1 Right on NC 194 at Todd	**85.6** Straight on NC 184 in Banner Elk
32.0 Left on US 221 North/NC 194 at Baldwin	**89.9** Arrive Beech Mountain, then turn around and follow NC 184
35.5 Left on US 221 Business North/NC 194 at West Jefferson	**98.3** Right on NC 105
38.7 Left on NC 88 at Jefferson	**102.3** Left on US 221 in Linville
	119.7 Arrive Blowing Rock via US 221 North

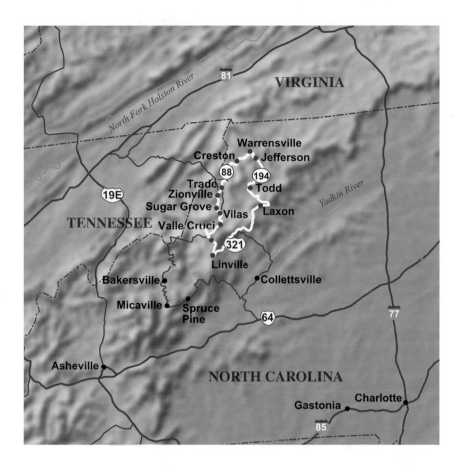

SOME AREAS OF the country still evoke a feeling of the glory years of motorcycling. Western North Carolina is one of them. Open country roads are lined with small farms set against a backdrop of low hills. Old road alignments pass buildings that once served as filling stations and country stores that are now converted to another purpose or stand empty and fallen into disrepair, mute testimony to the changing times. Surely the next bike you meet will be a 1927 Harley or a Henderson.

Our tour begins following the Blue Ridge Parkway north out of Blowing Rock, North Carolina. At the junction with US 421 at Deep Gap, exit the parkway and follow US 421 west. At Brownwood Road, turn right and follow the sign for the Todd General Store. Where Brownwood Road meets Railroad Grade Road, turn left and follow Railroad Grade. True to its name, this section of road follows an old railroad line. There is at least one bone-jarring dip on this road soon after you make the turn from Brownwood. It just comes out of nowhere and could be a real spring-buster if you hit it at speed. Where are those DIP signs when you need them?

As seen from the Foscoe community between Boone and Linville in North Carolina, the Grandfather profile depicts the silhouette of a bearded man facing the heavens. (Hugh Morton photo courtesy of www.grandfather.com)

Todd was a bustling timber center in its earlier days. As with many towns, it diminished when the timber ran out and many stores closed. **Todd General Store,** built in 1914, continues to serve the community as a tourist draw, museum, and functioning store. You can buy varied items such as brass tacks, beeswax, and Double Yellow Line-brand sun-dried canned possum. A fellow riding friend says they make great sandwiches here, too. Just be sure you count the cans of possum on the counter before and after they make your sandwich. Besides the general store, there are a few craft houses and emporiums to knock around in. You just might find an abandoned vintage machine hidden in the back of one of them.

When you arrive at the crossroad with Route 194, you'll need to make a difficult turn uphill and back to the right to get on track. It's a hard trick to do on big bikes and it's easier to take as a left turn, so you might want to follow Railroad Grade across 194, turn around in a flat spot, and return to the intersection to make your turn. Part of Route 194 is known as the Old Buffalo Trail, a route that herds of bison used to follow through the mountains. Biologists tell us that the great beasts would migrate east to spend winters on the coast where temperatures were milder, then return over the mountains during the summers. Some of the trails they left were used by early settlers and eventually incorporated into roads we still use. Nearby is a small village with the gruesome name of Meat Camp. That answers the question of what happened to the buffalo.

NC 194 north is freshly paved and good riding. After leaving Todd it crests a hill and settles down into a small valley dotted with a few small farms. Route 194 intersects with Route 221 at Baldwin and heads north to West Jefferson. You'll also find an older alignment of the road here that parallels the route into town. Follow the old road for less traffic and more curves.

West Jefferson is home to the **Ashe County Cheese Factory,** the lone survivor of a state-sponsored program from the early 1900s to promote cheese making as a way for dairy farmers to earn extra cash. Soon after the program started, cheese factories popped up all over. Making cheese was easy enough. Getting it to market over tall hills and bad roads was another matter, though, and soon put most would-be cheese kings out of business. One industry that did thrive during that time was moonshining. And the practice of 'shine running actually formed another industry: stock car racing. The ridge runners who drove souped-up cars with special tanks to hold the whiskey were the forerunners of today's racers. The early members of the National Association of Stock Car Auto Racing (NASCAR) who were the better drivers often started out running corn liquor along the narrow, dark roads of the Lost Provinces.

Mount Jefferson State Park is a good place for a picnic. It's just east of the town on Route 221. A short drive to the top rewards you with a nice view of the Stone Mountains to the west, the Blue Ridge to the east.

Follow Route 88 west out of West Jefferson along the north fork of the New. A few small villages are strung out along the banks of the river, interrupted by farms that manage to squeeze a few acres of crops in the narrow river valley. Eventually Route 88 meanders into Tennessee and becomes Route 67. A small sign announces your arrival into the Volunteer State in a matter-of-fact way. At the junction of Route 67 and 421, turn left, following Route 421 east. Just as you return into North Carolina, look for Old US 421 on your right and follow it.

Along Old 421, buildings that once served the traveling public abound, evoking a nostalgic feeling as you meander along. Around one corner you will pass an old filling station, now vine-covered and returning to nature,

Stopping to smell the flowers is not common on the famous Blue Ridge Parkway, although it might be fun to do so. (Photo courtesy of NC Division of Tourism, Film, and Sports Development)

Old as the Hills

while around the next an old store has been rescued from the same fate, now serving as a craft shop or home. Most of the activity around these buildings is gone, but the shadows they cast in the early morning light are unchanged. If you look into those shadows, you can see and hear images of the past—a tow-headed boy with a white cap putting "50 cents worth" in a 1949 Ford coupe or Joe the mechanic applying incessant banging and verbal torque to a stubborn bolt on a shiny Hudson. As you pass the station, your visions of the past vanish as quickly as they appeared, and the only sound that remains is the throbbing of your engine. If you still hear a banging noise now, it only means your tailbag has gotten caught in your rear wheel. Then again, it might be your stomach clanging the lunch bell.

The old route ends on Route 321 just a few miles west of Vilas. Make a right and continue on Route 321 until you reach Vilas where Route 194 joins. Turn right to follow 194 west. You'll see a sign of things to come: "Warning: Steep winding road . . . not recommended for vehicles over 35 feet in length." They aren't kidding either. Wing riders with trailers might want to make sure their rigs don't exceed the recommended length! This is more of a paved goatpath than a road, but it is always fun. There are some incredibly tight switchbacks here that have you looking fully back over your shoulder while you are still negotiating the current turn. If you aren't comfortable with looking fully through a turn and counter steering, stay on the interstate and off of this road.

The big twisty stuff lasts for a few miles, then you are deposited into Valle Crucis. Stop at the **Mast General Store** (www.mastgeneralstore.com), established in 1883 and the oldest continuously operating general store in the country. The heavy wooden front door displays a plaque indicating the store is on the National Register of Historic Places. The front room is where the hardware and groceries are kept. The center of the room is dominated by a huge pot-bellied stove that looks big enough to burn a cord of wood at a time. Other rooms are filled to the ceiling with crafts and a lot of outdoor gear.

Mast General Store in Valle Crucis, North Carolina, is only two days older than the beans on its back shelf. (Photo courtesy of NC Division of Tourism, Film, and Sports Development)

The post office has finally settled at the Mast store. In earlier times, you might have picked up your mail here or down the road at the Farthing's place, depending on whether the local politburo was Republican or Democrat. It moved to the Mast store when a Democrat was elected or to Farthing's Republican stronghold when the GOP

Surveys show that the main reason people visit Grandfather Mountain, in North Carolina, is to enjoy the beautiful mountain scenery. The second is to cross the famous Mile High Swinging Bridge. (Hugh Morton photo courtesy of www.grandfather.com)

won a local election. It went on this way until H.W. Mast married Mary Hazel Farthing near the turn of the century. After that the post office stayed at the Mast store, since it was now in the family.

More twisty road awaits your ride to Banner Elk. Another section of nearly 180-degree switchbacks, then another valley ride. Pavement markings along the way click off the distance in kilometers, remnants of the Tour DuPont bicycle race. Some of the steep uphill climbs on this section will make you rejoice in the fact that your two wheels aren't powered by your two legs alone! In Banner Elk, follow the road signs for **Beech Mountain** (www.skibeech.com) to complete your ride to the top. Beech Mountain is a ski resort and at 5,506 feet it's also eastern America's highest town.

When you start rolling back down the hill, just imagine what it would be like to blast down this mountain on a bicycle, with contact patches the width of your pinkie finger, wearing no more protective gear than a half-helmet and skin-tight spandex clothing, wheeling through a crowd of others hell-bent on getting down ahead of you. And people think motorcyclists are crazy?

Route 184 south out of Banner Elk has a moderate amount of traffic, mostly the Florida set. It ends on Route 105. Turn right and follow 105 into

Linville. In town, turn left on Route 221. You'll find the entrance to Grandfather Mountain (www.grandfather.com) just a few miles up the road.

Grandfather Mountain got its name from Indians who thought the mountain looked like the face of an old man. Unlike some other natural attractions where you have to stretch your imagination to see a familiar shape,

You'd think picking through a bucket of rocks would get tiresome after a while, but it's actually a lot of fun. And you do find some quality gemstones.

this one really does look like the profile of an old man outlined in the rock. Grandfather Mountain is unique in two other respects. It is formed of some of the oldest exposed rock found in the Blue Ridge chain and is the highest summit in the chain. Grandfather Mountain is privately owned and there is an admission charge. At the top there are 25 miles of hiking trails, a nature museum, and the famous mile-high swinging bridge. If you cross it, you can climb a moderately difficult trail to get to Linville Peak and 360-degree views of the area.

Moses Cone was known as "the Denim King." He used his money to, among other things, build Cone Manor and practically adopt the growing town of Blowing Rock, North Carolina. (Photo courtesy of NC Division of Tourism, Film, and Sports Development)

The route is finished off with a 19-mile dash into Blowing Rock along Route 221. The stretch between Grandfather Mountain and Blowing Rock is pristine motorcycling road, mostly flat and very curvy. This section parallels the Blue Ridge Parkway and was used as a connection during the years when the Linn Cove Viaduct (the last link in the Parkway) was being built. The viaduct was finished in 1987 and Route 221 was abandoned by the touring set. Great! It's like having your own personal section of the Parkway, but with more and tighter curves.

The last stop of the day is the **Moses H. Cone Flat Top Manor House** where the Parkway and US 221 meet near Blowing Rock. Built by textile magnate Cone as a summer home, the manor house is now home to the **Parkway Craft Center** and features a wealth of finely crafted Appalachian goods. These goods are several notches above those at roadside craft stands. If

North Carolina's Grandfather Mountain Is steeped in legend. (Photo courtesy of NC Division of Tourism, Film, and Sports Development)

you carry a National Parks Passport, you can get a "Blue Ridge Parkway" passport stamp here. Outside, you can enjoy the cool breeze on the front porch while you pass the time in a straight-back rocker. Can't you just picture yourself living here, glass of lemonade in hand, admiring your vast estate?

If you're staying in Blowing Rock you have only to travel a few miles down Route 221 to reach your destination. If you're returning to camp at Ferguson, follow Route 321 south and then Route 268 east.

■ For more trips in this region see *Motorcycle Journeys Through the Appalachians* by Dale Coyner, available from Whitehorse Press.

14 Jasper to Jefferson

Text and photos by Neal Davis

■ **DISTANCE** *To Jefferson: 175 miles; to Shreveport: 195 miles*

■ **HIGHLIGHTS** *Good roads with many opportunities to stop and take in the natural sights, bright lights and gambling, and a sleepy old restored Southern town*

0.0 Leave Jasper, Texas, via Hwy. 190	**85.0** Turn right onto Hwy. 84
20.0 Turn right onto Hwy. 256	**86.0** Cross Sabine River into Louisiana, turn left onto Hwy. 169
33.0 Turn right onto Hwy. 69	
35.0 Turn right onto Hwy. 255	**89.0** Turn left onto Hwy. 31
54.0 Turn left onto Hwy. 1007	**127.0** Get onto I-20 west
59.0 Turn left onto Hwy. 96	**129.0** Exit onto Hwy. 59 north
70.0 Turn right onto Hwy. 83	**148.0** Turn right onto Taylor
75.0 Turn left onto Hwy. 3121	*Mileages are approximate
80.0 Turn left onto Hwy. 21	

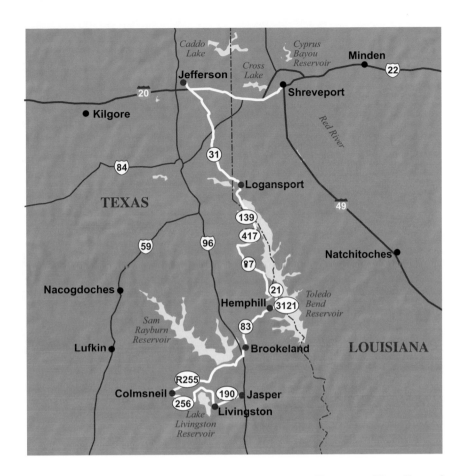

LEAVE JASPER, TEXAS, on Hwy. 190 west. The next 20 miles of high-speed road is a visual delight, especially in the spring when wildflowers line the sides of the roads. The many lakes and bayous containing giant cypress trees draped with Spanish moss run contrary to most folks image of Texas. After this run, turn right onto Hwy. 256, every rider's dream road running through the forest with gentle hills and numerous sweepers. Very fast riding is not safe, as your line of sight is limited by the heavy vegetation and healthy deer population.

After 13 miles, turn right onto Hwy. 69, go only two miles, and make another right turn onto Hwy. 255. For the next 19 miles, you can pick up your speed, as the sides of the highway have been cleared back a good distance and you can see through the curves. Turn left onto Hwy. 1007, proceed five miles, and turn left onto Hwy. 96.

For the last few miles, you will have had some excellent views of **Lake Sam Rayburn,** the largest lake in Texas, covering more than 114,000 acres. It is thoroughly enjoyed by fishermen and utilized for all water sports, which

Shreveport, Louisiana, is known for riverboat casinos, thoroughbred racing, and spicy cuisine. (Photo courtesy of Betty Jo LeBru, Shreveport-Bossier Film Office)

can add a lot of interest to your rest stops. As the road goes on, it passes the dam that creates this lake—truly an engineering marvel.

Eleven miles up Hwy. 96, turn right onto Hwy. 83, and follow signs as the road works its way through the small town of Hemphill. You may have noticed by now that the farther north you get in east Texas, the more frequent and pronounced the hills become. Five miles out of Hemphill, turn left onto Hwy. 3121, go another five miles, and turn left onto Hwy. 21. Five miles later, turn right onto Hwy. 87, a major road that is, nevertheless, a delight to ride. Although you are now going through the **Sabine National Forest,** some of the land along the road has been developed into pasture. After 16 miles, turn right onto Hwy. 139.

Slow down and enjoy the next 25 miles on Hwy. 139, as this is just about as good as it gets, with lots of hills, curves, and beautiful views. Turn right onto Hwy. 84 and cross the **Sabine River** into Louisiana at Logansport. Almost immediately after crossing the river, turn left onto Hwy. 169, proceed three miles, and then turn left onto Hwy. 31, which will take you back into Texas. Follow Hwy. 31 for 38 miles to the intersection with I-20—a pleasant ride with the potential for a good cruising speed.

When you reach I-20 you must pick your destination for the evening. If you would like to try your hand at some riverboat gambling, head east to Shreveport. If you prefer a small quiet old Southern town with an interesting historic district, take I-20 west.

If you're headed to **Shreveport,** just follow I-20 east for 39 miles. According to Louisiana law, all casinos must be on riverboats. It didn't take operators long to put the casinos themselves on permanent barges moored to the riverbank and build huge hotel complexes and support facilities on the adjoining bank. The two buildings are connected by covered "boarding walkways." In fact, you are given a "boarding pass" as you enter the casinos.

Almost all major gambling operators are represented off Exit 20, offering everything you would expect to find in Las Vegas. In addition to any losses your visit might incur, consider that the cost of the room will be around $100. Dining opportunities abound. I like the **Isle of Capri Casino** because it has nickel slots on the third floor. If you want to gamble, but would rather not spend so much on a room, head to Exit 21 and check out the **Motel 6** ($30). The cab ride back to the casino will only be a buck or two.

The massive swamps and bayous found in East Texas are a surprise to many riders. (Photo courtesy of Stan Williams/TxDOT)

If you're headed to **Jefferson,** take I-20 west for only a mile or two, exit onto Hwy. 59 north, and go about 19 miles. As you enter the city, turn right onto Taylor to get into the historic section of the city.

For a city its size, Jefferson has an amazing array of places to stay. If you prefer a standard motel unit, try the **Inn of Jefferson,** located on your right as you come into town, at 400 S. Wolcott ($45; 903-665-3983), a new motel within walking distance of the historic district. **The Excelsior House** at 211 W. Austin has been in continuous operation since the 1850s ($85+; 903-665-2513) at the center of things, and the interior has been faithfully restored and furnished in the period. To

The entrance to the Isle of Capri Casino in Shreveport, Louisiana, is hard to miss at night, even from space. (Photo courtesy of Betty Jo LeBru, Shreveport-Bossier Film Office)

narrow down the long list of historic B&Bs in the area, contact Jefferson Reservation Service (887-603-2535; www.jeffersonreservationservice.com). Try the fresh seafood, Cajun and Creole dishes at the **Black Swan** on 210 Austin. The helpings are abundant and the price is moderate.

There are no camping facilities in Jefferson proper. Fortunately, there are plenty nearby that are excellent. Try **Johnson Creek Park** located on **Lake o' The Pines,** which is operated by the Corps of Engineers (903-755-2435). There are 22 campsites sitting in a beautiful rural setting in the pines beside the lake. Facilities include flush toilets, showers, and grills. To get there, take Hwy. 49 west out of town, turn left onto Hwy. 729 for 15 miles, and go south on the park road for one mile.

Located on **Big Cypress Bayou,** the town of Jefferson was once a major river port that boasted a population of more than 20,000 people. Steamboats from the Mississippi River would come up the Red River through **Caddo Lake** and on up the Big Cypress Bayou to load and unload cargo. It was dubbed the **"Gateway to Texas."** During the Civil War, Jefferson exported cotton from the Southern states. After the Civil War, it served as the jumping

Louisiana is the place to be for old-time country fiddlin' and cajun music. (Photo courtesy Louisana Office of Tourism)

off point for many settlers headed farther west. The timber resources of east Texas went through Jefferson on their way to market.

Jefferson became a river port because of an act of nature: the New Madrid earthquake created a massive log jam on the Red River, known as the **"Great Raft,"** that raised the water levels in Caddo Lake and the bayou, allowing steamboat traffic. It is no longer a river port due to an act of man: in 1873, the U.S. Corps of Engineers removed the Great Raft, lowering the water levels. This change, along with the construction of railroads into Texas, led to a rapid decline.

Today, Jefferson is a sleepy little town of 2,500 people. Its gorgeous setting and the efforts of its residents to restore the town as it was in its glory days do attract visitors, however. Many antebellum homes and business establishments have been brought back to their former grandeur. Trolley tours, walking tours, boat rides, and even mule-drawn carriages cover the downtown historic district, making tourism the number one economic influence in the area today.

In places, Caddo Lake, in Louisiana, is more of a garden than a lake. (Photo courtesy of Betty Jo LeBru, Shreveport-Bossier Film Office)

■ For more trips in this region see *Motorcycle Journeys Through Texas* by Neal Davis, available from Whitehorse Press.

15 Fredericksburg to Austin

Text and photos by Neal Davis

- **DISTANCE** *241 miles*
- **HIGHLIGHTS** *Willow City Loop, Lime Creek Road, the historic city of Austin, the LBJ ranch, and views of the massive lakes north of Austin*

0.0 Leave Fredericksburg, Texas via Hwy. 16 north	**170.0** At T-intersection with Hwy. 165, turn right
20.0 Turn right onto Willow City Loop Road	**171.0** At T-intersection with Hwy. 290, turn left
33.0 Proceed straight ahead at intersection with Rural Road 1323	**174.0** Turn right onto Rural Road 3232
51.0 Turn left onto Sandy/Round Mountain Road	**181.0** Turn right onto Rural Road 2766
59.0 Turn left onto Hwy. 281	**181.0** Turn left into Pendernales Falls State Park
72.0 Turn right, in Marble Falls, onto Rural Road 1431	**181.0** Turn right onto Rural Road 2766
111.0 Turn right onto Lime Creek Road	**193.0** Turn right onto Hwy. 290
122.0 Turn left onto Rural Road 2769	**202.0** Turn left to continue on Hwy. 290
129.0 Turn right onto Hwy. 620	**217.0** LBJ Ranch is on your right
147.0 Turn right onto Hwy. 71	**218.0** Turn right onto Rural Road 1623
150.0 Turn left onto Rural Road 3238	**222.0** Turn left onto Rural Road 2721
155.0 Turn left onto Hwy. 12 toward Dripping Springs	**228.0** At intersection with Rural Road 1631, proceed straight onto 1631
160.0 Turn right onto Hwy. 290	**241.0** Turn right onto Hwy. 290 and continue straight into Fredericksburg
161.0 Turn left onto Creek Road	*Mileages are approximate
164.0 Turn right at intersection with CR 220 to remain on Creek Road	

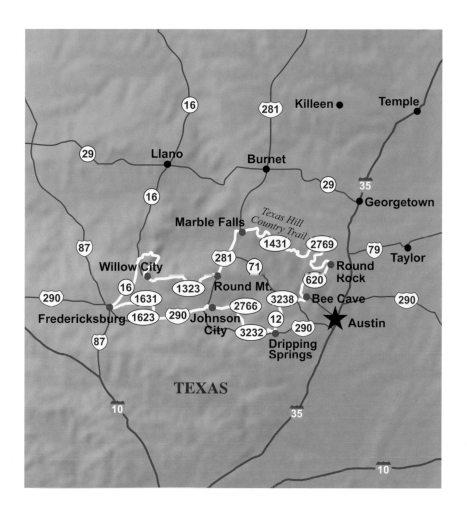

IN FREDERICKSBURG, TEXAS, take Hwy. 16 north for 20 miles and make a right turn onto Willow City Loop Road. Highway 16 is a good high-speed road with a fair amount of traffic for the Hill Country. Willow City Loop Road is one of the many one-lane, two-way roads you will find in this area, and it bounces up and down, twisting and turning through the countryside for all of its 13 miles. You should stay alert for oncoming traffic, keep a sharp eye for livestock out on the open range, and look for sand or gravel washes in the dips. Slow down and enjoy the ride.

As you come through Willow City, proceed straight ahead at the intersection with Rural Road 1323. After 18 miles of some of the best riding to be found anywhere, you will arrive in the one-store town of **Sandy.** Be extra careful along this stretch as it does have some extreme dips and a few tight curves that can sneak up on you if you are not paying attention. Clearing through the traffic and congestion of Sandy, take the first paved left onto

Texas Highways **magazine voted the Blue Bonnet Café the "Number One Restaurant for Breakfast in Texas" and ranked it among the state's overall Top 10 restaurants. (Photo courtesy of the Blue Bonnet Café)**

Sandy/Round Mountain Road, which quickly turns to good hard-packed dirt for eight miles through the countryside before intersecting with Hwy. 281 just north of Johnson City.

ALTERNATE ROUTE

If you do not wish to ride the dirt section, continue on Rural Road 1323 until it intersects with Hwy. 281 where you turn left toward Marble Falls. About 13 miles from Marble Falls, you rejoin the recommended route.

At the end of the Sandy/Round Mountain Road turn left at the T-intersection with Hwy. 281. Thirteen good, high-speed miles later you will cross the river and enter the town of **Marble Falls.** At the top of the hill on your right is the **Blue Bonnet Café,** famous for its down-home cooking and desserts. Try to arrive hungry!

In Marble Falls, take a right onto Rural Road 1431. Go 39 miles and turn right onto Lime Creek Road, a stretch that passes through several small towns and offers magnificent views of the rivers and lakes that make up this part of the Hill Country. As you approach the outskirts of Austin, the road becomes a four-laner.

Lime Creek Road runs for 11 miles along the lake, and it appears no attempts were made to grade or straighten when it was built, as it clings to the hillsides and meanders along. At the STOP sign turn left onto Rural Road 2769, go seven miles, and make a right turn onto Hwy. 620, which runs along the lakefront where there are many gated communities of million-dollar homes. This road also has several very sharp curves with recommended speeds of 15 to 25 mph. Believe the signs!

After 18 miles on Hwy. 620, turn right onto Hwy. 71 in Bee Cave; three miles later, take a left onto Rural Road 3238. After five miles, turn left onto Hwy. 12 toward Dripping Springs. You will have left behind the build-up surrounding Austin, as Hwy. 12 runs along a ridgeline almost its entire length. After five miles, turn right onto Hwy. 290, and follow the four-lane main road for only a short distance, maybe two blocks, and take a left onto Creek Road. It is easy to miss this turn; the road is directly across from the signs indicating Loop 64 off to the right.

Creek Road soon becomes a one-lane, two-way road, with several one-lane bridges along its nine-mile path. Three miles after the turnoff from Hwy. 290, turn right at the intersection with County Road 220 to continue on

Austin once served as the **national capitol** of the Republic of Texas; it was demoted to a mere state capitol when Texas joined the Union. Should you wish to visit this delightful city, continue on Hwy. 1431 past the Lime Creek Road turnoff to the T-intersection with Hwy. 183, where you should take a right. Follow Hwy. 183 to the intersection with I-35 and go south.

You will find hotels to fit every taste and budget along this route. For a real treat, try staying at the **Driskell Hotel** ($170; 512-474-5911) located at 604 Brazos Street. Constructed in 1886, the building served as a meeting place for the Texas government until the capitol was completed. Built to the highest standards of the day, the hotel retains it original décor while having all the modern amenities.

Austin, Texas, (metropolitan area population of over one million) has been picked as **one of the top five places to live** in the United States by both *Money* and *Fortune* magazines. The government of Texas and its employees form a large part of the city. The more than 50,000 students of the **University of Texas** also make up a large part of the local culture. And lastly, the electronics industry has contributed to the city's economic health: today, Austin is the home of Texas Instruments, Dell Computer, IBM, Hewlett-Packard, Apple Computer, and more than 200 other

The Governor's Mansion in Austin reflects the influence of the South in Texas. (Photo courtesy of Gay Shackelford/TxDOT)

high-tech companies, and is often referred to as the **Silicon Valley of the East.** As a result of the above, the people of Austin are the most highly educated of any city in the United States, with one-third holding college degrees.

Where but in Austin would you find a Stevie Ray Vaughan statue? (Photo courtesy of the Austin Convention & Visitors Bureau)

The Lyndon B. Johnson Library and gardens are a great spot to stop and stretch. (Photo courtesy of the Austin Convention & Visitors Bureau)

In addition, Austin is a major recording center to rival Nashville with its country music and Memphis with its blues. Whatever your taste in music, you'll have your choice of nightclubs with live entertainment every night of the week. While Austin is a major city with museums, art galleries, and cultural opportunities to match any other major city in the world, it does have some unique sites of its own.

The **state capitol building,** completed in 1888, is the largest state capitol in the nation and is even seven feet taller than the U.S. Capitol in Washington, D.C. Its exterior consists of pink limestone mined at Marble Falls only a few miles away. The more than eight acres of interior floor space are covered with a copper dome that is topped by a statue of the Goddess of Liberty. The rotunda, which houses the original **Texas Declaration of Independence** and the **Ordinance of Secession,** has a terrazzo floor featuring the flags of the six nations that have, at one time or another, claimed dominion over Texas: Spain, France, Mexico, the Republic of Texas, the Confederate States of America and the United States. Take a free, guided tour that includes the governor's offices and the chambers of the state senate and the house of representatives—just brace yourself to be bombarded by "Texas-sized" statistics!

By itself, the **Congress Avenue Bridge** is not much of an attraction, but during the summer, an estimated 1.5 million Mexican bats call the place "home." The bats migrate and nest here from May through October, and

THE SOUTH

their daily sunset exodus into the night sky is an amazing sight. Volunteers from **Bat Conservation International** are on duty to answer questions, or you can call the bat hotline (512-416-5700, ext. 3636) for information.

Austin is the center of the 14 campuses that make up the vast **University of Texas** system, which consistently ranks among the top 10 schools in the nation. Sitting on a 357-acre site in downtown Austin, UTexas is the home of more than 50,000 students; it is so large, one residence hall has its own zip code. The university library is the sixth-largest in the country, with more than six million volumes. The endowment of the University of Texas is one of the largest in the world, due to the fact that the state legislature gave the school more than two million acres of land in the west Texas desert, which were later discovered to contain vast oilfields. (It's no coincidence that the Petroleum Engineering Dept. is world class!)

There are several museums on the campus, but the most popular tourist spot is the **UT Tower** from which, in August 1966, **Charles Whitman** shot and killed 15 people and wounded 33 more before being shot to death himself. The second most visited spot is the

Dun nuh nuh nuh nuh nuh nuh nuh BAT BRIDGE!!! (Photo courtesy of the Austin Convention & Visitors Bureau)

Lyndon B. Johnson Library and Museum which contains four floors of memorabilia and a replica of the Oval Office during his terms as president.

For everything you ever wanted to know about Texas history, visit the state-of-the-art **Bob Bullock Texas State History Museum,** located at the corner of MLK Blvd. and Congress Avenue. Don't miss the **Texas Spirit Theater** showing of the film *Star of Destiny,* a Hollywood-class production that will have you charging into the streets screaming, "Remember the Alamo!" Plan on spending at least half the day here, enjoying the hands-on, interactive exhibits. Underground parking is available.

People of Hill Country are proud of their heritage.

Creek Road. At the T-intersection with Hwy. 165, turn right, and then at the T-intersection with Hwy. 290, take another left.

In approximately three miles, turn right onto Rural Road 3232 and proceed another seven miles to the T-intersection with Rural Road 2766. Take a right, and then an almost immediate left at the signs denoting the entranceway into the **Pedernales Falls State Park.** As you might guess by the name, the park adjoins the **Pedernales River** and has a view of the falls. In the summer, this is a popular spot to launch canoes for a pristine paddle in the wilderness.

After visiting the park, return to Rural Road 2766 and turn right. Continue

Along most Texas roads, you may encounter strange wildlife at any time. (Photo courtesy of Gay Shackelford/TxDOT)

THE SOUTH

on this road for 12 miles and then turn right onto Hwy. 290. After completing the run on Rural Road 2766, you may begin to wonder just how many excellent motorcycle roads exist in the Hill Country. Too many to count. Enjoy!

A block or so into Johnson City, turn left onto Hwy. 290, a high-speed, four-lane highway whose elevation affords overwhelming views. Fifteen miles later, the LBJ Ranch will be on your right.

Officially known as the **Lyndon B. Johnson State and National Historical Parks,** the complex contains the ranch house that served as the "Texas White House" during Johnson's term as president, a reconstructed cabin which represents his boyhood home, an active visitors' center detailing his life and accomplishments, and the family graveyard where he is buried. A 90-minute bus tour points out the

A series of dams near Austin have created beautiful lakes surrounded by upscale housing developments.

sights and explains what you are seeing. Note that this is no place for trotting out political opinions detrimental to the memory of the 36th president. To Texans, this is, after all, hallowed ground.

After your visit to the ranch complex, exit and continue onto Hwy. 290 for about a mile and make a right turn onto Rural Road 1623. After four miles take a left onto 2721, proceed to the intersection with Rural Road 1631, and go straight ahead. Thirteen miles later, turn right onto Hwy. 290 to downtown Fredericksburg.

■ For more trips in this region see *Motorcycle Journeys Through Texas* by Neal Davis, available from Whitehorse Press.

16 Galveston to Rockport

Text and photos by Neal Davis

■ **DISTANCE** *221 miles*

■ **HIGHLIGHTS** *The south Texas coast, riding on the beach, massive petrochemical plants, and one of the largest and most interesting wildlife preserves in the world*

0.0 From Galveston, Texas, ride west on Seawall Blvd.

35.0 Turn right onto Hwy. 332

40.0 Turn left onto Hwy. 523

47.0 Follow Hwy. 36 to the right

63.0 Turn left onto Hwy. 521

91.0 At T-intersection with Hwy. 60, follow Hwy. 521 to the left

112.0 Turn left onto Hwy. 35 toward Palacious

117.0 Enter Palacious and follow Hwy. 35 Business, if you'd like a view of the enormous fishing fleet

118.0 Return to Hwy. 35, turn south

144.0 Enter Port Lavaca

167.0 Turn left onto Hwy. 239 in Maudlowe

171.0 Hwy. 239 ends in Austwell; Turn right onto Hwy. 774

172.0 Turn left onto Hwy. 2040

179.0 Arrive Aransas Pass Wildlife Refuge

186.0 Return to Hwy 774, turn left

192.0 Turn left onto Hwy. 35

205.0 Turn left onto Park Road 13 into Goose Island State Park, at intersection, proceed straight

205.0 After your visit, return to Hwy. 35, turn left

221.0 Turn left onto Fulton Beach Road

*Mileages are approximate

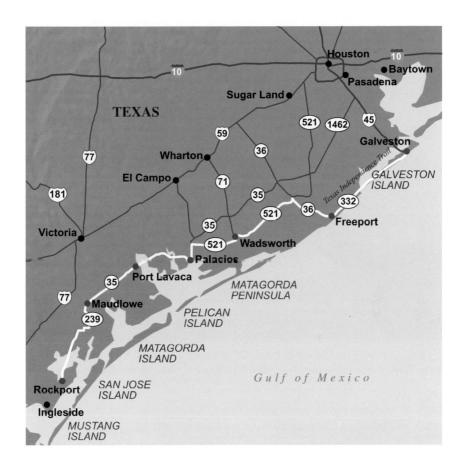

FROM GALVESTON, TEXAS, ride west on Seawall Blvd. You will soon leave the built-up zone of city services and find yourself passing by numerous beach homes built atop stilts. The area then quickly turns to open sand dunes and marshland. After roughly six miles, **Galveston Island State Park** straddles the entire island. The park headquarters on the left is a good place to get off the bike and take a stroll on the beach to enjoy the fresh sea breezes. If you turn right here, there is a nice, short loop through the marshes to the bay with campers and RVs dotted about.

At the end of the Galveston Island you'll have to pay a $2 toll to cross over the **San Luis Pass Bridge** onto **Follets Island.** From there, the next 13 miles to the resort town of **Surfside Beach** is a beautiful ride along the ocean. At several points, you can access the beach with your motorcycle and once there, you can amble along with the sea lapping at your wheels. Most of the access points consist of good hardpack, but you should probably avoid the ones where you can see loose sand before reaching the beach. The beach surface between the high and low tide marks is good and many motorcyclists

Yeah . . . but . . . what's on the other side? Nothing. And that's the point at Galveston Island State Park. (Photo courtesy Friends of Galveston Island State Park)

and automobiles travel it everyday. This place is almost deserted during the week and has very few people on it even on the weekends.

At the traffic light you should take a right onto Hwy. 332. Keep your eye out as you approach this light as there are usually **giant offshore drilling rigs,** known as "jack-up" rigs. You can ride up to them and see just how big and complicated these monsters are.

After crossing over the bridge to the mainland, you will enter the town of **Freeport,** a heavily industrialized area thick with petrochemical plants. At the first traffic light, turn left onto Hwy. 523 (a sign also points to Hwy. 36). Continue to work your way through this developed area following signs to Hwy. 36. After about seven miles, Hwy. 36 takes off to the right at the yellow flashing light. It is obvious that Hwy. 36 was built by dredging the marshes. As a result, it has nice stretches of water along both sides. Many people will be fishing or casting nets in an attempt to catch the bounty contained therein.

Soon you will cross the **Intracoastal Waterway** and gradually gain a small amount of altitude. As you do this, the marshland gives way to woods and an occasional farm. After about 16 miles, turn left onto Hwy. 521. The next 28 miles makes for a very pleasant ride through lush vegetation with many stream crossings and pecan groves. While this road is primarily straight, there are quite a few S-curves scattered along to keep your attention.

THE SOUTH

At the T-intersection with Hwy. 60 in Wadsworth, Hwy. 521 goes to the left, and after a very short distance, leaves Hwy. 60 to the right; stay on Hwy. 521. The landscape for the next 21 miles will consist of huge farms reaching as far as the eye can see.

The most dramatic feature along this ride, a **nuclear power plant** with high-voltage power lines stretching to the horizon, has a nice roadside stop explaining its history and operation. Guided tours are also available.

Shrimping is a major industry along the Gulf Coast of Texas. The fleet works at night and rests during the day. It doesn't get any fresher than this! (Photo courtesy of Jack Lewis/TxDOT)

From this point, turn left onto Hwy. 35 and continue five miles to the small town of **Palacious** (pop. 4,500). This small town lives on because an enormous fishing fleet calls this home. Seafood processing plants here get the catch ready for market. To get a good look at the fleet as you come into town, take Hwy. 35 Business and then turn left at the sign indicating the public boat ramp. At the end of the street that runs along the bay, retrace your route and make a left onto Hwy. 35 Business to continue on your way. Hwy. 35 Business shortly rejoins Hwy. 35 where you should turn left (south). The next few miles offer attractive views of the many bays along which the road runs.

After approximately 26 miles you will cross over a long bridge and enter the town of **Port Lavaca.** As one would assume while traveling along a stretch of road bordering the gulf, you can get good, fresh seafood in every town. Just after leaving the bridge in Port Lavaca, however, there's a place on your right that is unusual for the area. **Gordon's Seafood Grill** doesn't

Evidence of the oil industry will be all around you as you ride the Texas gulf coast. This semi-submersible drilling rig is headed for offshore waters to continue the search for resources and riches. (Photo courtesy of Randy Green/TxDOT)

look like much from the road, but the interior is very upscale and the seafood is prepared in an epicurean fashion. If you desire something other than the usual fried or boiled fish, shrimp, or crab, try this place. Be forewarned—it is somewhat pricey.

Continue on Hwy. 35 south for about 23 miles and make a left turn onto Hwy. 239 in Maudlowe. The first few miles of this run pass through farmland and then become marshier. There are many wildlife preserves through here which resemble the Florida Everglades.

The turns to the **Aransas Pass Wildlife Refuge** are well-marked: after about four miles, Hwy. 239 ends in the small town of Austwell. Make a right turn onto Hwy. 774. Continue for one mile and then turn left onto Hwy. 2040. After seven miles of riding on this increasingly narrow road, with the terrain growing swampy, you will find yourself at the park headquarters. Aransas is the winter home of the **whooping crane,** which is making a slow comeback from near extinction. The estimated worldwide population of these birds in 1945 was 15; the present count numbers more than 400. Five miles into the preserve there is an observation tower that allows one to look out over part of the park's 59,000 acres.

If you wish, you may return to the entrance via an eleven-mile one-way paved road through the backlands, which gives you an opportunity to see close-up the varying landscapes that make up this wonderful place. Please honor the 15 and 25 mph speed limits as the park is inhabited by deer, javelinas, bobcats, raccoons, alligators, turtles, frogs, snakes, and hundreds of bird species. The deer have become especially accustomed to the traffic and you may find the road around any curve completely blocked. If you plan to take any of the many hiking trails or spend a good deal of time off your bike, pick up some bug repellant at headquarters.

Leaving the refuge, retrace your route to the intersection with Hwy. 774 and make a left turn. While this road proceeds mostly flat and straight through farmland, it does have a few unmarked 90-degree turns along its nine miles. Stay alert. Turn left onto Hwy. 35 south at the intersection and

Gordon's in Port Lavaca is an excellent example of the many fine seafood restaurants that are to be found along the Texas Gulf Coast.

This seawall was constructed after a hurricane in 1900 wiped out Galveston. The city never regained its former prominence as the major city in Texas.

proceed approximately 13 miles to the left turn on Park Road 13 into **Goose Island State Park.** At the STOP sign, go straight ahead. This small road meanders around and then goes to the left along the seaside.

As the road turns left away from the ocean, the **Big Tree,** also known as the Lamar Oak or the Bishop Oak, will be on your right. The largest oak tree in Texas, it has a circumference of 35 feet, stands 44 feet tall, and has a crown of 89 feet. It is estimated to be more than 1,000 years old, and sitting as it does right on the gulf, one can only wonder how many hurricanes it has survived.

After your visit, continue on the small road through the oak groves, turning left at the T-intersection, and right at the four-way stop. Then retrace your route to Hwy. 35 where you

A visit to the Fulton Mansion in Rockport will give you an idea how the "rich and famous" cattle barons lived in an earlier era. (Photo courtesy of Bill Reaves/TxDOT)

should turn left. This little loop down to see the tree is only two or three miles and will not take much time.

If you are camping, sites are available in the **Goose Tree State Park** itself, with almost all the services you will need for a wonderful night nestled in a live oak forest. There is no food here, however. If you prefer to be in a more urban setting, continue on to Rockport to the **Ancient Oaks RV Park** located at 1222 Hwy. 35 south; their facilities include a laundry room, fishing pier, and swimming pool.

While exploring the wildlife refuges along the south Texas coast and the bayous of east Texas, be aware the waters may not always be friendly. (Photo courtesy of Jack Lewis/TxDOT)

The whooping crane population is making a nice comeback wintering in the Aransas Park Wildlife Refuge and co-existing with the oil industry nearby.

After 13 or so more miles on Hwy. 35, you will come to a long bridge spanning **Copano Bay.** Another three miles will bring you to a left turn onto Fulton Beach Road. You will soon be running along the seafront with modern condominiums sharing the area with several old mansions.

A more than adequate "mom and pop" place to stay is the **Bayfront Cottages** located next to the Fulton Mansion ($45; 512-729-6693). Should you prefer more modern accommodations, continue to the intersection with Hwy. 35 and turn left into Rockport proper where you will find all the national chains represented.

There are plenty of good places to eat, but for a unique treat, try the **Boiling Pot** located on Fulton Beach Road at Palmetto Street. Shrimp, crab, and raw fish are boiled in water rich with Cajun spices and then deposited directly onto your paper-covered table for your further handling. For an extra treat, try a cup of the gumbo.

The cities of **Rockport** and **Fulton,** separated in name only, abut each other with no noticeable boundaries. With a combined population of approximately 7,000, the mainstay of the economy is fishing. Originally developed by the **Morgan Steamship Company** as a port for shipping Texas beef to the

Sights such as these bring birders from around the world to south Texas. (Photo courtesy of TxDOT)

northeast, the advent of the railroad put it into a quick decline. The old mansions along the coast are the only reminders of the glory days. The **Fulton Mansion State Historical Structure,** located on Fulton Beach Road just after entering the Rockport city limits, is the most magnificent of the examples. Built in the 1870s by a cattle baron, it has been restored in all its grandeur. Guided tours are available to show you around and explain the history and uniqueness of this home.

These days, Rockport considers itself the premier **artists' colony** in Texas and many galleries showcase the local wares. Tourism is also becoming more and more important, and all the usual beach activities are well represented. If you want to see more of the **Aransas Wildlife Refuge,** several boat tours leave regularly from the beachfront.

■ For more trips in this region see *Motorcycle Journeys Through Texas* by Neal Davis, available from Whitehorse Press.

THE ROCKY MOUNTAINS

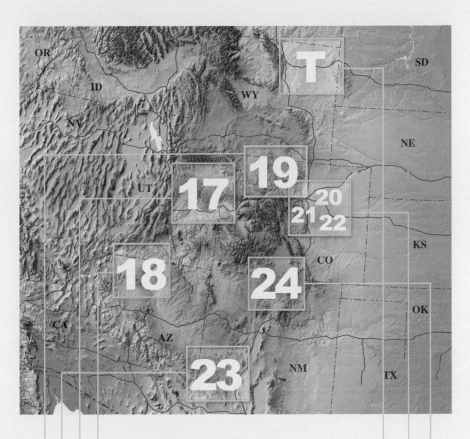

TRAVELOGUE: ROCKY MOUNTAINS

Into the West

Text and photos by Dr. Gregory Frazier

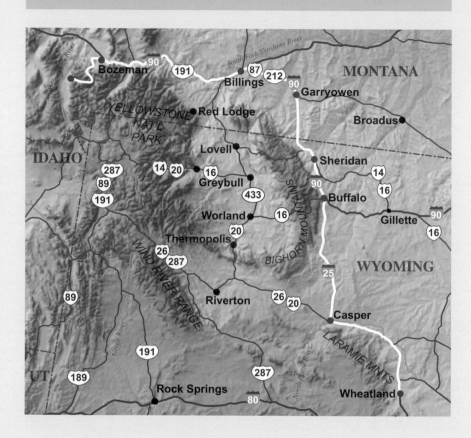

RIDING UP AND down the gentle hills of the Great Plains westward across Nebraska, it seems the terrain never varies.

Miles roll by as you traverse endless fields covered in prairie grass. In spring, the fields are green, dotted with yellow and purple flowers. During summer, the sun has burned the grass brown. By late fall, after the crops are harvested, you see tumbleweeds and dust, blown by unobstructed winds.

Through it all, there's the wide-open landscape, where a lone tree can serve as a landmark for miles.

Then, as you cross into Wyoming and reach the small town of Fort Laramie (not to be confused with the larger city of Laramie), on the banks of the North Platte River, you catch your first glimpse of mountains, 50 miles ahead. Near here, you reach a spot that is a decision-point on our journey, just as it was a century-and-a-half ago.

You can follow the Platte around the Laramie Mountains and then west, as travelers did on the old Oregon Trail. Or you can turn north at Casper and go ghost riding in search of Jeremiah Johnson, Chief Red Cloud, General George Custer, John "Portugese" Phillips, and Ernest Hemingway along the Bozeman Trail.

Between the 1840s and the 1860s, it's estimated that a half-million Easterners made their way west through the heart of Indian Territory over the Oregon Trail. During the early years, there was little trouble between the native Americans and the emigrants. But as the number of outsiders passing through tribal lands swelled, tensions developed.

In an effort to reduce confrontations, in 1851 the U.S. government entered into a treaty with several tribes of Indians, including Oglala and Brule Sioux, Arapaho and Cheyenne. The treaty identified 123,000 square miles of land, principally north of the Oregon Trail, where any "invasion" by white Americans was forbidden.

For their part, the tribes agreed to quit attacking forts, wagons, and travelers along the Oregon Trail, while the government agreed to pay the Indians $50,000.

Between 6,000 and 10,000 Indians were said to have been present when the treaty was signed at Fort Laramie. And you can visit the spot where that ceremony took place, just across the Platte from the town of the same name.

Fort Laramie isn't your typical fort. One of it's duties was to keep settlers from wandering into Native American lands.

Fort Laramie National Historic Site doesn't exactly fit the image of western forts from the movies. There's no wooden stockade around the place, and never was. Instead, this "fort" consists of a collection of restored buildings you can wander through. These served as a stop on the Pony Express Trail and home to troops charged with guarding travelers along a section of the Oregon Trail.

Theoretically, their role also involved keeping settlers from straying into Indian lands protected under the treaty. But that agreement was doomed practically from the beginning. First, travelers, hunters, and mountain men ignored the treaty and roamed through the forbidden territory at will. Second, the U.S. government failed to deliver on its payments to the Indians. And third, gold was discovered in Bannack and Virginia City, two towns in what is now the southwest corner of Montana, resulting in a wave of new settlers.

Worse, that gold discovery came at a time when the United States "back East" was being ripped apart by the Civil War. Many of the individualistic Westerners who had made a home for themselves in the Montana Territory shared secessionist sympathies with the South, but the Union desperately needed that gold to back its currency.

So, in the winter of 1862–1863, John W. Bozeman and J.M. Jacobs started from Bannack in search of a quick route back to the Oregon Trail from the gold fields. Unfortunately, their route, which became the Bozeman Trail, cut right through the prime hunting grounds of the Indian Territory set aside in the Treaty of 1851.

The restored forts along the former frontier are a great place to experience the Old West.

Following the general course of that route today is simple: just jump on Interstate 25 west of Fort Laramie and take it north and west, toward Casper. You can cruise along at 75, realizing you're covering more miles in a half-hour than wagon trains could traverse in a long day.

However, the traffic on this lonely stretch of interstate seems unlikely to match the thousands of horses, cattle, oxen, and people who tramped through the Indian hunting grounds in the 1860s, killing and scattering game along the way. In a few years, the Bozeman Trail was hundreds of yards wide in places, as goldseekers headed north along the

When one sees the rudimentary barricades surrounding Fort Phil Kearny, it's hard to believe they kept anything out.

eastern edge of the Big Horn Mountains straddling the Wyoming-Montana state line.

The Indians, particularly the Sioux, led by Chief Red Cloud, began to attack the wagon trains and anyone else moving through their hunting grounds. And the government responded by building forts along the route, manning them with the glut of troops left over when the Civil War ended.

These strongholds—Fort Fetterman outside present-day Douglas, Fort Phil Kearney north of Buffalo, and Fort C.F. Smith across the state line in southern Montana—were located progressively farther into Indian lands.

This move led to a quick response. Various Sioux, Cheyennes, and Arapahos, mostly under the leadership of Chief Red Cloud, launched a series of attacks on these forts that were generally successful.

The site of one of the pivotal battles is just off Interstate 90, three miles from Fort Phil Kearney. Parts of the fort, which once had a stockade enclosing 17 acres, have been rebuilt, and there's a visitor center where you can get directions about three miles up the road to the site of the Fetterman Fight.

On December 21, 1866, Captain William J. Fetterman, who claimed he could "ride through the Sioux Nation with 80 men," ignored direct orders and rode into a swarm of Sioux, Cheyenne, and Arapaho warriors whose numbers have been estimated between 800 and 3,000. In a half-hour battle, all 80 men, plus Fetterman, were killed, most by arrows, spears, or clubs.

After the battle, Fort Phil Kearney's commander asked for a volunteer to ride to Fort Laramie, some 230 miles to the south, for help. The weather was incredible, with temperatures well below zero and howling winds. But John "Portugese" Phillips, a civilian, volunteered for the mission.

Three days later, Phillips successfully arrived at Fort Laramie on the evening of the Christmas Ball, completing a truly heroic ride through incredibly adverse conditions. In fact, the weather was so bad that a reinforcement mission to Fort Phil Kearney could not be mounted until January 6.

Riding along Interstate 25 and 90, you have to appreciate the enormity of Phillips' task. He plowed his horse through snow drifts and survived achingly cold temperatures, day and night, to complete the ride.

Some say another civilian, Daniel Dixon, accompanied Phillips on his ride. Others say his companion was a mountain man who stopped 20 miles from Fort Laramie and told Phillips to go on alone, telling him the ride would "make him famous." That mountain man, rumored to stand 6-foot-2 and weigh nearly 250 pounds, eventually became pretty famous himself.

The forts were built with two purposes in mind: to hold a lot of troops, and to keep an eye (apparently every eye) on the frontier.

His name was John Johnson (or perhaps Johnston), and from the 1840s through the 1880s, he hunted and trapped in the area that would become northern Wyoming and southern Montana. Legend says that on a May morning in 1847, Crow Indians killed and scalped his pregnant wife, a Flathead Indian, while Johnson was away. Johnson declared a personal war on Crow warriors and reportedly killed many in the years that followed.

He became known as Dapiek Absaroka, or the "Killer of Crows" in the Crow language. It was said that he would cut out the livers of his victims and eat them to scare his enemies, earning him the name "Liver-Eating" Johnson among white settlers.

Over the years, stories grew around Johnson, with some suggesting that he eventually killed as many as 300 Crows. That number may be doubtful, but this larger-than-life man did inspire such legends. Eventually, the story of "Liver-Eating" Johnson was made into a movie. But Hollywood, apparently put off by his actual nickname, released the film as "Jeremiah Johnson."

Meanwhile, battles like the Fetterman Fight eventually caused the U.S. government to rethink its strategy regarding the Bozeman Trail. In 1868 federal officials entered into another treaty with Chief Red Cloud and his warriors, under which Forts Phil Kearney and C.F. Smith would be abandoned, with the army retreating to Fort Fetterman, along the Oregon Trail.

Although the government officially pulled up stakes in 1869, the migration of emigrants did not stop, nor did the confrontations between Indians and settlers. By the mid-1870s, the government had started a new campaign to force all of the Indian tribes onto reservations.

One of the most famous battlefields of that war is just ahead, across the Montana state line on a small knoll overlooking the Little Bighorn River. Here, on June 25, 1876, Brevet Major General George Armstrong Custer led some 230 men into a valley where an estimated 15,000 Sioux and Cheyenne Indians were camped along the river. That folly catapulted Custer into fame, albeit through his demise and that of the men he led.

The Little Bighorn battlefield is preserved as a national monument within the Crow Indian Reservation. It's just off Interstate 90 at U.S. Route 212. You can follow a five-mile tour that brings to life the events of that day, which ranks as the worst defeat suffered by the U.S. Army in the Indian wars.

Of course, the battle of Little Bighorn represented only a temporary victory for the Plains Indians. Over the next 20 years, these tribes were subdued through sheer military might as the United States kept growing and the West was "tamed."

But the remoteness of this area, and its legendary hunting, continued to attract new visitors. And by 1892, the Burlington and Missouri Railroad extended a spur north along the general route of the Bozeman Trail.

The Little Bighorn Battlefield Monument protects the men who fell in the battle. (Photo courtesy of the National Park Service)

One of the best places to get a glimpse of that era is the historic Sheridan Inn in Sheridan, just a little south of the Montana state line. This inn, built when the railroad reached Sheridan, quickly became a landmark of the West. Colonel William F. "Buffalo Bill" Cody used it as his home when he was in the area and signed up acts for his "Wild West Show" from the inn's huge porch. It was also the first building in Wyoming to have electric power and a telephone.

The Sheridan Inn was a hotel and restaurant. But its fame rests in the bar, which was built in England and shipped to Wyoming by rail. It was said to have been a gift from Queen Victoria for a performance of the "Wild West Show" in England.

In the early years, the bar's patrons would occasionally witness local cowboys riding their horses directly into the establishment in celebration. Later, they could look for famous visitors like Will Rogers, Calamity Jane, President Herbert Hoover, Gen. Jack Pershing, and even Bob Hope.

You, too, can visit the Sheridan Inn's bar, which is part of a restaurant still operating in the building. It, and the city of Sheridan, are a great place to go searching for what remains of the Old West.

But for a look into a more recent past, travel just a few miles down the road to the tiny town of Big Horn, Wyoming, where Ernest Hemingway spent time in the late 1920s.

Today, the town of Big Horn is little more than two bars, a post office, a museum, and a couple of stores. When Hemingway was in the area, it was one bar and a post office, both of which he frequented. The locals say that one day he received a manuscript in the mail and proceeded to a corner in the bar where he spent the next few hours making changes requested by his publisher. Once done, he paid his bar tab, put the manuscript in an envelope and walked back to the post office, where he set in motion the process of publishing "A Farewell to Arms."

Riding along the Bozeman Trail, it's easy to see why this area has been coveted by so many, from native Americans to travelers along the original Trail, the Burlington and Missouri Railroad and even today's interstates. Here, at the far end of the Great Plains, the West had its last stand. Squeezed between the mountains on the west and encroaching civilization on the east, history played out along a few hundred miles.

Listen closely while riding the route of the Bozeman Trail, and you can practically hear the whispering of ghosts through the trees and buffalo grass. The ghosts of those who lived, hunted, and fought here generations ago.

17 Dead Horse Point to La Sal Mts.

Text and photos by Marty Berke

■ **DISTANCE** *185 miles*

■ **HIGHLIGHTS** *From the 9,000-foot highs of the La Sal Mountain Loop Road to the lows of the Colorado River at 4,000 feet, with plenty in between*

0.0 Depart Dead Horse Point State Park, near Moab, Utah, heading on Route 313 east	**76.3** Take a left onto La Sal Mountain Loop Road (just after Ken's Lake)
22.5 Turn onto Route 191 south to Moab	**105.3** Take Route 128 north to Cisco and turn around
29.5 Turn onto 300 south	**149.3** Take Route 128 south
33.0 Turn onto 400 east	**160.3** Follow Route 191 north
33.5 Take your first left onto Mill Creek Drive	**180.8** Route 313 west
46.5 Turn onto Spanish Valley Drive	**185.0** Arrive Dead Horse Point State Park
	*Mileages are approximate

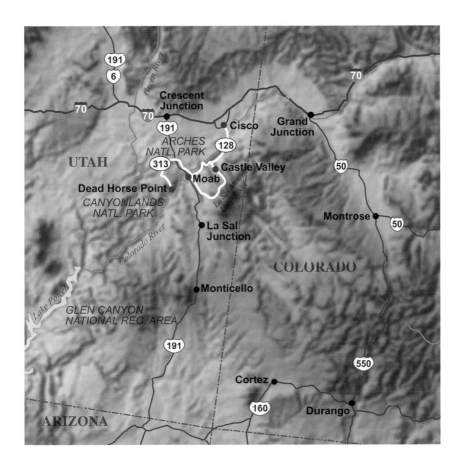

SPANISH VALLEY DRIVE, which parallels Route 191 south, starts its climb up the La Sal Mountains just after Ken's Lake. The La Sal Mountains are the second largest mountain range in Utah, with Mount Peale rising to an elevation of 12,721 feet.

The La Sal Loop Road reminds you of the way back roads used to be, an old-fashioned ride where riders take responsibility for themselves. Hairpins, 14 percent grades, and blind corners, all without DPW "two-bumps-22.5-miles-per-hour-for-the-next-3.2-miles-in-third-gear-only-please" signage. It is paved the entire way, but watch out for a couple of hundred-yard, road-damaged gravel sections (no sweat). The road is a scenic ascent into the **Manti-La Sal National Forest.**

Dotted with meadows, lakes, and trees, with peaks in the 12,000- to 13,000-foot range, the forest is perfect for a refreshing vista picnic after a hot desert ride. The climb begins with piñion and juniper, gives way to oak, then to larger pines and aspen. At the top are spruce and fir. The challenging climb ends with a panoramic view of **Castle Valley,** a popular filming location for

The Colorado River is one of the most traveled rivers in the world. (Photo courtesy of the National Park Service)

movies and commercials. On the way down the northwest end of the loop, you run into the Colorado River.

Known locally as the "River Road," Route 128 is a dazzling road of colors, light, and shadow, with the Colorado River on one side and sheer red-rock cliffs on the other. The Colorado also offers another kind of scenery: rafters and floaters heading downstream to **Moab.** Don't worry about turning around, the road is a beauty both ways.

By the way, that suspension bridge to nowhere is **Dewey Bridge,** a single-laner that was used until 1986. Now open only to foot traffic, it is on the National Historic Register.

There are no facilities in Cisco, so fill up in Moab before beginning the La Sal Mountain climb. (P.S. The "River

The view from Dead Horse Point showing the Canyonlands and the Colorado River. (Photo courtesy of the Utah Travel Council)

The Dewey Bridge was built in 1916 and spans 153 meters across the Colorado. (Photo courtesy of www.recreation.gov)

Road" is a great alternative to super-slabbing between Moab and **Grand Junction, Colorado.)**

Overheating? On the opposite bank, at the intersection of 128 and 191, is an old, abandoned cement building. Pack a bathing suit and swim there with the local kids.

The way back to **Dead Horse Point State Park** climbs **Seven Mile Canyon** from the 4,000-foot floor to the 6,000-foot point. If you're making this trip at night, watch out for the abundant nocturnal wildlife. A herd of deer live on the mesa and twice I had to hit my brakes for eight- and 10-point bucks. In late summer and early fall, violent thunderstorms give a dazzling, deadly display of fireworks. Five people were struck and killed on the mesa in 1987.

■ For more trips in this region see *Motorcycle Journeys Through the Southwest* by Marty Berke, available from Whitehorse Press.

18 Grand Canyon to Glen Canyon

Text and photos by Marty Berke

■ **DISTANCE** *124 miles*

■ **HIGHLIGHTS** *Descend from a chilly 8,000 feet to a hot 4,800 feet, riding below Vermillion Cliffs, through Marble Canyon, to Lee's Ferry, across Navajo Bridge, up Echo Cliffs, over Glen Canyon Dam, and beside Lake Powell*

0.0 Leave the North Rim of the Grand Canyon on Route 67 north	**101.0** Turn onto Route 89 north
49.9 Turn onto Route 89A south	**124.0** Arrive in Page, Arizona
	*Mileages are approximate.

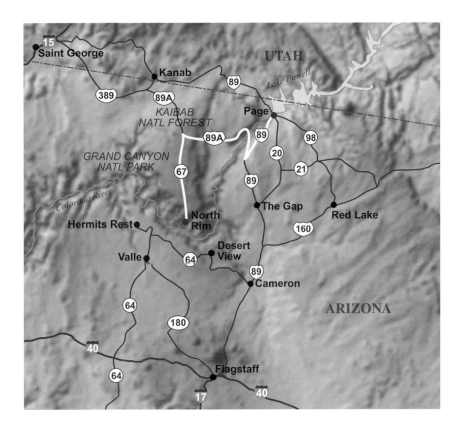

THIS IS A short scenic ride full of natural and man-made structures to enjoy. Crossing the Kaibab Mountains and coming off the **Kaibab Plateau** are lots of curves and a corkscrew onto House Rock Valley, then a straight desert run below the eye-catching Vermillion Cliffs. Cliff Dwellers is an oasis named after the original trading post built into the rock formations in the early 1900s. The original trading post is a quarter-mile past the new one.

Marble Canyon features brilliant crayon-colored cliffs, appearing washed out lemon in the morning and fiery orange, lipstick red, and deep magenta in the late afternoon. Take the short side trip, off Route 89A, at **Marble Canyon** to **Lee's Ferry,** established in 1865 as the only crossing of the Colorado River for hundreds of miles. Overturned and lost downstream in 1928, it never reopened because the 500-foot-high Navajo Bridge was finished the following year.

The **Lee's Ferry Campground** in the National Recreation Area, down-river from **Glen Canyon Dam,** is the launch point for rafting and kayaking the Colorado River. Approximately 14,000 people make the 280-mile expedition yearly. The Colorado River drops 2,000 feet during the passage and runs through 160 major rapids.

Rapids are caused by debris from side tributaries which constrict the river flow. When the average depth drops from 35 feet to just a few inches, the water speed increases from four to five mph to over 12 mph. Rapids are measured on a scale of one, a small riffle, to 10, the maximum a river-runner will attempt. Just below Lee's Ferry is Hermit Rapid, rated a nine. It's a hell of a start.

The day I was there, a six-raft party was departing for the 18-day run through the Grand Canyon. I couldn't help but notice the pallet load of beer in their provisions. At 95 degrees Fahrenheit, my curiosity got the better of me.

"Are you bringing a fridge with you?" I asked. Someone looked up, knowing exactly what provoked the question, and replied, "We'll let nature do it for us." The water, released from the bottom of 560-foot Glen Canyon Dam, is a constant 45 degrees Fahrenheit. Although I prefer my cool ones at 42 degrees, I'm always amazed at how nature provides.

On the other side of Glen Canyon Dam is the **Page/Lake Powell area.** The second largest man-made reservoir in the world has 1,986 miles of shoreline (more than the entire Pacific coast of the lower United States), five marinas spaced 50 miles apart, and numerous shoreline campgrounds. The National Park Service calls this "a dramatic example of the combination of one of nature's most inspiring settings and one of man's most ambitious projects."

From the rim of the Grand Canyon, it isn't hard to believe the power of the Colorado River. (Photo courtesy of the National Park Service)

THE ROCKY MOUNTAINS

The **Glen Canyon Bridge** is the second highest steel arch bridge in the world. Before it opened on February 20, 1959, the trip from one side of the canyon to the other was 197 miles. The Glen Canyon Dam and its power plant required 5.1 million cubic yards of concrete, poured round the clock for three years, to complete. The dam's crest is 1,560 feet long. It sits on top of 710 feet of bedrock and is 583 feet above the original river channel.

Wind and rain have sculpted the walls of the Canyon. (Photo courtesy of the Arizona Office of Tourism)

At its full pool capacity, Lake Powell holds 27 million acre-feet of water 560 feet deep at the dam. It took 17 years to fill the lake, and what was started on March 13, 1963 was completed on June 27, 1980. The dam backs up the Colorado River for almost 200 miles to Hite Marina in Utah (imagine how much bran it would take to relieve this problem).

Page, begun as a construction camp for Glen Canyon Dam, is the gateway to Lake Powell. Sitting on Manson Mesa, it has a perfect view of the lake. Lake Powell's **Wahweap Marina and Campground** is a large National Rec-

The beer castle at the launch point at Lee's Ferry.

reation Area complex below Page, on the shores of the red rock, blue water lake. With the water at 75 degrees Fahrenheit and days between 85 and 90 degrees during late September, this is an excellent destination for a last gasp of summer's breath.

Swimming at the Coves is a unique experience. The flooding of Glen Canyon enables you to step off 30- and 40-foot cliffs into 500-foot waters. If that's a little steep, you can wade a few feet into the water and swim off the ledge. Looking under water while swimming the edge of a canyon is a freaky experience. You can even swim up a canyon from the Coves. How steep is the edge you swam off? Check out the river side of the dam!

■ For more trips in this region see *Motorcycle Journeys Through the Southwest* by Marty Berke, available from Whitehorse Press.

19 Continental Divide Loop

Text and photos by Marty Berke

- **DISTANCE** *190 miles*
- **HIGHLIGHTS** *The Continental Divide with mountain curves and alpine scenery the whole way*

0.0 Leave Hot Sulphur Springs, Colorado, on Route 40 west	**99.6** Take a left onto Route 14 east
21.4 Turn onto Route 134 west	**133.8** Turn onto Route 125 south
47.9 Turn onto Route 131 north	**183.2** Turn onto Route 40 west
81.3 Turn onto Route 40 east	**190.0** Arrive in Hot Sulphur Springs
97.4 Turn onto National Forest Service 315	*Mileages are approximate
98.7 Return to Route 40 east	

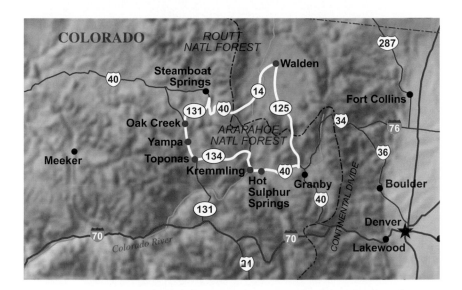

KREMMLING, COLORADO, NESTLED at the confluence of the Colorado and Blue Rivers, is a small town with a big heart. Hosting BBQs on the town green, it's a strategic stopping place for the annual three-day "Ride The Rockies" bicycle event. If you're using **Hot Sulphur Springs** as home base and approaching from the west, stock up on food, drink, and essentials.

Route 134 is a crooked road that travels through the **Arapaho and Routt National Forests.** Gore Pass, at 9,827 feet, is an early challenge on this loop. You can camp at the pass, but snow is *always* a possibility.

The town of **Oak Creek** is small but has a laundry and two restaurants with excellent food and daily specials. The bean burrito with green chili is out of this world at the Cantina. Have some liquid handy before you take that first bite.

Route 131 melds with Route 40 just below **Steamboat Springs.** Climb over Rabbit Ears Pass, crossing the Continental Divide, on a civilized, anti-climactic, wide, three-laner complete with a climbing lane. Near the crest, take National Forest Service (NFS) 315 to a high alpine meadow NFS campground and access road to the rock formation that inspired the pass's name. In June I had to plow through a few frozen snow streams to get to the view but . . .

Route 14 north plays peekaboo with Grizzly Creek most of the way to **Walden.** Route 125 gives the swivel-headed rider a 360-degree snow-capped, mountain panorama. Entering the Arapaho National Forest, the valley road tightens from sweepers to S-turns to hairpins, topping the Continental Divide at 9,621-foot **Willow Creek Pass.** Over the pass, Willow Creek keeps you company to Route 40. Pick up essentials in **Granby.**

■ For more trips in this region see *Motorcycle Journeys Through the Southwest* by Marty Berke, available from Whitehorse Press.

20 Top of the Paved Continent

Text and photos by Marty Berke

■ **DISTANCE** *200 miles*

■ **HIGHLIGHTS** *Canyons, creeks, lakes, rivers, and three life zones, and the highest paved North American road*

0.0 Begin at Golden Gate Canyon State Park in Golden, Colorado. Follow Route 119 west to Route 279 south

8.5 Route 279 south (Oh My God Rd.) to right on Business 1-70 west

15.4 Business 1-70 west to Route 103 south

16.0 Route 103 south to Route 5 south

28.8 Route 5 south to Mt. Evans

45.1 Return Route 5 north to Route 103 south

61.3 Route 103 south to Route 74 north

78.8 Route 74 north to Interstate 70 west

81.3 Interstate 70 west to Route 6 east

88.2 Route 6 east to Route 58/93 north (follow Route 93 north)

100.7 Route 93 north to left on Golden Gate Canyon Road (turns into 70 Road west)

102.3 70 Road west to Route 46 west

110.1 Route 46 west to Route 119 east

118.8 Route 119 east to Route 72 east

129.4 Route 72 east to Route 93 north

146.9 Route 93 north to Route 119 west

158.2 Route 119 west to entrance of Golden Gate Canyon State Park and home base

200.0 Arrive at Golden Gate Canyon State Park

*Mileages are approximate

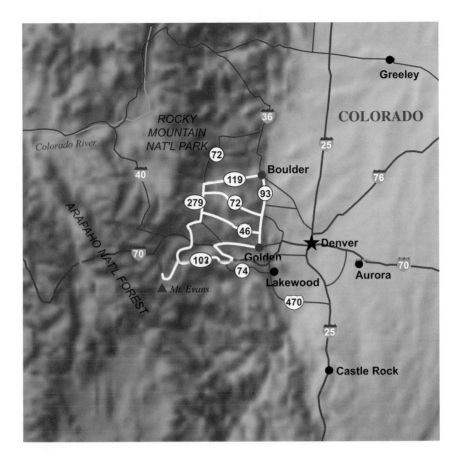

ROUTE 119 IS nicknamed the **Peak to Peak Highway.** Although there are plenty of mountain peaks surrounding the area, most, like the highway, are anonymous. Heading west (it feels south) on Route 119 from home base is only a warm-up, albeit one of the best warm-ups, for a ride.

Entering Black Hawk and starting just above **Central City** is Route 279. It's obscure through Central City, so if you miss it, just ask in downtown for the **"Oh My God Highway."** The name is far more intimidating than the road. Even shiny cruisers can do this one-time stagecoach road.

Being a backroad, Route 279 doesn't appear on many maps, but is an excellent dirt road that cuts through Virginia Canyon and into **Idaho Springs** from the backside. Along the way are many abandoned mines honeycombing the hillsides. The green hillsides dotted with the sandy beige old mine dumps and shaft houses conjure up an army of giant ants building their colonies. Some of the road gets narrow, but with little traffic it's not a biggie.

The next stop is a biggie, really the biggest. The ride to **Mount Evans** is a climb to 14,260 feet. This is the top of the paved world—or at least North

America, depending on who's talking. This is an adjustment in altitude and attitude. Cool all the time, snow any time, this 28-mile roundtripper passes lakes named Echo (go ahead, try it), at 10,600 feet, and Summit, at 12,830 feet. The eight-foot snow banks mean snowball fights in July. The Mount Evans Crest House, built between 1940 and 1941, sits at 14,260 feet. With views of the **Continental Divide** and the **Front Range,** the top of **Mount Evans** redefines the word vista.

Back down Route 5 at the junction of Route 103 is the **Echo Lake Lodge,** a friendly place to warm the cockles from a cold ride. The fun heats up again riding through **Pike National Forest,** up and over Squaw Pass at 9,807 feet. With the circulation returning to your extremities, start warming up for the canyon rides.

Begin with **Clear Creek Canyon,** 15 miles beside Clear Creek, then through 13 miles of **Golden Gate Canyon,** and finally, end run down the 20 miles of **Coal Creek Canyon.** Just when the forearms need a breather from all that countersteering comes Route 93 north.

Route 93 tries to be a challenging road to **Boulder** but the DPW smoothed out many of the curves and left a few sweepers of what could have been. Boulder is a manageable city of good food, diverse lifestyles, and stunning

"Oh My God" Highway sounds more intimidating than it is—even big cruisers can handle the hard-packed gravel surface.

THE ROCKY MOUNTAINS

You'll have a chance to meet new friends along the way. Here, a group of locals take a refreshing stroll.

beauty. It also appears to be an enlightened city, given all the "motorcycle only" parking areas near the promenades.

The **Boulder Harvest Restaurant** can recharge the internal tank with ease and variety. From a tofu and eggless spaghetti dish, for all the cholesterol watchers, to a choice of homemade cinnamon and raisin muffins, and a wide variety of entrees, you can't do better for the bucks or body. If you're a smoker, pick another stop. Gassed up (not a gastronomic comment about the food), work it off with a run through **Boulder Canyon,** climbing the 14 miles beside Boulder Creek.

■ For more trips in this region see *Motorcycle Journeys Through the Southwest* by Marty Berke, available from Whitehorse Press.

21 Rocky Mountain High Loop

Text and photos by Marty Berke

- **DISTANCE** *184 miles*
- **HIGHLIGHTS** *The finest views in the United States, and Rocky Mountain National Park*

0.0 Begin in Golden Gate Canyon State Park in Golden, Colorado, then take Route 119 east to Route 72 west

10.6 Route 72 west to Route 7 west

33.1 Route 7 west to Route 34 west

51.9 Route 34 west to Route 40 east

111.9 Route 40 east to Interstate 70 east

156.3 Interstate 70 east to Route 6 east (left lane exit)

171.9 Route 6 east to Route 119 east

174.4 Route 119 east to Golden Gate State Park

184.0 Arrive at Golden Gate Canyon State Park

*Mileages are approximate

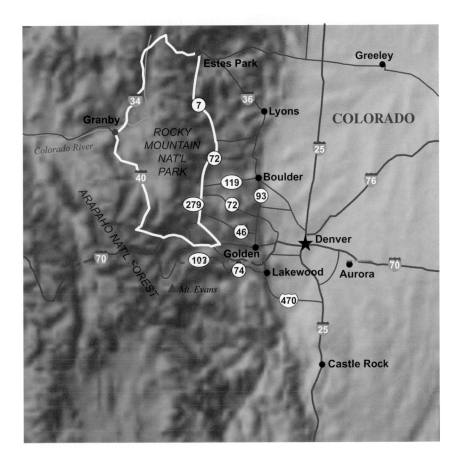

LIKE AN OVERTURE to a symphony, the routes to **Rocky Mountain National Park** prepare the rider for what's ahead. As mentioned, Route 119 is nicknamed the **Peak to Peak Highway.** Renaming it the Many Peaks Highway would be more accurate. Wandering through the **Roosevelt National Forest,** Routes 119, 72, and 7 have many peaks and valleys. All are conquered with tight curves, lots of hairpins, sideways esses, and cresting turns. Your first crest is entering Nederland.

Nederland, a small mountain town with a history of shipping and distribution during the gold rush days, offers the closest grocery, gas, and eateries to **Golden Gate Canyon State Park.** The Mining Company Nederland of the Hague bought the mill and surrounding mining properties sitting on Middle Boulder Creek, hence the town's European name. The Assay Office Saloon offers a range of pub grub from Rocky Mountain Oysters to a Philly Steak Hoagie and homemade pies. Complete with pool tables, a pinball machine, two TVs, and a full complement of local color, including target practice in the men's room—it's worth a stop.

Expect to share the road with creatures more unpredictable than automobile drivers. (Photo courtesy of National Park Service)

Former home of Enos Mills, "father" of Rocky Mountain National Park.

Peaceful Valley, a name reflecting the road as much as the terrain, is the next bottoming-out spot. Just after Meeker Park is the cabin of **Enos Mills,** the naturalist, writer, and conservationist who is known as the father of **Rocky Mountain National Park.**

Mills, declaring, "The Rockies are not a type, but an individuality, singularly rich in mountain scenes which stirs one's blood and which strengthen and sweeten life," began a campaign for the preservation of the area. He succeeded in 1915 when Rocky Mountain National Park was created.

Rocky Mountain National Park is a spectacular wilderness ranging from deep canyons to alpine meadows to craggy mountain peaks, 76 of which are above 12,000 feet. The park's 415 square miles straddle the **Continental Divide,** where snow melt and rain flow west to the Pacific or southeast to the Gulf of Mexico.

Trail Ridge Road, cutting through and riding the top of the park, is one of the great alpine highways in the United States. Connecting Estes Park with Grand Lake, it takes three or four hours to cover the "Roof of the Rockies." It can be crowded in the summer months, with three million visitors traveling through the park each year. On a clear day, average visibility is 83 miles, so relax and enjoy the 50-mile road which rises to 12,183 feet above sea level. Trail Ridge Road is usually open from Memorial Day to mid-October depending on the weather. It snows every month of the year here. Full-dresser applies to rider and scooter alike.

One-third of the park and 11 miles of Trail Ridge Road are above tree line and tundra. The tundra is a harsh world where five-year-old plants are smaller than your fingernail, and foot traffic takes hundreds of years to repair. The park offers a variety of plant life, varying with the altitude and sunlight. Open stands of ponderosa pine and juniper grow on the south-facing slopes; cooler north slopes are home to Douglas fir. Stream-side are blue spruces intermixed with lodgepole pines. Wildflowers paint the meadows with a full pallete of

THE ROCKY MOUNTAINS

colors. More than a quarter of the plants that grow in the upper regions of the park are also native to the Arctic.

After crossing Milner Pass at 10,758 feet, my favorite picnic spot appears on the right. If the snow has melted, Lake Irene is a serene spot away from the crowd. From Lake Irene, Trail Ridge Road slowly descends through Farview Curve, passing the Colorado River headwaters, Never Summer Ranch, and the Kawuneeche Visitor Center before leaving the park for Grand Lake.

Grand Lake, named after the county it's in, is the largest natural lake in Colorado. It was formed by the Colorado River, which before the turn of the century was called the Grand River. As the river flowed south, it created the canyon which also bears its name.

The Utes controlled the area around Grand Lake in the early 1800s, fighting off the marauding Cheyenne and Arapaho who traveled from the Eastern Plains to these rich hunting grounds. The Ute, to protect their women and children during a battle, would float their families onto the lake on a raft. One unfortunate time, a storm with high winds capsized the raft, drowning the entire village. The grieving Utes named the waters Spirit Lake, left the area, and never returned.

It's hard to see from the road, but follow the signs (it's a left) to **Grand Lake Lodge.** An international clientele enjoys the lodge's full-length

Oh beautiful, for spacious skies . . . Colorado's majestic vistas can be downright inspirational, but must be experienced in person. (Photo courtesy of National Park Service)

veranda view of Grand Lake and Shadow Mountain Reservoir, backdropped by verdant, tree-covered mountains. It is sometimes called "Colorado's Favorite Front Porch." Three vintage cars and a directional signpost with mileage to Rio de Janeiro, Tokyo, San Jose, (Argentina, Chile, or Costa Rica, but definitely not California), and other international destinations sit outside the office. Worth a free view. If you can afford the lodge, it's a peaceful, luxurious splurge.

Back on Route 34, the ride stays on the high alpine meadow until the T-intersection at **Granby.** Hang a left and follow the Fraser River into the ski resort of Winter Park. From the ski resort, Route 40 climbs and climbs up to Berthoud Pass at 11,315 feet. Crest the pass and descend into the small mining town of Empire. The **Peck House** in Empire is the state's oldest hotel still in operation. It's a genteel place to have a cool drink on the veranda overlooking the Empire Valley. **Empire** is also home to the original Hard Rock Café, on Main Street a.k.a. Route 40. It is easy to see that the sign and structure predate all those T-shirts. It closes at 2:00 p.m. and serves breakfast.

At Empire, merge with Interstate 70, and exit left onto Route 6 for a 15-mile tight, twisting, enveloped-by-towering-cliffs ride along **Clear Creek Canyon.** The existing roadway is built on the roadbed of yesterday's trains, which brought gold seekers up to the mining camps of **Black Hawk** and **Central City.** The last freight train ran up the canyon on May 5, 1941. It was

Peck House, in Empire, is the oldest hotel in Colorado still in operation.

THE ROCKY MOUNTAINS

only after the tracks were pulled and the canyon walls blasted that the road was built.

Route 6 also passes through three tunnels. Tunnel Number 2 is 1,168 feet long and the second-longest in Colorado. The longest is **Eisenhower Tunnel** on Interstate 70, 9,941 feet long.

Route 119 east is 10 miles from the gambling towns of Central City and Black Hawk. In gold mining days these two towns were nicknamed the "richest square mile on earth." Central City, like Cripple Creek, has renovated Victorian buildings packed with gamblers and slot machines. Central City also boasts a few firsts: the first gold strike in Colorado, at Gregory Gulch by John H. Gregory, and the first Stetson Hat, produced in the 1860s by John B. Stetson.

The Glory Hole Saloon and Gambling Hall offers the best non-gam-

Rocky Mountain National Park in the spring is awash in color and life. (Photo courtesy of Eric Wunrow/CTO)

bling attractions in town. The nightly prime rib dinner special is excellent and very inexpensive. It's served up with a free nightly dance review and vaudeville act. Both dinner and the show can be had for less than the price of a movie ticket.

For more trips in this region see *Motorcycle Journeys Through the Southwest* by Marty Berke, available from Whitehorse Press.

22 Cache la Poudre Trail

Text and photos by Marty Berke

- **DISTANCE** *230 miles*
- **HIGHLIGHTS** *Canyon roads, and the only designated "wild and scenic river" in Colorado*

0.0 Begin at Golden Gate Canyon State Park in Golden, Colorado, then take Route 119 east to Route 72 west

10.6 Route 72 west to Route 7 east

33.1 Route 7 east to Route 36 north

47.5 Route 36 north to Route 34 east

60.6 Route 34 east to Route 287 north

80.0 Route 287 north to Route 14 west (left on Mulberry Street in Fort Collins)

108.1 Route 14 west to Walden

230.0 Arrive in Walden

*Mileages are approximate

Alternate Route

Route 119 east to Route 36 (turn left at 28th Street in Boulder). It's an alternative way to Estes Park via a valley road along the foothills outside of Boulder.

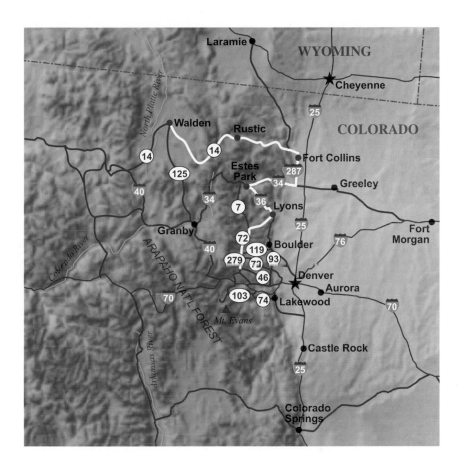

THIS IS CANYON country. The height of the canyon walls, the straining to see around the next curve, and the quick look at the rivers make you feel like one of those back window gooney head bobbers with brake light eyes. Be prepared for an aching neck.

Boulder Canyon and **Big Thompson Canyon** are delightful appetizers to begin this full course canyon meal. Follow **Boulder Creek** out of the university town of the same name, with twists and turns tantalizing the senses and whetting the appetite. Leaving Estes Park via Route 34 east, travel the Big Thompson Canyon beside the Big Thompson River, happy to be on sticky rubber crossing the slick crack-filling tar. In 1984, the Big Thompson received 11.5 inches of rain in less than five hours. Normally a couple of feet in depth, the river rose to 20 feet within hours, scouring the canyon of anything in its path, and washing away 139 people and countless homes. It is easy to imagine how the river could rear its head for this devastation, because of the narrowness of the canyon walls and the water level nearly to the road even during normal times.

The Cache la Poudre is the only river in Colorado to be officially designated "Wild and Scenic."

The Scorched Tree Bed & Breakfast offers their guests six-course gourmet meals and two private dining rooms.

Route 287 to **Fort Collins** is motel city. Plenty to choose from and a full complement of retail stores and restaurants to go with them. It is a small price to pay for the gourmet and gourmand blend of asphalt spices being cooked by Route 14.

The outstanding 101-mile **Cache la Poudre-to-North Park Scenic Byway** demonstrates Colorado at its best. Steeped in local history of mountain men, pioneering, and early stagecoach days, the Cache la Poudre (French for "hide the powder") "Wild and Scenic River" is the first and only river in Colorado to earn this national designation. The Byway runs from Ted's Place, just west of Fort Collins, to **Walden** in the North Park Region, just below Wyoming.

The **Roosevelt National Forest** surrounds the river and Route 14 literally cuts through the heart of it. Baldwin Tunnel, bored in the fall of 1916, eliminated the need for traveling the old North Park Stage Line road to **Livermore** and then down Pingree Hill to **Rustic.**

Offering tourists and wanderers a wide range of places to stay, Rustic aptly describes the town. Campgrounds, rustic cabins, lodges, and fancy inns abound. Food along **Poudre Canyon Trail** is also varied, from simple nightly roadside specials to gourmet six-course meals at the **Scorched Tree Bed & Breakfast.** The Scorched Tree B & B offers two private dining rooms for guests of the establishment.

After Rustic, Route 14 leads to the Big Narrows, a forbidding granite chasm made passable by convict labor blasting through the rock in 1919. Old Man's Face (Profile Rock) is on the left, 1.7 miles past the Poudre Canyon fire station. There are several parking areas to grab that obligatory tourist shot. After **Chambers Lake,** the climb through Cameron Pass peaks at 10,276 feet. Next, Route 14 slowly descends into Gould at 8,000 feet and, while paralleling the Michigan River, shoots into Walden. Staying above 6,000 feet through mountains reaching over 12,000 feet and then easing back down to 8,000 feet, it's easy to understand why the Cache la Poudre area is referred to by the locals as the "hideaway where the natives play."

Walden is a crossroads town. Head north to Wyoming through the pristine North Park area on Route 125 and close the book. Head west on Route 14 to **Steamboat Springs,** through the Rabbit Ears Mountains and Pass, or south, on Route 125 beside the Never-Summer Range, and set up a new home base in **Hot Sulphur Springs.**

■ For more trips in this region see *Motorcycle Journeys Through the Southwest* by Marty Berke, available from Whitehorse Press.

23 Gila Cliff Dwellings Loop

Text and photos by Marty Berke

- **DISTANCE** *116 miles*
- **HIGHLIGHTS** *Tight S-turns, hairpins, and climbs through deep river-carved canyons to vistas on cliff-hugging sweepers*

0.0 Leave City of Rocks State Park, in Faywood, New Mexico, on Route 61 north

19.9 Take Route 152 west

21.1 Turn onto Route 35 north

46.0 Take Route 15 north

57.8 Arrive at Gila Cliff Dwellings National Monument

69.6 Return to Route 35, but turn south

94.5 Turn onto Route 152 east

95.7 Take Route 61 south

115.6 Arrive back at City of Rocks State Park

*Mileages are approximate

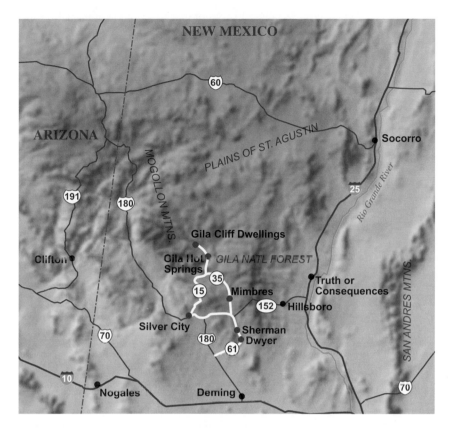

STARTING OUT FROM **City of Rocks State Park** in Faywood, New Mexico, Route 61 and Route 35 follow the Mimbres River Valley. The well-marked roads climb 45 miles through Mimbres Canyon. Staying at river-level, the sweepers stretch from 25 to 55 mph. When the road branches away from the Mimbres River, the climb becomes steeper and signs for Lake Roberts start to appear. Fed by the Gila (HEE-la) River, the lake provides a scenic backdrop for picture or picnic.

Just beyond **Lake Roberts,** joining the Gila River on the left, is the Route 15 intersection. The Middle and West forks of the Gila River seem to fade to streams as the road pulls up and away, hugging the cliff wall. Cresting 10 miles before the cliff dwellings, the steady third gear (sometimes second) descent allows vista viewing.

Gila Cliff Dwellings National Monument, another city of rocks, was last occupied more than 700 years ago. The earliest inhabitants found the nearby creek a dependable year-round source of water. They lived in seven naturally formed caves, six of which contain ruins of these prehistoric (because they left no written record) dwellers. Perhaps 40 to 50 people lived in the 40 rooms from about 1280 to the early 1300s, tilling soil and hunting small game.

Gila Cliff Dwellings Loop

Pueblo is a Spanish term applied to Southwestern Indians who built communal houses, farmed, and made pottery. This area was occupied by the Pueblo Indians of the Mogollon (mug-ee-YOWN) culture. Today's Northern Pueblo Indians are direct descendants of these people.

The original inhabitants used stone tools to level bedrock floors, then plastered the floors with mud for a hard, even surface. The vigas (VEE-gahs), large beams for the roof, were cut with stone axes and fire. They supported smaller poles and finally, a mud roof.

The Gila National Forest. (Photo by Jim Orr courtesy of the New Mexico Department of Tourism)

The dwellings were used by the Apaches who came into this area many years later, but the first recorded visit by a European was credited to archeologist-historian Adolph Bandelier in 1884.

Retracing Route 15 about 12 miles south, a quarter of a mile of rough dirt road leads to **Gila Hot Springs** (small sign on Route 15) and Berke's-Best-

The City of Rocks National Park is small, but interesting with huge sculpted boulders. (Photo by Mark Nohl courtesy of the New Mexico Department of Tourism)

THE ROCKY MOUNTAINS

At the Gila Cliff Dwellings National Monument you can tour ancient cities built into the walls of the earth. (Courtesy of the New Mexico Department of Tourism)

Buy-for-a-Buck (honor system). The water leaves the ground at 165 degrees Fahrenheit. To accommodate everybody, the water flows through three shallow cooling pools. For $2.50 a night, the visitor gets primitive campsites with his and her pit toilets, fishing, and soaking rights, opposite a huge canyon wall on the Gila River.

After the intersection of Route 35, Route 15 south blossoms into a series of fourth, third, second, and occasionally first gear hairpins through pine and cedar forest. Choosing this path provides the most climbing miles.

Silver City is a good place to gas up, buy provisions, or eat the mother lode at Kountry Kitchen on the cheap. Route 152 east, past the **Santa Rita Open-Pit Copper Mine,** Silver City's main source of income, is a wide stretch of highway back to home base.

▪ For more trips in this region see *Motorcycle Journeys Through the Southwest* by Marty Berke, available from Whitehorse Press.

24 New Mexico's Rocky Mountains

Text and photos by Marty Berke

- **DISTANCE** *257 miles*
- **HIGHLIGHTS** *Two-laner heaven. Vast alpine meadows, tight mountain passes, old-time narrow-gauge railroads, natural red-rock formations, raging rivers, little streams, and a living museum make this a memorable ride.*

0.0 Leave the Abiquiu Lake in Abiquiu, New Mexico, on Route 96 east	**215.9** Take Route 84 south
2.4 Turn north onto Route 84	**254.7** Turn onto Route 96 west
55.8 Take Route 17 east	**257.0** Arrive back at camp
121.5 Turn onto Route 285 south	*Mileages are approximate
159.7 Take Route 64 west	

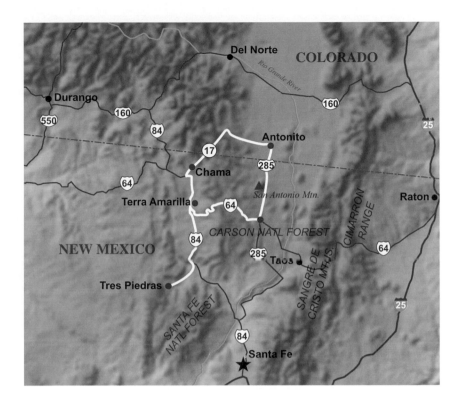

BARELY GETTING INTO fifth gear, the first stop on this loop is **Ghost Ranch Living Museum.** There are a number of stories about how Ghost Ranch got its name. Many years ago the Hispanics called the area El Rancho de los Brujos—the Ranch of the Witches. Tales of wailing babies, a giant snake, a flying red cow, and a murderous brother are all part of the local legends. The **Piedra Lumbre (rocks afire) Land Grant** is the setting for this unique National Forest Service Museum.

If you see flying cows, see a doctor, but giant snakes are a real possibility. Brought to the ranch as orphans or injured, here are animals of the wild rarely seen, never mind this close. A mountain lion, red fox (not the comedian), golden eagle, bald eagle, and Mandy, the bobcat, are but a few of the characters in this cast. Two favorites are Horendo, the black bear, found as a cub by the side of the road where her mother was killed by a car, and Kiki and Kino, two of only 65 Mexican wolves left in the world.

Ghost Ranch Living Museum also encompasses **Beaver National Forest.** Less than one acre, it is the smallest National Forest in the United States. There are plenty of smaller animals, birds, snakes, and a stirring historical display of the Northern New Mexico region and its people, in word and photography. Next, briefly stop at **Echo Canyon Amphitheater.** Naturally

This view from Ghost Ranch makes the terrifying witch stories almost worth it. (Photo by Jim Stein courtesy of the New Mexico Department of Tourism)

carved by erosion, this theater of sandstone is a 10 minute walk from the parking spot. It is also a campground and picnic area.

After **Echo Canyon,** the road narrows and climbs toward alpine country. The white, snow-capped Colorado San Juan Mountains loom ahead in the distance.

Chama is the western terminus for the longest and highest narrow gauge steam railroad in the United States, the Cumbres & Toltec Scenic Railroad. Built between 1880 and 1882 to serve the mines of southwestern Colorado, the railroad is now a Registered National Historic Site. It runs for 64 miles, climbing a four-percent grade and cresting at **Cumbres (Summit) Pass** at 10,015 feet. After passing through groves of aspen and pine, through the spectacular Toltec Pass of the Los Pifios River, the train rumbles down into **Antonito, Colorado,** the eastern terminus.

Did I mention this trip parallels the train most of the climb? The train leaves **Chamber** at 10:30 a.m. If you're on the road between then and noon, there are a number of pullouts to photograph the old beast billowing black coal smoke and whistling white steam. It's worth planning.

After Cumbres Pass, continue to climb to La Manga Pass Summit at 10,230 feet and then parallel the Conejos River. If it's spring, the melt usually peaks between the last week in May and the first week in June. The river runs high and fast for even more drama. **The Conejos River Guest Ranch** sits on the river and offers rustic cabins and solitude. The cabins are fully-equipped housekeeping units with one or two bedrooms plus living rooms with hide-a-beds, so three bikes gets the price down to motel prices per bike. Dinner menus are wide and reasonably priced, considering the diners are a captive audience.

The Rio Chama meanders across the valley. (Courtesy of the New Mexico Department of Tourism)

Road, river, and railroad end in Antonito, Colorado. **The Narrow Gauge Café,** although next to the terminal and unassuming, serves loaded tostadas and superb four-alarm green chili with ground pork at non-tourista prices. Route 285 is the only portion of the trip that feels highwayish. Passing San Antonio Mountain at 10,935 feet saves you from the full super slab feeling. This 30 miles is worth the ride to get to Route 64 at Tres Piedras.

The next 50 miles is the quintessential alpine mountain ride. Long sweepers over emerald green meadow vistas are dashed with yellow, purple, and

The Cumbres & Toltec Railroad will take you back in time. (Courtesy of the New Mexico Department of Tourism)

white wildflowers bordering mountain streams and lakes. Wild and domestic animals graze on the background carpet that shades from spring yellow-green to mature, deep pine-green. The road stays high for 25 miles. **The Brazos Cliffs** overlook, just before dropping dramatically off the meadow, is the place to rest the fanny and energize the mind.

A dramatic drop means 45 mph switchbacks, the fastest posted switchbacks in the Southwest. This is four miles of drop and finally levels out before connecting with Route 84 and back home. The loop is designed to go against the traffic. There's a loss of two miles of steep climb on the east side of Cumbres Pass and four miles on Route 64 east for the Alpine Meadow backside ascent. Turn around for those spots rather than enduring exhaust.

■ For more trips in this region see *Motorcycle Journeys Through the Southwest* by Marty Berke, available from Whitehorse Press.

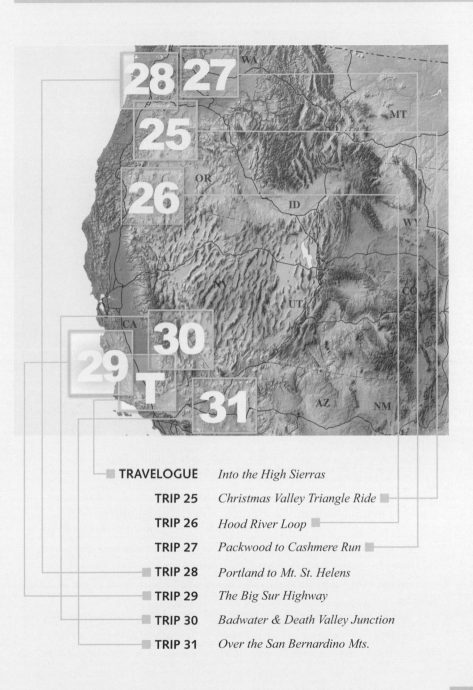

Into the High Sierras

Text and photos by Grant Parsons

I HATE TO nit-pick, but this is not exactly what I had in mind.

If you happen to live in Southern California, where perfect, sunny days are as predictable as stopped traffic on the 405, this foggy, overcast sky is perhaps a welcome novelty.

But I don't, and it's not. I live in Ohio, and I didn't need to travel 3,000 miles to get weather like this.

So, after two days of riding around under the kind of dull overcast that would be more at home in a Midwestern winter than a California spring, I've had it. I want sun, and I don't care if I have to go to the high Sierras to get it.

Hey, wait a minute, I think as I sip an overpriced latte in an espresso bar in fog-shrouded Santa Barbara, *the high Sierras...*

I unfold a bit more of the map laid out on the table in front of me and consider my options.

I had planned to take this loaner Honda ST1300 up the coast, which the weatherman is predicting will be socked in with fog for the next few days. The Pacific Coast Highway is one of the great roads in America, but not if you only see 50 feet of it at a time.

On the other hand, if I make a hard right about there, I can cut across California's Central Valley and be standing on top of a 9,200-foot pass sometime tomorrow.

I look out at the gray ocean and the even-grayer sky, pondering the vastness of time and space, and the little slices of each that we have here on this planet, while a fly buzzes against the coffee-shop window.

Ah, what the heck. I'm outta here.

Climbing out of Santa Barbara on California Route 154 a few minutes later, I've got several things going for me.

First, I've got no real plan—just a half-baked notion of heading in the direction of the Sierras. So I've got nothing to lose.

Second, as I'm heading out of town, there's a heck of a lot more traffic coming at me out of the Santa Ynez mountains than there is going my way. This is always a good sign. And third, it's still early—like 7 a.m.—meaning I've got the whole day in front of me.

All of this contributes to a wonderful sense of well-being as the thick fog along the coast gives way to thinner clouds and the occasional glimpse of blue sky. It's still cool, but behind the ST's big fairing, I'm plenty comfortable.

Tight mountain curves turn into wide sweepers as I near the top of a ridge. Finally, I round one last bend to find crystal blue sky extending in all directions. Now, this is what I'm talking about.

Soon, I roll through Santa Maria, whose main claim to fame is its proximity to Vandenberg Air Force Base, the West Coast's answer to Florida's Kennedy Space Center. Both serve as launching sites for America's space program, but while missions from Kennedy are usually accompanied by a great deal of publicity, the ones that originate here tend to have classified military objectives.

Even before the heightened security of recent years, you couldn't ride onto the base. Now, I suspect that anything moving in the general vicinity is closely watched.

That's OK, I'm headed east, over the low Sierra Madre range and out into the southern edge of the Central Valley.

The mountains provide a great escape from schedules, appointments, and stress.

The giant sequoia trees are awesome. (Photo courtesy of the National Park Service)

It's warming up significantly as I roll along the aptly named Caliente Range, and by the time I stop for something to drink at the only store I've seen for about 40 miles, the temperature is already in the high 80s. I sip Gatorade under a tree and look out over a landscape that shimmers in the heat, soaking up the California warmth I've been seeking for days.

I dial the ST's front windscreen down to its lowest position to get as much cooling wind as possible, and the bike and I hum along a ribbon of asphalt through sand and rocks.

It's pretty barren landscape for about 60 miles, and when I get to the bit of civilization known as Taft, it has an appropriately end-of-the-world feel. Oil well pumps nod slowly in the heat, and the town looks like it's in the midst of a decade-long siesta.

Turns out this area was the site of one of California's most infamous oil successes, or environmental disasters, depending on how you look at it. Back in 1910, a well-driller with the unfortunate nickname of "Dry Hole Charlie" turned his luck around in one giant swoop with the Lakeview Well, just outside of Taft. Drilling deep into the earth on the afternoon of March 15, Charlie hit paydirt at 2,220 feet.

A roaring column of sand and oil 20 feet in diameter blew the top off his derrick and spouted 200 feet into the California sky. The gusher could not be contained, and it just got stronger for an astounding seven months, while pooled oil was collected and pumped off. Finally, a massive sandbag dike 100 feet in diameter was built around the well, and the weight of the above-ground oil slowed the gusher to a trickle.

All those pumps show that there's still plenty of oil left here, though. And as I top off the ST at a gas station, it strikes me that this is the motorcycle equivalent of sampling the local product in the tasting room of a winery.

*   *   *

I confess that my solo motorcycle travel habits may seem a bit strange—particularly to those who like to take it easy. Generally, when I'm by myself, I don't. To me, riding a motorcycle is about the best state of being there is, and I seldom want the experience to end. So when I'm by myself, the day is never over until I say it's over.

Which is why, when I check into a roadside hotel in Tulare room just long enough to dump my gear and refold my maps bet back out.

I've got about four hours before dark, and it looks like if I h make it up to Sequoia National Park and back before it gets to what's another 160 miles beginning at 4 p.m.?

I gas up in Visalia (there's no fuel available in the park), and turn north on California Route 245. At first, the road is nothing special, but once I'm north of Woodlake, the easy sweepers turn into ever-tightening 15-mph twisties.

A few miles later, I have to admit it's about the best section of road I've seen in a long time—and there's no one on it. Barely wide enough for two cars, and with no painted lines, it threads among pinon trees and auburn-colored, grassy hillsides for more than 20 miles.

It's the asphalt equivalent of an enduro course, and a stretch that I thought would take about 30 minutes takes nearly double that before I reach the entrance to Sequoia and Kings Canyon National Parks. The only bummer is that I don't have time to turn around and ride it again.

Instead, I pay my money and head into the parks, where I find a well-maintained, serpentine road that's lined with soaring trees and a ton of fun at the posted 35-mph speed limit. Amazingly, it, too, is empty of traffic, so I get a gorgeous ride through a spectacular national park all to myself. How often does that happen?

The coast may be nice, but on this trip, the real California is in the mountains.

Into the High Sierras

I'm enjoying myself so much that in typical fashion I blow past a lot of cool stuff, with my attention on the road and a smile on my face.

What kind of stuff? Well, when I read a brochure later, I learn that one of those really big sequoias just off the road is the General Sherman Tree, the largest tree, by volume, in the world. It's 2,000 years old, 275 feet tall, and 36 feet in diameter at the base.

It's probably pretty impressive. Next time, I'll definitely stop.

It's 8:13 a.m. I've been riding for nearly two hours. I've got a good map, a full tank of gas, and it's another beautiful day.

If there's a better feeling than that, I don't know what it is.

I'm headed for the high point of the day, Sherman Pass, which tops out at more than 9,000 feet. By the time I stop in Camp Nelson for breakfast, I'm halfway there, and a hot meal seems perfectly in order.

A couple of BMW riders in the booth next to me say they've just come from where I'm heading. They report that the road over Sherman Pass, which is often closed in winter, is open and in good shape.

Back on the bike, I cruise through the communities of Quaking Aspen and Johnsondale, then hook a sharp left onto Sherman Pass Road, headed toward the pass itself, about 15 miles away. Over that distance, the terrain changes dramatically.

Until now, I've been skirting the mountains, but as I ride east, I'm pointed at the sky on tight switchbacks strung together by short straight stretches. With every turn, the temperature drops and the wind picks up.

It was looking like spring down low, with new, green leaves on the bushes. By the time I reach the turnout at Sherman Pass, I've traveled back in time to late winter.

The best place to see and be seen on the Angeles Crest? Newcomb's Ranch.

I park the bike and take a minute to breathe in the thin, clear air. Then I check out the view, unobstructed by any other vehicles.

To the north are the higher mountains in the heart of the Sierra range. Somewhere out there, only about 40 miles away, is Mount Whitney. At 14,495 feet, it's the highest point in the contiguous states.

I enjoy the view for a while, then turn back and retrace my ride down to Johnsondale. It's just as good in the other direction.

*   *   *

I knew this would happen sooner or later. I'm just glad it was later.

After hundreds of miles on blissfully uncrowded roads, I run into traffic again heading into the town of Kernville. When I get there, I find out why. Turns out that this region is a mecca for hikers, kayakers, mountain bicyclists, and off-road motorcyclists. Even though I've arrived mid-week, they're out in force. I can't imagine what it would be like on a weekend.

The traffic gives me a chance to slow down and soak up the town, which looks like a pretty cool place to hang out. Ice cream shops, trendy gift stores, hotels, and plenty of good restaurants line the main drag, and from some of them, you can watch rafters bouncing off the rocks on the Kern River.

But I've got an appointment with one of the region's most recommended motorcycle routes—Caliente-Bodfish Canyon Road, which starts several miles south of Kernville. As I turn off heavily traveled California Route 178 to pick up this back road in the sleepy town of Bodfish, I'm thrilled to see that none of the traffic comes with me. Yee-ha.

Inside the first three miles, it's clear that the road's reputation is entirely deserved. Climbing sharply out of Bodfish on 180-degree switchbacks, the uneven asphalt immediately demands your complete attention. It then rises and falls over auburn hills and into wide, mountain valleys. In one curve, the scenery in the valley below is so beautiful I actually stop. Sipping water as my feet dangle over the edge of the pullout, I've once again got the world to myself.

The last major challenge of the day comes around sunset, as I'm blasting down four-lane California Route 58 toward my overnight stop in Palmdale.

Off to my right, among the Tehachapi Mountains, I see about a million stark white wind turbines, twirling madly on their stalks. Stare at them long enough, and they're hypnotizing.

With 4,600 turbines, the Tehachapi range is home to the largest concentration of wind-power generators in the U.S. In fact, this wind farm makes enough electricity to supply 500,000 people, which is more wind-generated electricity than the rest of the country combined.

Bring your sunglasses for those romantic rides into the setting sun.

What's odd, though, is that I can't feel any appreciable breeze. It doesn't strike me that this is because I'm on the lee side of the mountains until the road makes a final turn toward Tehachapi Pass. Instantly, I'm heading straight into a wind that's capable of powering a city of a half-million. And boy, can I feel it.

It only gets worse when I cross the gap in the mountains and curve south. Now there's a gale blowing steadily from my right, and the fully faired ST does its spinnaker impersonation, pushing me toward the centerline of the highway.

Over the next several miles, I discover a lot about how a motorcycle reacts in a crosswind. I learn, for instance, that the gusts hitting the right side of the bike are only partly responsible for pushing me left. The other factor is that when the wind catches my upper body, the natural reaction is to force myself right, into it. And how do I do that? By pushing against the left handgrip, which effectively countersteers the bike in that direction.

Eventually, I figure out that in this kind of wind, it's better to simply tip the bike about five degrees to the right and shift my butt so I'm sitting on the left edge of the seat. In that position, everything is close to neutral again.

You learn something new every day.

After a night in Palmdale, the only thing left is to return the ST to its home in the Los Angeles area. And fortunately, I've put myself in the perfect position to do that.

If you've heard anything about motorcycling in Los Angeles, you know that one of the roads you've got to ride is the Angeles Crest Highway. This asphalt ribbon winds over the San Gabriel Mountains from the desert into the Los Angeles basin. And I'm only about 20 miles from it.

I roll out of Palmdale at dawn on a Saturday. The sky is blue, the temperature is comfortable and I figure there'll be lots of riders and cars up on the Crest. But when I turn onto the Angeles Forest Road, which climbs up to join the Crest, I see exactly one Ducati, one VFR, and one Porsche in a dozen miles.

When I reach the Crest Highway, I discover why.

I turn right to start on the short downward journey into Glendale, on the L.A. end, figuring I'll turn around there and ride the road all the way to its eastern end in Wrightwood.

Within a quarter-mile, I descend into a solid wall of thick, soupy cloud. Visibility goes from unlimited to about 10 feet. Apparently, the coastal fog I left behind days ago is still here.

I hold my breath, trust to luck and make a U-turn, quickly re-emerging into bright sunshine that looks like it extends east from here all the way across the vast Mojave Desert. Apparently, it's only the western tip of the road that's getting the bad weather.

At a turnoff, I stop for Pop-Tarts and Pepsi, the breakfast of champions. A couple of sportbikes pull in moments later.

"Man, it's great up here, isn't it," one rider says. "I'm sure glad we went for it."

Turns out they're part of a mass of motorcyclists who gathered in fog and rain at a gas station in Glendale, trying to decide whether to venture up the road. Clearly, they'd be better off up here, but I'm not going down to tell them.

Instead, I turn east to enjoy the 50 miles or so of clear road in that direction. The pavement climbs steadily through sweeping corners, and since you're riding along the crest, the views to each side are incredible. This is one road that actually lives up to the hype. It's wonderful.

I roll along for miles, then round a corner to find a full-on motorcycle circus. The parking lot of a small store is jammed with maybe 80 motorcycles, mostly sportbikes. Their rainbow hues shine in the morning sun, and the aroma of bacon and coffee lures me in.

Welcome to Newcomb's Ranch, the best place to see and be seen on Angeles Crest. I squeeze in among the leather and Kevlar, buy an OJ and carry it back outside to watch. Motorcyclists mill around, reliving rides, planning others and congratulating themselves for braving the rain down in L.A.

Eventually, I tear myself away to ride the rest of the Crest. I work my way down to the eastern end at Wrightwood, then turn around and double back for a last run toward civilization that signals the end of a great few days on the road.

The Crest is just as good in this direction, except that by now, traffic is building. No problem. I'm content to roll along, not wanting this day to end. In fact, about 10 miles from Glendale, I pull over and settle on a rock to enjoy the sunshine.

I'm still well above the fog, and I can look out across sunlit cloud tops that fill the L.A. basin like a bowl of whipped cream. Somewhere under them is the hustle of the city. Traffic. Freeways. Reality. Funny. For the first time in the entire trip, I'm in no hurry.

25 Christmas Valley Triangle Ride

Text and photos by Bruce Hansen

- **DISTANCE:** *226 miles to complete the triangle.*
- **HIGHLIGHTS:** *Enormous alkaline lakes, tallest fault scarp in North America, dunes, beautiful earth colors and rock formations, rustic towns, huge cattle ranches, friendly people, and great food*

0.0 From Valley Falls, Oregon, go 61.5 miles north on State Highway 395

61.5 At Christmas Valley/Wagontire Road (also called County Road 514) turn left, this is well marked as toward Christmas Valley

88.0 If you are staying at the Outback B&B, look for their hand painted sign, other-wise, continue to the town of Christmas Valley

100.0 Continue through Christmas Valley, watch for the sign for Fort Rock

113.0 Turn right toward Fort Rock

129.0 From Fort Rock, continue west on County Road 511

135.0 Turn left (south) on Fremont Highway toward Silver Lake

IT'S A STORY I thought I'd never tell. Perhaps it's best that a suburbanite like me tell it. I've enjoyed riding in every climate the great Pacific Northwest has to offer: the rugged snowcapped mountains, the gentle grasslands, the soggy temperate rainforests, the high dry plains, the lonely coastal fog shrouded hills, but I've never viewed the desert as anything but an obstacle to where I'm going. I'd much rather hang out at Starbucks and watch people watch my bike than head off into the desert.

Perhaps that was because I'd only crossed the Oregon and Washington deserts riding in a car. The heat blast that hit each time the door opened made me long for the cool forests to the west. Then came my first motorcycle desert crossing. Some friends and I had picked what was to be the hottest week in Oregon history to make the journey. I feared the ending of the story before the first chapter began.

Always uncomfortable in high heat, I thought I'd spend my days miserable and bored—looking at mile after mile of sage brush. As the story unfolded, it was one of the best rides I've ever taken. The naked beauty of the desert, the silvery dawns, the horizon constantly tugging on my bike. I liked the genuine, flinty people who flourished in the harsh climate.

Christmas Valley Triangle Ride

A hunter's cabin snuggles into the high rocky hills surrounding Summer Lake.

When it came time to introduce my wife to riding, I chose to take our suburban lives to a world where the word latte is rarely heard and not fully understood: the southeastern high desert area called Christmas Valley. Looking at the map, it's a great, upside down triangle that now draws me like some kind of mystery force. Sturgis-bound Californians have long known about this special place.

To get to **Christmas Valley** from California, turn off from 395 about 62 miles north of **Lakeview.** Take the mostly straight road through sage brush country, past a giant super secret US spy radar array (Please don't tell anyone about it.), and up a steep 8% hill to a mountain enclosed plateau now called Christmas Valley.

Some people think John Fremont named this valley when he camped here on December 24, 1843. The true story is: he camped about 150 miles south of this area and some map maker mistakenly assigned the name to a place Fremont had never visited. The town of Christmas Valley has a lodge, which serves simple hardy meals and cheap strip motel rooms used mostly by migrant workers and sage rat shooters. These rooms were on the rustic side last time I looked. We stayed in the impossibly clean **Outback Bed and Breakfast** 12 miles east of town. Best breakfast I've ever had.

From the town of Christmas Valley, follow the signs west to **Fort Rock** to see one of few geological wonders in the area accessible by paved roads. Stay alert on the 29 miles from Christmas Valley to Fort Rock. Sometimes these roads take a 90-degree turn for no apparent reason. The straight part can lull a rider into thinking the highway will never turn.

Picture a wagon train pursued by hostile Indians. There is no refuge in the desert, or is there? According to legend, the wagon train headed toward a formation called Fort Rock—a natural, walled, citadel rising 325 feet from the floor of the desert. Recently, several pairs of 9,000-year-old sandals were found in a nearby cave. This interesting rock formation was formed five to six million years ago when volcanic material attempted to rise up from the floor of a lake. Fort Rock puts a visitor in touch with ancient peoples and events. It is a state park now and contains several trails to allow a visitor to explore the views and imagine the geological and human violence that formed the history of this special place. Just outside the park, the community of Fort Rock has a tavern with good food. You can enjoy a chicken dinner and think about the wagon train holding off the Indians.

Join State Route 31 just seven miles east of Fort Rock. From the junction, it's 68 miles north to **Bend** or a little over 18 miles to **Silver Lake** if you turn south. To complete the Christmas Valley Triangle, turn south on State Route 31. At the frontier town of Silver Lake, you can drive the four miles to one of the most famous steak houses in Oregon: the **Cowboy Dinner Tree** restaurant (reservations only 541-576-2426). The steak is known for its 26 to 30 oz.

It would be a mistake to think the Christmas Valley Triangle is just some pancake griddle ride. Mountains, valleys, lakes, cliffs, and sand dunes wait to entertain a rider.

Fort Rock shimmers in the afternoon. All the roads out to it are paved, but if you ride a dual-sport bike, more wonders like this open up to you in Christmas Valley.

Stand with your back to Fort Rock and look out over the valley floor. This is the place where a battle took place between wagon-bound settlers and angry native Americans.

weight—about the size of a football. If you have no way of dealing with leftovers, you might want to save this experience for later and just eat at the **Silver Lake Café and Bar.**

Leaving Silver Lake you will pass by ranches, an abandoned one room school, and the town of **Summer Lake.** The **Lodge at Summer Lake** has meals and several simple motel rooms. A couple of miles later you'll find the **Summer Lake Inn Bed and Breakfast,** a more upscale family resort. After you pass the **24 Ranch,** you'll see more and more of the alkali portion of Summer Lake as well as the high brown and gray basalt mountains on the right. These are often snow-capped in winter and spring.

THE WEST

State Route 31 takes you past Summer Lake an into an interesting desert floor decorated by volcanic monuments. Twenty-nine miles after Summer Lake you roll into **Paisley.** Named after the town in Scotland, it's had a post office for over 100 years. I like the little city park—perfect for a picnic. Often hunters and fishermen stay at their RV park, motel, and eat in their restaurant. When you step into the gas station you will think you've gone back into time—just like the 1950s gas stations my daddy told me about. Closed on Sundays.

On the east side of the triangle that makes this loop, we stopped at the highest and most exquisite fault scarp in North America. Turn to your right; you see a sheer slab of amazingly hard dark basalt rising abruptly 2,500 feet from the desert floor. Turn to your left, there is a beautiful blue lake surrounded by perfect white alkaline

Climb up to the top of Fort Rock if you dare. Hundreds of feet below an ancient lakebed appears fuzzy with sagebrush.

shores. Hundreds of birds gather to feast on the brine shrimp that miraculously survive in the caustic waters. My coffee-shop mind was unable to grasp the terrible and fragile beauty of this desert no matter how often my eyes shouted, "This is beautiful!"

To finish this Christmas Valley triangle, you will motor 23 miles south from Paisley on State Route 31 to Valley Falls. Your tale of a desert crossing could have a happy ending like mine. All the yokels at the coffee shop will hang on every word as you tell your desert tale.

Before starting a Christmas Valley story of your own, be aware of local weather conditions: high winds, heat, or frigid night air can affect how your desert story ends. Be aware that the best time to travel is early morning when the winds are usually quiet but the animals are most active. After a wind storm, parts of the highway could be covered with drifted sand or alkali dust. Does this make you want to linger near the neighborhood Starbucks instead of heading out to the desert? I understand.

■ For more trips in this region see *Motorcycle Journeys Through the Pacific Northwest* by Bruce Hansen, available from Whitehorse Press.

26 Hood River Loop

Text and photos by Bruce Hansen

- **DISTANCE:** *146 miles*
- **HIGHLIGHTS:** *Charming rural highways, deep forest twisting roads, unbelievable views of Mt. Hood and the Oregon fruit tree industry, and Lost Lake*

0.0 Leave Portland, Oregon, going east on Interstate 84 toward The Dalles

65.0 Exit I 84 toward Highway 35 (Mt. Hood)

67.0 Look for sign toward Panorama Point on the right side of the road, then turn left and follow signs to Panorama Point.

72.0 Leave Panorama Point and continue south on Eastside Road

75.0 Turn left onto Wells Drive

76.5 Turn left onto Fir Mountain Road and go until the pavement ends

79.0 Back track past Wells Drive; Fir Mountain Road will veer west toward Highway 35

89.0 Turn left (south) onto Highway 35

95.0 Turn right and stay on Cooper Spur Road toward Parkdale (this has excellent twisties,) watch for possible gravel in spots

100.8 Arrive at Cooper Spur Inn, then do the Lost Lake tour, retrace your route to Parkdale

106.9 From Parkdale it's easy to follow the signs to Lost Lake. I'll give you the directions, but I suggest you just follow the signs. There are plenty of them and the road is so pretty. Turn left on Baseline

107.5 Right onto Old Parkdale Road

108.6 Left onto National Forest Road 16 (Red Hill Road)

112.0 Right onto Tony Creek Road

112.5 Sharp left onto Carson Hill Road (this will become Lost Lake Road)

119.6 Stay on Lost Lake Road

125.1 Arrival at Lost Lake.
From Lost Lake to Hood River, take Lost Lake Road toward Dee

145.9 Lost Lake Road becomes Dee Highway (Hood River Highway), follow this right into Hood River

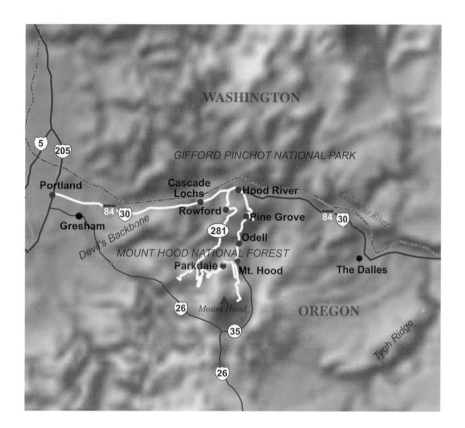

IN 1924, Wells Bennett, with most of his daredevil racing days behind him, roared up Mt. Hood to the 8,500 foot elevation on his four-cylinder Henderson. A group on foot started out on the same July 4th morning and easily out-paced him due to the abundance of piano-sized boulders which constantly presented themselves in front of him. Although eager to reach the summit, after four days of scrambling, he was finally defeated by a stinging snow storm and blinding winds. No one has ever made it higher on a motorcycle.

This journey is told from the point of view of a traveler coming from Portland, since most visitors approach the Hood River area from **Portland** by driving through the **Columbia River Gorge**—a dream of a journey. Local bikers like to make any excuse to take the Columbia River Scenic Highway when in the gorge, but sometimes we are in a hurry.

Going the shortest way and about 65 miles from Portland, you turn off Interstate 84 on Exit 64 going toward state Highway 35. Morning is the best time for this trip due to the high winds that usually pick up during the afternoon. The trip can be exhausting when the gorge winds are at 50 mph.

After leaving the interstate, stay on the route toward State Highway 35. About a mile from the exit and just after the last stop sign, look for the turn

The never-ending line of fruit trees point to Mt. Adams. Travelers from Portland often come out in the spring to gawk. In the fall, they come to buy apples and pears.

These apple trees are kept short by pruning. This makes the apples reachable and causes dense blossom growth.

on your left toward **Panorama Point.** Some signs designate this Panorama Point Road and others show it as East Side Road. Don't feel bad if you miss this turn. There's no pull-out lane and you may have traffic behind you. It seems I miss it about 50% of the time. It's worth backtracking to see the view. Snaking up to the **Panorama Point Park,** you will be teased by twisty little roads spidering off here and there. Most of these end in gravel, but I still enjoy exploring them.

If you can manage to visit Panorama Point in the morning, you are in for a fantastic view of **Mt. Hood** and the apple-tree-filled valley before it. In the afternoon, the view becomes back-lit and not as nice for photos. After snapping pictures and using the restroom, continue south on East Side Road. After a couple of miles, follow Wells Drive to Fir Mountain Road. This narrow road takes you past glorious views of Mt. Hood until the pavement ends. How I long to have a good gravel bike at this point! Instead, I turn around, retracing my route for a mile until I can turn left on Ehrck Hill Road. Take Ehrck Hill Road to SH 35. Turn left.

SH 35 will take you past miles of apple and pear trees. In the spring the blossoms draw thousands of tourists. Motorcyclists get to smell the fragrance. In the fall, the air is sweet with the heavy sugary smell of apples and pears. We never buy enough since they taste so good, and an apple shopper can go far beyond the five varieties carried by most supermarkets. Stop, sample, and buy apples if they are available.

About six miles from Ehrck Hill Road, you will see the **Cooper Spur** turnoff. Follow this to the **Cooper Spur Ski Area.** When you go through the tiny berg of Mount Hood, look for the house just north of the big beautiful barn. That is the former home of Wells Bennett, the famous motorcyclist, who would race his 40-horsepower Henderson against early airplanes and anything else fast.

For a couple of miles after the village of **Mount Hood,** you will be amongst row after row of fruit trees. As they end, the road becomes sinuous with intermittent pot holes and fir trees thickening as you gain altitude. Occasional picturesque ranches backed by high rounded hills appear along the way.

At the top, just after a set of glorious twisties, you can find a restaurant and clean guest cottages called **Inn at Cooper Spur.** If you want to brave the gravel roads of the area, you can get to the **Cloud Cap Inn.**

My bike is strictly for the pavement so about a half-mile from the ski area, I can take a wooded road east to connect to SH 35 if I want to blast out of the Hood River Valley, but if I have the time, I like to head north to the lazy, and heavily-wooded roads leading to Lost Lake.

This is going to sound complicated, but if you want, toss the book into the tank bag and just follow the signs to **Packwood,** then to **Lost Lake.** If you like directions, here goes. To get to Lost Lake, retrace your way down the Cooper Spur Road for four miles until you can turn left at Evans Creek Road. After a half mile, turn right onto Clear

In the 1920s, engineer John A. Elliott built this part of the Old Columbia River Highway so that it had a maximum five percent grade and no turn had a radius of less than 100 feet. Bikers have been known to spend all day running these perfect roads.

Creek Road and run into the little artsy town of **Parkdale.** Besides art, the two main industries are packing apples and providing nice homes for retirees. From here the fastest way to get to Lost Lake is to proceed the 3.5 miles to the town of **Dee** and follow the signs to Lost Lake Road.

If you love to spend time on lonely deep forest roads, at Parkdale, turn left at Red Hill Drive and follow it for a quarter-mile until it becomes County Road 16. Stay on this twisty narrow county road for about 15 miles until you come to County Road 18. Stay on this for two miles. You get to cross the West Fork of Hood River just less than a mile before County Road 13. What a view! Turn left onto County Road 13 and enjoy it for five miles.

The north side of Mount Hood shines brightly in the morning light. Portland residents need to get up early to see this view.

This sounds complicated, but few people have ever gotten lost just looking for the plentiful signs pointing the way to Lost Lake. Once you are at **Lost Lake,** you can get snack foods at

How nice it would be if this ride were "undiscovered." But it's likely you will meet fellow bikers on a weekend trip to Lost Lake.

their little market, have a picnic with a perfect view of lake and mountain, take the spongy fern trail around the lake, rent a boat or canoe (no power boats allowed) and fish, swim in the clear waters, and take a camp site for the night (reservations recommended). Once while eating sandwiches in the picnic area, we watched a daddy and his young son catch a 20-inch rainbow trout from a rented row boat.

Indian legends hold Lost Lake as a place of bad luck. It is told that at a great gathering on the lake, a host of Indians were about to enjoy a feast when a snow white doe, pursued by wolves, jumped into the clear waters. It swam out to the middle, dived beneath the surface and was never seen again. The medicine man judged this to be an omen of bad luck. The whole group left immediately.

You can find fireweed growing in the open places left by clear cuts or along roads.

When you leave this lake, follow the Lost Lake Road toward **Dee,** not really a town, but more of a location on a map. Driving through this area, I could never figure out why it has a name. Once on the Dee Highway, follow the signs toward **Hood River.**

If you want romance, try the **Hood River Hotel,** a pretty, restored hotel in the center of the charming town of Hood River. If you want elegance, and cost is no object, the **Columbia Gorge Hotel** offers stunning luxury to soothe tired bones. Affordable, clean lodging can be found at the Comfort Suites. Get breakfast at **Bette's Place** or a gourmet dinner at **Brian's Pourhouse.**

The well-maintained buildings of Hood River might charm you or transport you back to the era of Wells Bennet and the barnstorming days of the 1920s. A day in the Hood River Valley is a day surrounded by rustic and geological beauty.

■ For more trips in this region see *Motorcycle Journeys Through the Pacific Northwest* by Bruce Hansen, available from Whitehorse Press.

27 Packwood to Cashmere Run

Text and photos by Bruce Hansen

- **DISTANCE:** *169 miles one way.*
- **HIGHLIGHTS:** *Mountain views, deep forests, cliff-hugging rural highways, rapid climate changes from temperate rainforests to desert sage brush, geological wonders*

0.0 Start in Packwood, Washington, going east on US Highway 12

72.0 Merge onto Interstate 82 North toward Ellensburg/Selah, get into the left lane

73.7 Take exit 30a onto Washington Highway 823 North toward Selah (This is a left exit ramp)

77.2 Stay on 823 North, merge onto 821 North

101.7 Turn right onto Thrall Road toward the freeway

102.3 Take the US 97 North/ I 82 N ramp

110.2 Take the US 97 North exit (exit number 106)

162.4 Turn right onto US 2 toward Cashmere

168.7 Arrive in Cashmere, Washington

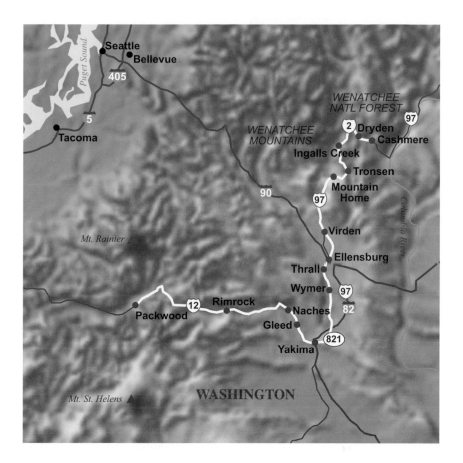

REMEMBER NOAH? FIRST there was the flood. Washington State slept under the sea. As the Teutonic plates lifted the Evergreen State out of the waters, the area was flooded with basalt lava the thickness of cold pancake syrup. Basalt is so hard; erosion can hardly make a mark on it. Perhaps the only thing left to do to change the endless basalt is to cover it up. Glaciers, gigantic floods, and windblown dust did it. To complete this picture, throw in some volcanoes. Voila! Washington State.

Into this geological wonderland a bike comes wandering. Your bike. You can see all these wonders in this next journey from **Packwood** to **Cashmere.**

From Packwood you will journey east on US 12. You will roll down the shoulders of **Mt. Rainier** over its much drier east side. The forests dramatically change from ferns and douglas firs to pines and alpine firs. Descending from White Pine pass, a winter ski area, you can see smaller volcanoes and folded mountains far below.

The first time I rode this highway, I was perched on an unfamiliar rented bike. The highway has only a thin guardrail between the highway and deep

When the road through Mt. Rainier National Park was constructed, builders created art with stone.

canyon below. I nervously carved each turn, trying to watch the scenery and still maintain a safe speed. Somehow I noticed I was going faster and faster and seeing less and less. Knowing I was exceeding the highest possible speed with which this road could be navigated, I was surprised when a chopper with ape hangers passed me on a blind turn. I kept waiting to see the remains of his bike attached to the front of an oncoming SUV or a smear of orange paint on a guardrail somewhere. I'm guessing the fellow made it safely down to **Yakima.** But I decided to slow down and enjoy the forest and mountains more.

Soon you will be on the edge of **Rimrock Lake,** a six-mile-long reservoir formed in 1925 when the **Tieton Dam** was built. At one end a tiny store,

The golden hills northwest of Yakima hold their secrets. Geologists believe these are piles of gravel left behind by floods and glaciers.

with a well-used bathroom around back, made me wonder if it was built the same year as the dam.

Soon after leaving Rimrock Lake, you will notice the trees almost disappear and desert shrubs pop up. **Mt. Rainier** keeps most of the Pacific moisture on its west side. **Naches** has services like gas, food, and lodging. If you want anything other than the simplest food and lodging in this area, turn left (west) onto WA 410. About 20 miles up the road is **Whistlin' Jack Lodge** with a chef, cabins, and motel rooms.

Pulling out of Naches go east on US 12. You may find this road busy with big trucks and increasingly suburban traffic as you approach **Yakima.** About 12 miles outside of Naches, keep an eye out for I 82, toward **Selah/Ellensburg.**

Passing through Mt. Rainier National Park will treat your senses: forest smells, gentle air, and smooth pavement.

Stay on I 82 for about two miles and take the WA 823 N exit (exit 30a) toward Selah. Stay on WA 823 as it merges to WA 821 north toward Ellensburg. You are in for a treat.

Most of the automobile traffic is running parallel to you on I 82; you are sweeping through the Yakima River Valley on a graceful riverside road. The golden grass-covered hills to the west look fuzzy and soft. There are huge heaps of glacial gravel left by the ice age. I never get tired of seeing the cold blue river, golden hills, and clear blue sky. The state police drive tan, dust-colored patrol cars with friendly, helpful troopers who do not tolerate speeding. Watch for rocks on the road near cliffs.

Ellensburg was built in the **Kittitas Valley** and prides itself for its location central to touring the many **Yakima Valley** wineries. Remember that basalt flow I told you about covering most of the state of Washington? Here the basalt is covered by ancient and glacial gravel. The Kittitas Valley allows the winds to blow through here fiercely at times. It was here I found out that a Harley Road King is superior to a Honda Goldwing in serious crosswinds.

As you approach Ellensburg from the south on 821, keep in mind your goal is US 97 north toward **Wenatchee.** Stay on 821 north until you get to Thrall Road. Turn right here, go about a half mile and merge onto US 97 north (also called I 82 north). After eight miles on this highway, you will take the US 97 north exit toward Wenatchee.

Be sure to stop and enjoy those thousand-dollar mountain views.

An Indian Paintbrush. As the snow retreats, these blossom across the mountains all summer.

Once you are on 97 north, the winds seem to quickly fade as you pass by pretty farms and rural scenes. You are on your way to **Blewett Pass.** US 97 in this area has broad sweeping turns with pretty views of forests and mountains. It's all four-lane, quick driving unless you get behind a clump of RVs or heavy trucks.

Blewett Pass, famous for 55 million year old fossilized palms and flowers, (in earlier times) thousand-dollar gold nuggets and beautiful mountain views. It's about 60 miles from Ellensburg to the junction of US 2. Turn east (right) onto US 2 and take the second **Cashmere** exit (Cotlets Way) to find the motel. I always stay in Cashmere because nearby **Leavenworth** has so many tourists that the room prices are often higher.

Cashmere used to be called Mission, but changed its name in 1904 to its present name after the beautiful Vale of Kashmir in India. The best food in this part of Washington is the **Walnut Café** (reservations recommended—even for lunch) about two blocks from the motel. It's a bit on the gourmet side. If you want simple, down-home food and don't mind a little smoke in your eye, **Barney's Tavern** has great breakfasts and big simple dinners.

Another place with good home cooking is the **Big Y.** Get back on US 2 north toward Leavenworth. You'll see the Big Y about five miles up the road on the right just past **Drydon.**

Located on a major fault (called the Leavenworth Fault) and surrounded by sharp mountains, the nearby town of Leavenworth is a marvel of geological

You could get dizzy with the rapid climate changes from deep forests to rocky deserts and back to forest. The roads on this ride aren't busy, but the motorcyclists on them will be.

and economic wonders. Several years ago Leavenworth decided to go with a Bavarian theme rather than turn into a ghost town as the timber industry started to fade. The results are startling. What started as a few Bavarian-style false fronted stores is now a booming Bavarian business center. You may not find pot holders and ceramic plates celebrating Noah and the flood, but lots of items with the image of King Ludwig II.

For more trips in this region see *Motorcycle Journeys Through the Pacific Northwest* by Bruce Hansen, available from Whitehorse Press.

28 Portland to Mt. St. Helens

Text and photos by Bruce Hansen

■ **DISTANCE:** *242 miles round trip from Portland. 300 miles round trip*
■ *from Seattle.*
HIGHLIGHTS: *Excellent views of the volcanic destruction and renewal of the Mt. St. Helens area, and perfectly designed sweeping roads up the mountain*

0.0 Depart Portland, Oregon, taking I 5 North toward Seattle, Washington	**65.5** Turn right onto WA 504
65.0 Take the WA 504 exit (Exit 49) toward Castle Rock/Toutle	**121.5** Keep on WA 504 toward Coldwater Lake/Johnston Ridge

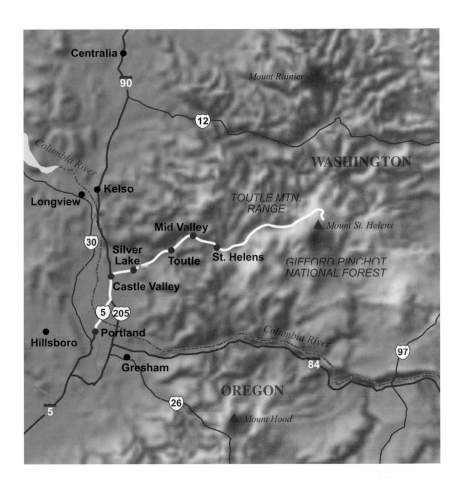

ON MAY 18TH, 1980, the bulging north flank of Mt. St. Helens collapsed. Magma and super heated gas and ash, kept for centuries under unimaginable pressure, exploded outwards at speeds over 800 mph. In five minutes over 230 square miles of forest were flattened. As a result, many of the roads had to be rebuilt. Lucky for motorcycle travelers.

Locals know this region to really be two distinct trips. One is the tame and lazy western side of the mountain. Here you are likely to pass a Crown Victoria with gray-haired tourists out for a pleasant drive and a look at the stunning views of the volcano. You are also able to cruise some of the best engineered and most beautiful roads in all the state of Washington. On a typically clear day you should get excellent volcano photos and, depending on how much time you spend in the museums, a great understanding of the volcano we call **Mt. St. Helens.**

Beginning riders like this trip for the wide and forgiving roads. If you are on a rental, this is a great place to get used to your bike. Experienced riders

The trees are small here, but are recovering nicely. Part of the 1980 blast flattened everything. Oh no! Is that smoke coming from the peak again?

Many of the roads in this area had to be rebuilt after the volcano blew, creating the ideal ride for motorcyclists.

enjoy the banked turns, views, and photo opportunities, as well as the interpretive museums. Often I bring visitors to this place just to make sure they have a great experience.

The eastern side of Mt. St. Helens is a dark and twisty ride where few mini-vans dare to travel.

A journey to the tame side involves some interstate travel through gentle valleys and billboard-framed small towns. Once off the interstate you can view such roadside attractions as an A-frame house partly buried in volcanic ash and a 30-foot-tall statue of **Big Foot.** This is the place to be to see the 1980 eruption interpreted through well-financed Federal museums. Keep in mind you will be ascending over 4,000 feet from base. It's typical to find temperature variations of 20 to 40 degrees from sea level. Bring gear to stay comfortable on this beautiful ride.

My favorite way to do this trip is to leave fairly early on a sunny Sunday morning. No traffic, no crowds, and a chance to eat a great breakfast in **Woodland, Washington.** If you must travel midweek, be aware that the Portland area rush hours can be hard on a biker, especially on hot days. I've found myself inching along, tire-to-bumper, at five mph for 10 miles. Portland has about 20 to 30 hot summer days each year, but many more slow freeway traffic days. Leaving **Portland** is better in the mornings since so many Washington residents commute to Portland each morning and return in the evenings. As you leave Portland in the morning, notice all the Washington plates going the opposite direction.

Once you are in Washington State, and out of the city of **Vancouver, Washington,** you can start to enjoy the scenery. Interstate 5 parallels the Columbia River for 40 miles or so and you get occasional glimpses of the mighty river.

This part of the Pacific Northwest has pretty rolling hills, some grassy and some forested. Sadly, the little towns are nearly all framed in ugly billboards that clamber for your attention. Some visitors like to swing off the road and visit the poker parlors of hilly **La Center.** I always like to take a break in **Woodland.** Many riders will make Woodland a stop if they are planning a trip up to the eastern side of Mt. St. Helens. The best breakfast in town is at the **Oak Tree Restaurant.** To find this place, take the Woodland exit and turn right like you are taking 503 north. You will see it on the left about 300 yards off the freeway.

Continuing north on Interstate 5, make sure you take the 504 exit (exit 46) toward Silver Lake. There's a fine **Mt. St. Helens museum** near **Silver Lake** offering video and still images of the eruption that sent billions of pounds of ash all over the globe. I've noticed that most motorcyclists are so eager to see the mountain, they slip right past it. Highway 504, also called the **Spirit Lake Memorial Highway,** offers 52 miles of world-class motoring, but part of the fun is to stop along the way. On my way to the road's end, I always stop at three places: the **Hoffstadt Bluffs Visitor Center,** the **Forest Learning Center,** and the **Coldwater Ridge Visitor Center.**

The hot gases, traveling hundreds of miles per hour, actually cooked the trees stubborn enough to resist the blast.

Hoffstadt Bluffs Visitor Center offers you a chance to see the devastation and recovery in a way unique to most mountain views. With the trees gone, the naked slopes show their streams, boulders, and hills in a way you can't see in other places.

Clouds trail off the summit of the sleeping volcano and shade a devastated area. Inside the cone, the lava dome continues to bulge. No telling how much longer one has to ride these roads.

Take out your binoculars when you stop at the Forest Learning Center, because you will likely see the resident herd of Roosevelt's elk, one of only four subspecies of elk to survive exposure to modern civilization.

At the Coldwater Ridge Visitor Center you start to find yourself at some serious altitude—3,091 feet. Here you can learn how the mountain's slopes, practically sterilized of all living things in 1980, are recovering. There is a video wall presentation that gives visitors a good overview of the whole cataclysmic eruption. You can also stop at their café

Stand with your back to the mountain and try to picture a 200-mph wind made up of oven-hot poison gases, ash, sand, and rocks blasting through this area. Miles of once lush forests were flattened.

THE WEST

for a sandwich, soup, salad, or drink—or check out the gift shop, book store, and a staffed information desk. I usually pick up my parking pass here.

The apex of this trip is the **Johnston Ridge Observatory** (elevation 4,255 feet). Here you can visualize the blast zone, get the best view of the lava dome and pumice plains, as well as the most close-up view of the mountain. Camera buffs, this is it! There are also interpretive exhibits that focus on the geological forces behind the eruptions. I like to toss some hiking boots in my bags so I can take one of the many hikes and stretch my legs before the trip back. No food available here.

You can check out the view in real time by visiting this web cam address:

The contrast between the sweet, roadside flowers and the hot, colorless blast of ash adds interest to riding near volcanoes.

(http://www.fs.fed.us/gpnf/volcanocams/msh/) Be careful. Viewing this pretty place may want you to drop what you are doing, in a most uncivilized way, and blast off toward Mt. St. Helens.

■ For more trips in this region see *Motorcycle Journeys Through the Pacific Northwest* by Bruce Hansen, available from Whitehorse Press.

29 The Big Sur Highway

Text and photos by Clement Salvadori

- **DISTANCE** *251 miles*
- **HIGHLIGHTS** *The Big Sur coast, Carmel Valley, the west side of the Salinas Valley, Monterey peninsula. and some of the very best motorcycling in the world*

0.0 Begin in Cambria, California. Turn north onto CA 1	**151.0** Turn right onto US101
34.0 One mile past Gorda, turn onto Los Burros Road, follow to South Coast Ridge Road, then to Plaskett Ridge Road, then to South Coast Ridge Road	**161.0** Exit onto G14/Jolon Road
	182.0 Turn right across from the Lockwood Store to remain on G14
	202.0 Turn right at STOP sign to remain on G14
47.0 Rejoin CA 1 in Lucia	**212.0** Turn right onto Chimney Rock Road
76.0 Opposite Andrew Molera State Park, turn right onto Old Coast Road	**218.0** Turn left onto Adelaida Road
84.0 Old Coast Road rejoins CA 1	**220.0** Turn right onto Vineyard Drive
99.0 Turn right onto Carmel Valley Road/G16	**229.0** Turn right onto CA 41
140.0 Turn left to remain on G16	**246.0** Turn right onto CA 1
147.0 G16 becomes Elm Avenue after you cross the Arroyo Seco River	**251.0** Arrive back in Cambria

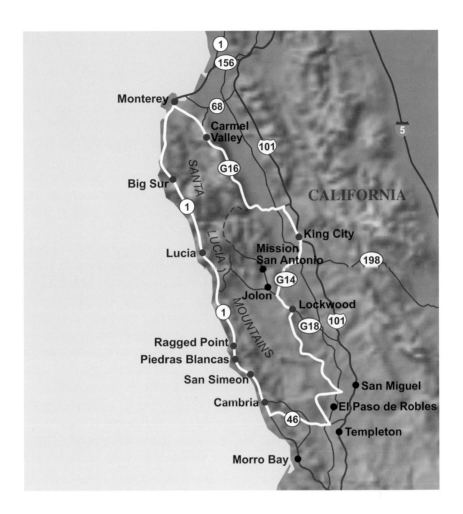

FOR THOSE NOT familiar with pre-American California, the Spaniards used Monterey as their capital, and to them, that big wilderness to the south, which was virtually impossible to traverse, became known as El Sur Grande. Or, as the Kingston Trio sang in the 1950s, "The south coast, the wild coast . . ."

At the traffic light, head north on CA 1 where the road starts running along the edge of the flatlands that stretch from the Santa Lucia foothills to the sea (good for cattle). Very fast motorcyclists will enjoy the long curves, but you could spot the CHP along this stretch.

You will have reached the so-called community of **San Simeon,** which is nothing more than a dozen motels scrunched in on each side of the highway. The only reason for existence is its proximity to Hearst Castle.

If you look up on the ridgeline to your right, you will see the towers of **Hearst Castle.** A big sign indicates a right-hand turn, should you wish to get a closer look at this marvel (see Hearst Castle sidebar, page 252).

THE HEARST CASTLE

William Randolph Hearst's father, **George,** made a lot of money from mining interests in the late 1800s and bought most of the land around the little seaside community of **San Simeon.** He also purchased a failing newspaper, the **San Francisco Examiner,** for his son, who turned it into a sensationalist paper with lurid headlines and pictures similar to the tabloids you'd find by the supermarket check-out counter today.

Willie made his money a quarter cent at a time selling his newspapers, but he did sell a lot of them. In fact, he got to be very rich and very powerful, and when he was 50-something he fell madly in love with a showgirl named **Marion Davies,** who just happened to be more than 30 years younger than he was (how predictable). He built his

When William Randolph Hearst wanted to impress his mistress and friends, he did it in a big way, building a veritable castle at the south end of the Big Sur.

castle on the coast so his mistress could throw great parties, and the construction went on from 1919 to World War II. He called the place **La Cuesta Encantada** (The Enchanted Hill), but it is now better known as Hearst Castle; the main section has a mere 40,000 square feet of living space in more than 100 rooms.

Mrs. Hearst, his official wife, was an understanding woman who stayed in New York, spending lots of his money, and having her own version of a good life. Hearst died in 1951, and in 1958, the Hearst heirs realized that they had a great white elephant on their hands and gave the place to the state. It has since become a serious money-maker, as thousands of tourists troop through every week at $14 a head.

The castle is worth a visit, if only to see what excess wealth can do to good taste. After buying a ticket, you can walk around and think about how nice it would be to have all that money. You should allot a half day to this little adventure. There are different tours you can take, including one at night. To get more information, call 800-444-4445.

Opposite the castle, on the sea side, are the actual remnants of the whaling station of San Simeon, with a small store and sandwich shop.

You will come up on **Piedras Blancas** ("white rocks," thanks to the guano). The lighthouse (no visitors, please) which you passed after the sea-lion beach had gas and a ramshackle motel.

After the White Rock business center, the road develops a couple of straightaways, then comes around a vicious curve to drop down to **San Carpoforo Creek,** with a house belonging to the national forest on the right just after you cross the bridge. From this point, the **Santa Lucia Mountains** go straight down to the ocean. This is where the serious riding begins, the road twisting up sharply and steeply.

Ragged Point has a very pleasant 20-room lodge ($90+; 805-927-4502) and a very good restaurant, as well as a coffee shop, hamburger joint, and small store that also sells gas.

From here, the road gets occasionally fast—and occasionally hazardous. If you are a first-timer, take note of the 15-mph signs you will occasionally see posted. I think that one should ride the Big Sur slowly in one direction to admire the view and get the feel of the road, go back slowly the way you came—and then you can ride it at any speed you wish.

The real hazard on this road is not the road itself, but the gawking tourists who are constantly wandering over the center line, slowing abruptly to gaze out to sea, and driving in and out of scenic viewpoints.

The town of **Gorda** will have gas, food, and half a dozen cabins to lodge in. Beyond Gorda a mile will be the

Looking north from Hurricane Point to Bixby Bridge—this is the Big Sur at its best.

A troop of motorcyclists come south along the Big Sur Highway, a road that every motorcyclist should ride at least twice in his or her lifetime—once in each direction.

If you can honestly tell me that this isn't motorcycling heaven, I'll follow you. (Photo courtesy of David Gubernick/Monterey County CVB)

turn onto Los Burros Road (dirt) which scrabbles up to the South Coast Ridge Road (dirt). A couple of miles farther on, Plaskett Ridge Road (dirt) also climbs up to South Coast Ridge Road. Beyond the turn-off, you'll see a campground at Plaskett Creek, and then the road opens up into the **Pacific Valley.** There was a store out there for many years, but it burned down in 1997, and as of January 2000, there had been no attempt to rebuild.

You will drop down to the **Mill Creek Picnic Area,** start back up and there will be a sign for Nacimiento Road, with a 300-degree turn back to your right, over a cattle guard. **Kirk Creek Campground** will be almost across the road. It is definitely worth going up Nacimiento Road for a couple of miles, as there are stupendous views of the coast in both directions. Remember, you are in no hurry.

Cross over the bridge at **Lime Kiln Creek State Park.**

You have come upon the not-so-bustling community of **Lucia,** with nought but a small store and restaurant, usually open for early lunch and breakfast on the weekends. The 10 motel rooms of Lucia Lodge sit in a row, one out on the edge of the cliff over the sea, the rest coming inland. You'll want to stay in #10, right at the end; it's expensive, but the view is worth it ($100+; 408-667-2391).

Beyond Lucia, you'll find more fast road, often improved by CalTrans in an effort to defeat the landslides of the winter.

Pass the **Esalen Institute,** with a sign reading BY RESERVATION ONLY. This place is a very pleasant hangover from the 1960s, one of those holistic feel-good resorts where you can check in for a couple of nights, eat vegetarian food, attend soul-searching seminars, and, best of all, hang out in the natural hot springs that are on the cliff high above the water (408-667-3023).

Coming up, the **Julia Pfieffer Burns State Park** has good hiking and a wonderful waterfall falling into the ocean. Just north of here, in 1983, a landslide came down from **Partington Ridge** and closed the highway for more than a year.

From here, the road sweeps around the outside curves of the hillside, then cuts inland for even tighter curves around the watercourse. Soon, however, you will see signs of civilization, such as art galleries, inns, and even the **Henry Miller Museum.** You will be approaching the community of Big Sur.

Nepenthe—loosely translated as "the place to lose oneself in"—is probably the nicest lunching spot on the coast. Go up on the high terrace and order an ambrosiaburger—the view will be worth the 10 bucks.

Crest the rise to the two fanciest places on the Big Sur coast; the **Ventana Big Sur Inn** is inland ($260+; 408-667-2331; 800-628-6500), and the **Post Ranch Inn** is on the edge of the sea. Choose the latter if you have a spare $365+ to spend (408-667-2200).

Down in the community of **Big Sur,** there will be other options, including the comfortable **Big Sur Lodge** at the **Pfeiffer Big Sur State Park** ($100+; 800-424-4787; 408-667-3100), as well as a half a dozen commercial places to stay along CA 1.

Just south of the entrance to the state park, you'll find the turn down Sycamore Canyon Road to **Pfeiffer Beach;** it used to have free access, but in 1998 the state began charging five dollars.

When I'm not staying at the Post Ranch, my favorite spot is the **Ripplewood Resort,** with a dozen cabins down by **Big Sur River** that were built

Beware of high winds and stunning views on the Bixby Bridge along the Big Sur Coastline. (Photo Courtesy of Monterey County CVB)

THE MONTEREY PENINSULA

The Monterey Peninsula is a Tourist Destination, so ordinarily I wouldn't be too keen on it. Although there is lots to do and see, it is not really motorcycling—with one exception: the national and international motorcycle races that are held every year out at the **Laguna Seca Raceway,** a few miles east of town on CA 68.

The big show pieces on the peninsula are **Cannery Row,** with the **Monterey Bay Aquarium** at the west end and a dozen restaurants serving overpriced food. The glorious tourist trap of **Fisherman's Wharf** is very picturesque. And let's not forget the gated community of **Pebble Beach** and its overrated **17-Mile Drive.** Motorcyclists cannot pay at the gate and cruise the 17 miles unless they have dinner or room reservations somewhere inside the fence. Or a friend who can buzz them in.

Food is everywhere. Down on Cannery Row, **Trattoria Paradiso** (654 Cannery) serves everything from California cuisine to Calabrese-style Italian food. On Fisherman's Wharf, I gravitate to **Abalonetti's Seafood,** which has the most scrumptious fried calamari. You'll find more good seafood at the **Monterey Fish House,** 2114 Del Monte Avenue. If someone else is picking up the tab, try **Club XIX** at **The Lodge** in Pebble Beach.

For fine accommodation, check in at the **Monterey Plaza Hotel** on Cannery Row, with 290 rooms and suites, and prices starting at $200 (800-334-3999; 408-646-1700). On the more economical end, you can go to North Fremont Street, where a long line of motels await your business, such as the **Best Western De Anza Inn ($65+; 43 rooms; 2141 North Fremont; 800-858-8775; 408-646-8300).**

The Corkscrew at Laguna Seca Raceway, home of Reg Pridmore's CLASS Motorcycling School (www.classrides.com). (Photo courtesy of Ian Donald)

Bixby Bridge, the keystone to the success of the Big Sur Highway, was completed in 1932 and made briefly famous in the opening shots of the TV series, "Then Came Bronson."

to house workers back in the 1930s ($75+; 408-667-2242). Ask for #8 or 9, right on the river's edge.

Andrew Molera State Park will be on the left, giving pedestrians access to four miles of unblemished beach; it's worth the hike. Opposite the park, off CA 1, a dirt road goes up to the right, the Old Coast Road, where a sign reads IMPASSABLE IN WET WEATHER. True, but it's a great ride on a dry day.

Pass the **Point Sur Light Station** (begun in 1887), now a state historic landmark with guided tours on weekends (408-625-4419), and head down to **Little Sur Creek,** to a curving bridge that would beg speed—were it not for those concrete rails.

At **Hurricane Point,** it can get righteously windy. Ride over **Bixby Bridge,** made mildly famous in the opening credits of the 1960s TV show, **"Then Came Bronson."** On the north side of the bridge, the Old Coast Road will reconnect with CA 1. This bridge, finished in 1932, was built with the help of prisoners who wanted to take time off their sentences. I'd say their labor was put to good use, and we should do something similar today.

The road will straighten out a bit as it tears over **Rocky Creek Bridge,** past Palo Colorado Road, over **Garrapata Creek,** and past **Garrapata State Park,** to cross **Malpaso Creek** and enter **Carmel Highlands.** The show is almost over.

Off to the left will be **Point Lobos State Reserve,** a very nice, but very crowded park where the hordes from Monterey come to see a bit of wildlife.

From there, you will pass the **Carmel River State Beach** and a Carmelite nunnery.

After crossing the **Carmel River** you will come to a traffic light. You are now on the southwest edge of the **Monterey (King's Mount) Peninsula.** A left would take you into Carmel; straight up the hill heads into Monterey. For lots of info, go directly to the Visitors Center (831-649-1770) at 380 Alvarado Street in downtown Monterey (see Monterey Peninsula sidebar).

At the traffic light turn right onto Carmel Valley Rd./G16, where the sign points toward Carmel Valley.

Stay straight as Los Laureles Grade/G20 goes off to the left, which is, by the way, a good way to get to Laguna Seca Raceway.

Carmel Valley Village will provide your last chance to gas up for a while. There will be great riding for the next 40 miles, down Carmel Valley, over a rise, and down toward the **Salinas Valley.**

At the STOP sign turn left following G16; the right turn goes to **Arroyo Seco.**

Turn left at the sign reading GREENFIELD; head down to the girder bridge, cross over the **Arroyo Seco River** and keep going, now on Elm Avenue, running through flat farmland.

Monterey Marina looks a little like a commercialized Blue Lagoon. Try the chowder. (Photo courtesy of Monterey County CVB)

Turn right onto Central Avenue—a turn that is hard to anticipate right out there in the middle of those flat, flat fields; you will be headed south, paralleling US 101. Turn right onto US 101 as Central Avenue ends.

Exit right onto G14/Jolon Road, where there will be gas and a convenience store. Pass the turn to Fort Hunter Liggett and the **San Antonio Mission** (see Trip 8), to stay on G14. Turn right opposite the **Lockwood Store,** following G14 down Interlake Road. At the STOP sign turn right, fol-

Monterey Bay under a California sunset. (Photo courtesy of the Monterey County CVB)

lowing G14 and dropping down to the **Nacimiento Dam.** At the STOP sign turn right, leaving G14 and going onto Chimney Rock Road, a very nice piece of under-utilized asphalt. Turn left at the **Adelaida Cemetery** onto Adelaida Road. Stay left on Adelaida Road as Klau Mine Road goes off to the right. Then turn right onto Vineyard Drive. At the next STOP sign turn right onto CA 41. Then at the following STOP sign turn right onto CA 1.

■ For more trips in this region see *Motorcycle Journeys Through California* by Clement Salvadori, available from Whitehorse Press.

30 Badwater & Death Valley Junction

Text and photos by Clement Salvadori

■ **DISTANCE** *127 miles*

■ **HIGHLIGHTS** *If you want to get on the throttle, you could do this in a few hours, but most people who have never been here before will take all day.*

0.0 Begin at Furnace Creek Ranch, in Death Valley, California, then head east onto CA 190/178

0.5 Turn right onto CA 178/Badwater

72.0 Turn left onto CA 127

90.5 Turn left onto CA 190, back toward Death Valley

127.0 Arrive back at Furnace Creek Ranch

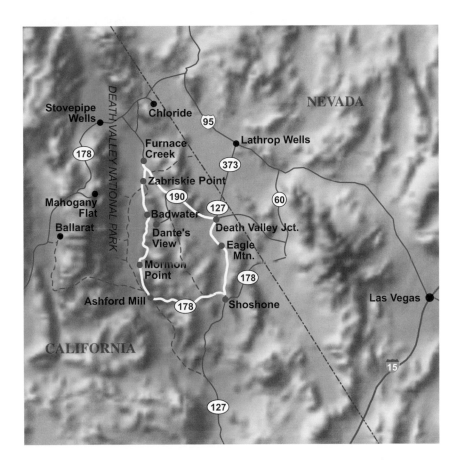

TURN RIGHT COMING out of **Furnace Creek Ranch** to head east on CA 190/178. Turn right as you come on a rise, with the **Furnace Creek Inn** up on your left. A well-marked road, CA 178/Badwater, will cut sharply to the right; that will be the one you want. CA 190 will go straight ahead to Death Valley Junction.

At the entrance to **Mosaic Canyon,** there is a left turn up a short dirt road to a parking area where you could start a very pretty, very geological hike up to **Zabriskie Point.** Being a lazy cuss, I recommend you ride two-up to Zabriskie and walk back downhill to where you left the other bike. It is one of the more popular hikettes in the park, and you will pass lots of people.

On your left, you will see the north end of one-way Artists Palette Drive; this is the end not to enter.

At about mile seven, on your right, will be the northern entrance to the **West Side Road.** This is 35 miles of sometimes good, sometimes bad dirt road, depending on the past winter and the amount of repairs done. If it has been raining, forget it, unless you have a dual-sport motorcycle and are

WEST SIDE ROAD

If you take the **West Side Road,** you'll see a couple of smaller roads shooting off to the west which are good for dual-sport bikes. After five miles, you'll spot Trail Canyon Road, which used to climb up to **Aguerebery Point** some 20 years or so ago, but a big slide took out a big chunk of the road and left nothing but a steep mountainside. In another five miles, **Hanaupah Canyon** will go off to the left and dead-end after a few miles. And in another 10 miles, after passing the grave of **Shorty Harris** and the remains of the **Eagle Borax works, Johnson Canyon** will go off to its own dead end, becoming impassable long before you get to the ruins of **Hungry Bill's** ranch. Yet another five miles farther on, by some old tanks, **Galena Canyon** goes west a short way to an old talc mine.

Seven more miles beyond Galena Canyon, Warm Spring Canyon Road will cut back to the west; if you were to follow it for about 33 miles, it would take you right out of Death Valley and into **Panamint Valley.** I'd advise you to reset your tripmeter to 0 at the turn. From there, you would beat up a long, rocky wash and come into **Striped Butte Valley.** At 15+ miles, keep to your left; in another five, also keep left. The only possible problem you might have would be climbing the little cliff right at **Mengel Pass** (4,326 feet); it's not for the faint of heart, but *lots* of people do it. That will lead you into **Goler Wash,** which runs out to Panamint Valley and Wingate Road, going north to **Ballarat.** Good dual-sport exercise.

If you are staying strictly on the West Side Road, you will be back on CA 178 just three miles beyond the turn-off to Warm Spring Canyon Road.

If you think it's fun to look at the painted mountains, try riding them! (Photo courtesy of the National Park Service)

THE WEST

Badwater is more than 270 feet below sea level. If I could just dig a ditch from the Pacific Ocean to Death Valley and stick in a couple of water turbines to generate electricity, I could let gravity make me rich. (Photo courtesy of Craig Erion)

willing to get dirty. If it's dry, however, a Gold Wing could go through (see West Side Road sidebar, page 262).

On your left, you'll see the entrance to Artist Drive, which is a very pleasant one-lane, one-way jaunt for nine miles through the foothills of the **Black Mountains,** one of the many smaller groups that make up the **Amargosa Range.** There's lots of attractive geology to see out there, especially in the afternoon when the western sun is striking the rocks.

To the right will be the turn to the **Devil's Golf Course,** which is located a mile down a good dirt road. Over a couple of million years, the wind and rain have left neatly formed stacks of salt and gravel scattered all along the old lake bottom. If you will be needing salt for your picnic, just take a pinch of the white stuff.

To the left will be a turn up a two-mile dirt road to the parking area for the **Natural Bridge.** A short quarter-mile hike will bring you beneath the 50-foot arch. The road develops a few twists and turns along about now, as it hunkers in under the steep cliffs to the left (east), avoiding the potentially marshy bits of the **Salt Creek Basin.**

You can park your bike at **Badwater,** 270 feet below sea level, where a white sign up on the cliffs will remind you of where you would be if somebody

SHOSHONE

Go right one mile into the tiny town of **Shoshone** if you are interested in gas, food, information, or a place to sleep. Shoshone, which flourished briefly as a mining center, has become a small stop on the back way into Death Valley. You can get a room at the **Shoshone Inn,** an old-fashioned motel with 16 units; prices start at $50 (760-852-4335).

Next door, you'll find the **Charles Brown General Store;** Mr. Brown, a local politician, basically owned the town, and he passed the whole thing along to his grand-daughter Susan when he died. Across the road, you will see the **Red Buggy Café & Crowbar Lounge,** otherwise known as **Brown's Bar,** serving solid food seven days a week from 7:00 in the morning to 9:30 at night.

Don't miss the **Shoshone Museum,** which has a bit of everything that has withstood the ravages of a hundred years of use and exposure to the elements.

dug a 200-mile trench from the **Pacific Ocean**—if you put some turbines along there you could generate some real electricity as the ocean rushed in. If you want to get the full impact, you could walk out onto the saline flats about three miles and stand at 279.8 feet below sea level.

South of Badwater, the quality of the road deteriorates a bit, as it is not heavily used and the USNPS has only limited funds. But it is still a good road, although it has a lot of patches, and it swoops around the edges of the slag that has come off the hills—great honking curves of a mile or more, where the last guy can see the first in a chain of 20 fast-moving sportbikes.

As you come around **Mormon Point,** the road will begin a gentle, barely perceptible climb. By mile 43 you will have reached the southern junction of the West Side Road.

Enter **Ashford Mill,** or better put, the small remains of the old borax mill. It's not the sort of place you'd want to vacation in, although I have slept on the picnic tables there, much against park regulations, and the place has a pleasantly eery aura about it.

After a few miles Hwy. 178 makes a sharp left to the east, to take you up over **Jubilee Mountain,** while Henry Wade Road goes straight (see Mr. Wade's Road sidebar, page 267).

The road gets right twisty as you come up on **Jubilee Pass,** cut deep through the mountain at a modest 1,290 feet. The road will then slip down into a valley and immediately start to climb again.

Once you are up at **Salsberry Pass,** at a somewhat more lofty 3,315 feet, you will drop down into **Greenwater Valley** (I'll leave you to figure out where that name came from) and leave the park.

Off to your left will be a small collection of unmarked dirt roads heading north into Greenwater Valley. They all more or less congeal into one 28-mile

DEATH VALLEY JUNCTION

Death Valley Junction began as the town of **Amargosa** in 1907, but after the **Tonopah & Tidewater** and the **Las Vegas & Tonopah** railroads arrived about 1914, it became Death Valley Junction. Population then soared to 300. The railroad was used to haul borax out of nearby mines until 1928, and then things went into a slow decline. When World War II came along, the railway tracks were torn up to help the war effort.

In the middle of town, you'll see the large, one-story, U-shaped complex which used to house railroad workers, but is now owned by **Marta Becket,** the ballet dancer. At one end of the U, you'll find the **Amargosa Opera House,** where Marta has been putting on superb performances since 1968, always on Saturday night, and sometimes on Mondays, depending on the season. It's a cultural event you should not miss; call (760-852-4441) for full information. She also has a dozen rooms available in her **Amargosa Hotel,** which is in the complex, with prices starting at $45. For food, you could go to the **Serenity Ice Cream Parlor,** located at the other end of the U, open at 10 a.m. on most days. And that will be it for businesses in DV Junction. For serious food, you will have to go seven miles north to the Nevada state line, where the casino serves 24 hours a day.

Meet up with the other two-wheelin' boys and girls at Death Valley Junction.

Right after the turn, you will notice an operating borax mine off to your left, the **Ryan Mine,** just outside the somewhat gerrymandered national park boundaries. The road will continue up **Furnace Creek Wash** into **Greenwater Valley.** After seven miles, the road will turn sharply to the right, with a parking area for trailers, and off to the left will be the Greenwater Valley Road, 28 miles of dual-sport dirt that will connect you with CA 178 just east of **Salsberry Pass.** It is an entertaining dual-sport ride, climbing gradually to 4,050 feet, and then dropping slowly down to about 2,000 feet by the time you see pavement again.

The paved road starts a serious climb to **Dante's View,** first straight, and then winding through a delightful little canyon, followed by some serious squiggles to get to the top and the view. Of course, you know that Dante wrote *The Divine Comedy,* in which he describes visiting Heaven, Purgatory, and Hell—and this, according to some well-read namer of places, would be his view of Hell. You will be at 5,475 feet, directly above **Badwater,** right across from 11,049-foot **Telescope Peak** only 20 miles to the west, with Death Valley spread out to your left and right. It is a superior view, especially if you can catch it at dusk on a full moon, the sun setting in the west, and the moon rising in the east. Perfect. Just watch out on your way down.

Ah, yes, Dante's View, at 5,475 feet, is the best view in California, with Badwater below at −279.8 feet, and snow-capped Telescope Peak in the distance, at 11,049 feet.

dirt road that goes up the valley and connects with the road to **Dante's View.** More on that from the other end. At the STOP sign turn left, as CA 178 connects with CA 127. Our route goes left, but a short trip to the right, to Shoshone, might be in order (see Shoshone sidebar, page 264).

CONNECTOR

If you are interested in heading to **Palm Springs,** you can take CA 127 South to Baker, then continue straight across I-15 onto Kelbaker Road, going through **Kelso** and on to **Amboy** on old US 66. From there, the Amboy Road will go south to 29 Palms, and you could turn to Chapter 14 to figure out what to do next.

While cruising north on CA 127, you will be riding beside the **Amargosa River,** which flows (when it flows, which is very, very, very rarely) south past Shoshone to the **Dumont Dunes.** The 25-mile stretch from Shoshone to **Death Valley Junction** is known for its flatness and fast curves. Ahead of you will be **Eagle Mountain,** a great hunk of stone sticking up some 2,500 feet from the desert floor, out in the middle of nowhere. In the distance, you'll see a cluster of buildings; it will take a few minutes to get there, although it will seem as if they are just a mile away.

At mile 97, you have arrived at **Death Valley Junction.** (see Death Valley Junction sidebar). Just north of the Opera House, CA 190 turns to the left, back to Death Valley.

ALTERNATE ROUTE

If you wanted to skirt the east edge of the national park, you could go north on CA 127 to the Nevada state line and continue on to Beatty, Nevada.

Seven miles along, at the state line, where CA 127 morphs into NV 373, you will find the new **Longstreet's Inn & Casino,** with food, 60 rooms starting at $60 (702-372-1777), and some ordinary gambling. They also offer "Camel Rides," $45 for an hour's ride and breakfast, $75 for a ride and dinner; you could not pay me $45 to ride one of those blessed dromedaries for

---

MR. WADE'S ROAD

You could go straight on Henry Wade Road, a dirt and sand track that ties into CA 127 after 33 miles. The sign recommends high clearance and four-wheel drive; I recommend a dual-sport bike, although I watched **Jim Wolcott** run a Sportster over it years ago.

The road runs along the **Amargosa River,** which flows (?!) north into Death Valley; the river is usually dry unless very heavy rains have fallen, but at one point the road crosses the river and there is a stretch of soft sand. It's not a real problem for a d-p bike or a well-ridden naked motorcycle, however. Gold Wings and TL1000Rs might find it a bit much.

SERIOUS DUAL-SPORT RIDES

The 9+ mile **Echo Canyon Road** is a fun, but serious, dual-sport ride. A skid plate should be considered essential equipment. I knocked a hole in the sump of a V65 Sabre years ago trying to get there, and once crunched, twice shy. Otherwise, it is a great ride, but not for the faint of heart. You'll go about five rough miles up to the canyon, then have a twisty trundle over a lot of smooth loose rocks as you go through the narrow, winding canyon.

As you clear the canyon and come out into a small valley, a significant (i.e. you can't miss it) dirt road goes off to the left. Twelve years ago, I found an old map of Death Valley dating from 1951, and it showed a road going off from **Echo Canyon** and crossing over the **Funeral Mountains,** coming out at **Amargosa Valley** on the Nevada side. Of course, I took my KLR 650, with

my bride-to-be on the back, and went exploring. The only real problem, other than finding ourselves up a few dead-ends, was an eight-foot dry waterfall, but previous passers had built a loose-rock ramp which we negotiated with a good deal of care. Then we climbed to the top of the mountains and came down a long, long dry wash into the Amargosa Desert, with a far-off view of **Big Dune.** It was the best 20-mile trip I've ever taken.

If you wish to try it, do take a friend along on another bike, as well as some water, just in case . . .

Back in Echo Canyon, keep on going until you come to the site of the old **Inyo Mine,** very isolated and romantic, with a few decrepit old buildings slowly falling apart. Half a mile beyond the mine the road will be barricaded as it disappears into the mountains.

Occasionally, I do Death Valley on a dual-sport bike; that is Kurt "Baja" Grife and myself, taking our ease in Rhyolite.

THE WEST

Death Valley is not the place to run out of gas . . . nor water . . . nor courage. (Photo courtesy of National Park Service)

an hour. Across the road you'll find the old **Stateline Saloon & Gambling Hall,** right next to **Mom's Place,** which offers beer, gas, and packaged food.

Continuing north, you will come into **Amargosa Valley,** where Mecca Road goes off to the west. Here, you'll find **Rosa's Mexican Restaurant,** open 8 a.m. to 8 p.m. every day except Monday, and a hundred yards behind the restaurant, the **Desert Village Motel,** a two-story affair with 17 units starting at $45 (702-372-1405). Curious place, this valley, with good and plentiful well water right here in the middle of the **Amargosa Desert.** There is even a turf farm and a 5,000-cow dairy nearby.

After 23 miles, NV 373 ends where it butts into US 95 at **Lathrop Wells,** where a really ugly, cheap, fake-front joint called the **Amargosa Saloon & Casino** will try to take your money. Take a left, and you will be headed toward Beatty, Nevada. The road is quite open and straight, going through the Amargosa Desert. Other than the **Yucca Mountains** to your right, the **Funeral Mountains** to your left, and lots of dirt roads disappearing into the mountains, there is not much here. A monstrous sand dune will be off to your left. After 52 miles you will arrive in **Beatty.**

Back at **Death Valley Junction,** head west onto CA 190, a long, straight road with a slight climb. You will cross the nameless saddle (3,040 feet) between the **Funeral Mountains** and the **Greenwater Range,** to begin the long,

Twenty Mule Team Canyon is five miles of good dirt road that any bike can deal with.

20-mile descent to Furnace Creek Ranch. It would be right easy to pick up a serious head of speed along here.

There will be a turn to the left which will take you 13 miles up to **Dante's View**—and it is a must-do (see Dante's View sidebar, page 266). Pass the east (NO ENTRY) end of the one-way road through **Twenty Mule Team Canyon.**

To your left will be the start of the Twenty Mule Team Canyon Drive, a well-maintained dirt road a little less than three miles in length which weaves through the hills; any good rider can do it. They say that if you are there in the evening as the land cools off, you can hear some sort of snap, crackle, and pop. By the way, the old 20-mule borax hauling wagons never came through here—it's just a catchy name.

Ah, **Zabriskie Point.** Old man Zabriskie happened to be a superintendent at the borax mines a long time ago, and now his name lives on, attracting mobs of tourists. The huge buses in the parking lot are likely full of French and German tourists (though never in the same bus). Park your bike, climb the hill, and look out over the other-worldly scene. I'd suggest you skip it during the day when crowded, and come up late at night instead. It will be purely ethereal.

Look for a small sign off to your right indicating ECHO CANYON, with a dirt road running off from **Furnace Creek Wash** toward the Funeral Mountains (see the Serious dual-sport Rides sidebar, page 268).

The road will swoop around a couple of curves, and **Furnace Creek Inn** will appear on your right. The building to your left used to be a garage that could actually do repairs, but that closed up about 10 years ago. Just beyond the defunct garage will be the left turn down CA 178 to Badwater. Follow CA 190 back to **Furnace Creek Ranch.**

■ For more trips in this region see *Motorcycle Journeys Through California* by Clement Salvadori, available from Whitehorse Press.

31 Over the San Bernardino Mts.

Text and photos by Clement Salvadori

■ **DISTANCE** *181 miles*

■ **HIGHLIGHTS** *A lot of desert, a good deal of mountain, and a good ride which will last you the better part of a day*

0.0 Begin in Indian Canyon and Ramon, in Palm Springs, California, then head north via Indian Canyon Drive

6.0 Cross over I-10. Indian Canyon Drive becomes Indian Avenue

14.0 Turn onto CA 62. Head for Yucca Valley

26.0 Turn left onto Pioneertown Road

30.0 Arrive Pioneertown

32.0 Turn right onto Pipes Canyon Road

39.0 Turn left at CA 47, also known as Old Woman Springs Road

45.0 Arrive Old Woman Springs

79.0 Turn left onto Rock Camp Road

84.0 Turn left onto CA 18

89.0 Arrive Cactus Flats

95.0 Turn left. Join CA 38 south

96.0 Follow CA 38 left

106.0 Arrive Onyx Summit, Continue onto CA 38

118.0 Arrive Barton Flats, Continue onto CA 38

125.0 Arrive Angelus Oaks, Continue onto CA 38

130.0 Turn right, following CA 38

136.0 Turn left onto Bryant Street

141.0 Turn right onto Avenue F

145.0 Turn right onto Oak Glen Road

151.0 Enter I-10, head east

156.0 Take CA 111 back to Ramon and Palm Canyon

181.0 Arrive in Palm Springs

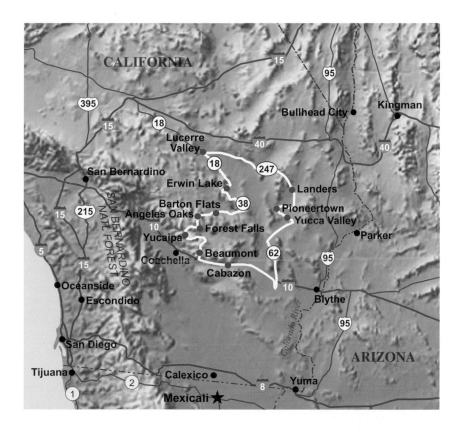

GO NORTH ON Indian Canyon, in Palm Springs, California. After 14 miles you'll come to an intersection with CA 62. Head on into **Yucca Valley.**

Turn left onto Pioneertown Road, which will take you up through rocky, brushy country.

Soon you'll arrive at **Pioneertown,** a collection of old buildings and wagons, with some newer additions, such as a motel, to attract the tourists.

After Pioneertown you'll want to turn right at a four-way, middle-of-nowhere intersection. Follow Pipes Canyon Road, a winding stretch along **Pipes Wash** with a few scattered houses and a lot of horse activity.

ALTERNATE ROUTE

A dual-sport rider might opt to go straight at the intersection. The pavement ends in a little over a mile, at **Rimrock,** then a rough dirt road continues past the **Farrington Observatory** for 17 miles (shortest version) to connect with CA 38 on top of the **San Bernardino Mountains.**

If you went left at the intersection, another dirt road would go for 16 miles to meet up with CA 38 at **Onyx Summit.** Although both versions have about a 4,000-foot climb, neither are terribly difficult.

Lake Arrowhead and the village rest quietly in the hills. (Photo courtesy of the Lake Arrowhead Communities Chamber of Commerce)

The community in Lake Arrowhead revolves around activities on the water. (Photo courtesy of the Lake Arrowhead Communities Chamber of Commerce)

At the STOP sign, turn left. **Pipes Canyon** ends at CA 247, also known as Old Woman Springs Road.

You will see signs for **Landers,** a desert community off to the right, where local residents have twice spotted the mysterious **Big Tread,** or Goldeman, a legendary, never-photographed creature that leaves Kenda tracks in the desert.

On your left, you will see what appears to be a row of statuary lining the road; that is **Moby Dick's** place. Dick moved out of The Big City (Los Angeles) in the late 1980s, and has found happiness here in the high desert. He makes his mildly bizarre sculptures out of anything he can find, but his main source of inspiration is old motorcycle parts. With a hundred or more decrepit and cannibalized bikes neatly lined up, and boxes of nuts and bolts under a protective roof, he could probably find you a carburetor for a DT1, though it might be a little corroded.

CA 247 will enter **Johnson Valley,** which looks rather barren, spread out between the **Big Horn Mountains** and **Iron Ridge.** People do live out here, but not many, and civilization as we know it has been left behind.

Old Woman Springs will be off to your left. Turn left onto Rock Camp Road at this remote intersection, where hardly a house or car can be seen. At the STOP sign, turn left as Rock Camp slides into CA 18. There'll be a huge Mitsubishi cement plant stuck in the hillside in front of you. What are the Japanese doing making cement in the California mountains? Obviously the global economy is beyond my comprehension. But CA 18 otherwise provides a great ride up the mountainside as you climb into the **San Bernardino National Forest.**

For trivia collectors, this was the second designated national forest in the country, signed into being by **Prez Ben Harrison** in 1892.

As you arrive in **Cactus Flats,** a dirt road goes off to the right; had you come up from Rimrock you might have ended up here. From here, you will start a gentle descent down the **Johnston Grade** to shallow **Baldwin Lake,** whose surface sits at 6,698 feet above sea level. The San Berdoo Mountains are pretty high, and they stretch for more than 50 miles east to west, though we are just going to cut across the eastern end.

In the middle of the mountains are several lakes, **Big Bear** and **Arrowhead** being the best known. Not only is the whole area a resort so people can escape the heat of the Los Angeles basin, a lot of people have chosen to live up here year round, which means it is often crowded.

Turn left as CA 18 enters a built-up area and meets head-on with CA 38, and both roads join to go to the right (south) on Greenway Drive.

At the STOP sign, turn left at the end of Greenway, following CA 38; CA 18 goes to the right.

From here, CA 38 is known as the **Rim of the World National Forest Scenic Byway.** Follow CA 38 as it leaves civilization, angling right and going past the Big Bear suburbs of **Erwin Lake** and **Sugarloaf.** You will leave the forest, climbing slowly.

Crest **Onyx Summit;** at 8,443 feet, it's the highest paved road in southern Southern California, which refers to that part of SoCal which begins just

If you are up in Big Bear City, high (6,700 feet) in the San Bernardino Mountains, and feeling peckish, Thelma will fill you up.

Over the San Bernardino Mts.

275

Looking up Mill Creek Canyon, you can see San Gorgonio Mountain, one of the San Bernardino Mountains, in the distance, standing 11,499 feet tall.

You may encounter some dual-sport riders in the area. These are from the Big Bear Trail Riders at Middle Control Road where it joins SR-38 just above Angeles Oaks. (Photo courtesy Ron Sobchik)

north of the Los Angeles basin. To your left will be the dirt road that could lead a dual-sport bike back down to **Pioneertown.** Up here high in the forest, it is hard to imagine that you are just 100 eagle-flying miles from the crowded heart of Los Angeles and the sun-soaked Pacific beaches.

From here, you will have a steep descent to Barton Flats and the stunning valley of the **Santa Ana River.** I promise you, once that river reaches the valley, the romance will be gone, but here in the wilderness it is a beauty. To the south will be **San Gorgonio Mountain,** the tallest peak in southern California at 11,499 feet.

After dropping 3,000 feet, you will arrive in the middle of **Barton Flats.** Glass Road goes off to the right, the pavement ending in a maze of dirt roads. Dozens of camps and private residences are scattered throughout Barton Flats, and in the summer it is virtually a city in the woods.

You will be in the center of the town of **Angelus Oaks,** which has a fire station, a general store, and a telephone—in case you want to reach out and touch someone.

Turn right, following CA 38, as the road comes down into **Mill Creek Canyon,** with a wide riverbed in front of you. If you turned left, the road, Valley of the Falls Drive, dead-ends after 4+ miles in the community of **Forest Falls.** CA 38 goes down along **Mill Creek,** an impressive sight as it cuts down through the mountains.

And all of a sudden you will be out of the mountains with the **San Bernardino Valley** in front of you.

Old Grey Back. This mountain hangs over the valley as you drop down from Onyx summit to Angeles Oaks. (Photo courtesy Ron Sobchik)

Turn left onto Bryant Street at the **Mill Creek Ranger Station,** where a sign points left saying YUCAIPA 4.

At the traffic light, turn right onto Avenue F after passing through downtown **Yucaipa,** following the road down **Wildwood Canyon** as it turns into Wildwood Canyon Road.

At the next STOP sign, turn right on Oak Glen Road, the road going alongside the **Little San Gorgonio Creek,** past the **Edward Dean Museum of Decorative Arts,** through **Cherry Valley,** and head due south to **Beaumont** ("Beautiful Mountain," in French).

At the intersection with I-10, cross over and head east.

After the Banning exit go past **Cabazon** and catch CA 111 back into **Palm Springs.**

■ For more trips in this region see *Motorcycle Journeys Through California* by Clement Salvadori, available from Whitehorse Press.

Index

About the Contributors

Marty Berke is a resident of Mexico Beach, Florida. He caught the two-wheeled touring bug with his first Schwinn, and graduated to the motorized species not long afterward with a 1955 Vespa, a driver's license, and a $50 IOU to Mom. Marty now focuses on finding good roads all over the world and new ways to share them with you. He is the author of *Motorcycle Journeys Through New England,* and *Motorcycle Journeys Through the Southwest.*

Dale Coyner's journeys through the Appalachians began out of a curiosity for what was "around the next bend." He came to riding later than some, purchasing his first motorcycle, a Yamaha Radian, after he finished college. He credits the open, freewheeling nature of motorcycling with firing a sense of wonderment about his surroundings that led to rediscovering his native region. He shares his best finds with you in his book, *Motorcycle Journeys Through the Appalachains.*

Neal Davis has traveled, over the past 35 years, by motorcycle through more than 21 countries. Many of the adventures of his growing family were on two wheels as well, and he succeeded in infecting them with the "bug." After selling his small business in 1980, Davis took up motorcycle touring with a passion. As a leader for

organized motorcycle tour companies in Europe and Mexico, he introduced others to the many motorcycling opportunities that exist around the world. He is the author of *Motorcycle Journeys Through Northern Mexico, Motorcycle Journeys Through Southern Mexico,* and *Motorcycle Journeys Through Texas.*

Dr. Gregory Frazier is a professional motorcycle adventurer, and has traveled around the world by motorcycle. He is also an accomplished motorcycle racer, having won races with both BMW and Indian motorcycles. When not adventuring, Dr. Frazier lives on his ranch in the Big Horn Mountains of Montana.

Bruce Hansen, when he isn't teaching, writes about motorcycle travel for *Rider, RoadBike, American Iron, Motorcycle Cruiser Magazine, Motorcycle Tour and Cruiser,* and *Motorcycle Escape,* and has written and photographed for *Paddler Magazine* and *Canoe and Kayak.* He lives in Portland, Oregon, and is the author of *Motorcycle Journeys Through the Pacific Northwest.*

Bill Kresnak is legal affairs editor for *American Motorcyclist* magazine. When he's not writing about bike bans and public land closures he enjoys exploring ghost towns and covered bridges, and riding historic routes like that of the Ohio-Erie canal. He rides a Suzuki GSXR1100.

Lance Oliver, the associate editor of *American Motorcyclist* magazine, has been riding motorcycles for 25 years, not counting trips to grade school as a passenger on his mother's Honda 50. Originally from West Virginia, he has since lived in New York, Florida, Costa Rica, and Puerto Rico, and currently works at the AMA headquarters in Ohio, where he stubbornly refuses to recognize winter and tries to ride in January and February, just like he did in the tropics. This makes him a source of amusement for co-workers.

Grant Parsons has been an enthusiast ever since he bought his first bike—a 13-year-old 1973 Honda CL350. His journey of fun and discovery was punctuated at first by frustrating electrical troubleshooting on the side of various roads, and, many years later, by stops along the same roads, but this time getting paid to do so as the senior editor of *American Motorcyclist* magazine. He and his wife, Charlotte, are proud to have recently given their 5-year-old son, Jake, his first motorcycle ride this year.

Clement Salvadori has written nearly 900 articles for several dozen motorcycle magazines during the past 21 years. One of motorcycling's most erudite observers, Salvadori served as a Foreign Service Officer with the State Department after receiving his master's degree in foreign relations. Salvadori realized he enjoyed traveling more as a motorcyclist than as a diplomat. So he resigned and took to riding around the world. He is the author of *Motorcycle Journeys Through California,* and *Motorcycle Journeys Through Baja.*

Photo Credits

pages 32 and 128: Photos courtesy of the American Motorcyclist Association

page 44: Photo courtesy of the Balsams Grand Resort Hotel

page 67: Matthew Cavanaugh photo courtesy of Shelburne Falls Area Business Association

page 85: Rich Cox photo

page 121: Photo courtesy of the USDA Forest Service

page 128: Kevin Wing photo

pages 138 and 144: Photos courtesy of the North Carolina Division of Tourism, Film, and Sports Development

page 152: Photo courtesy of the Texas Parks & Wildlife Department

page 166: Randy Green photo courtesy of TxDOT

page 182: Photo courtesy of the Utah Travel Council

page 186, 196, and 258: Photos courtesy of the National Park Service

page 190: Rick Athearn photo courtesy of BLM/Kremmling Field Office

page 202: Jerry Trottmann photo, courtesy of the Friends of the Poudre Organization

page 206 and 210: Photos courtesy of the New Mexico Department of Tourism

page 214: Clement Salvadori photo

page 248: Photo courtesy of the Monterey County CVB

page 268: Photo courtesy of the Lake Arrowhead Communities Chamber of Commerce

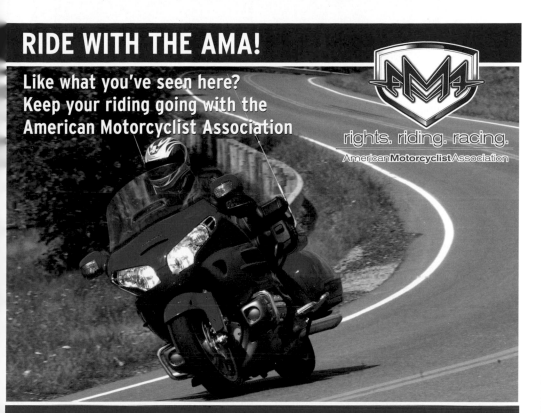

WHITEHORSE PRESS MOTORCYCLE JOURNEYS SERIES

Motorcycle Journeys Through California $24.95
Motorcycle Journeys Through the Pacific Northwest $24.95
Motorcycle Journeys Through the Appalachians $24.95
Motorcycle Journeys Through New England $19.95
Motorcycle Journeys Through Texas. $19.95
Motorcycle Journeys Through Northern Mexico $19.95
Motorcycle Journeys Through Southern Mexico $19.95
Motorcycle Journeys Through the Alps and Corsica $24.95
Motorcycle Journeys Through Baja $19.95

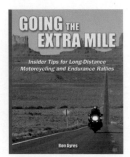

GOING THE EXTRA MILE

by Ron Ayres

Jam-packed with advice from long-distance motorcycle travel veterans,
and written by best-selling author Ron Ayres, this handbook can help you
extend your range on a motorcycle. Written for anyone who wants to com-
fortably spend more time in the saddle and less time waiting at the next
rest stop, this book compiles the proven techniques that can make your
next long motorcycle trip fun, safe, and comfortable.
GEM. . . . . Retail $19.95

MOTORCYCLING EXCELLENCE (2ND ED.)

by The Motorcycle Safety Foundation

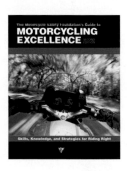

A remarkable source of riding wisdom, this all-new and expanded edi-
tion is the definitive reference for safe motorcycle riding techniques and
strategies. It helps brand-new riders learn safe riding habits and shows
veterans how to perfect their riding skills. The book describes train-
ing-tested techniques for riding well—the culmination of what the MSF
has learned about teaching students of all ages and experience. "The
More You Know, The Better It Gets!"
MCX2 . . . . Retail $24.95

MOTORCYCLE CAMPING MADE EASY

by Bob Woofter

Motorcycle camping offers an inexpensive and relaxing way to see the country, enjoy nature, and share stories with your friends around a campfire. With
the wide choice of high quality products now available, camping by motorcycle has never been easier. But camping by motorcycle isn't just a matter of
buying high-tech equipment. This book is loaded with practical information to
help you enjoy the whole experience.
WFT· . . . . Retail $19.95